EDITING
THE HARLEM
RENAISSANCE

AFRICAN AMERICAN
LITERATURE SERIES

The earliest African American writings frequently bore witness to the trauma of the slave trade, resistance to bondage, and fight against oppression, but these literary expressions also reflected cultural traditions created by fusing African, European, and American artistic practices. As the tradition developed, writers embraced multiple genres, including songs, poetry, sermons, speeches, narratives, antislavery tracts, letters, and petitions. This series, the first university press series devoted to the African American literary tradition, invites proposals for monographs, edited collections, and annotated editions that feature innovative new research from a variety of historical, theoretical, and critical perspectives.

Series editors

Valerie Babb, Emory University
Rhondda Robinson Thomas, Clemson University

EDITING
THE HARLEM RENAISSANCE

Edited by
Joshua M. Murray
& Ross K. Tangedal

CLEMSON
UNIVERSITY
PRESS

© 2024 Clemson University
All rights reserved

First Edition, 2021
This paperback edition published 2024

ISBN: 978-1-949979-55-8 (hardback)
ISBN: 978-1-83553-873-9 (paperback)
eISBN: 978-1-949979-56-5 (e-book)

Published by Clemson University Press
in association with Liverpool University Press

Clemson University Press is located in Clemson, SC.
For more information, please visit our website at www.clemson.edu/press.

Names: Murray, Joshua M., editor. | Tangedal, Ross K., 1986- editor.
Title: Editing the Harlem Renaissance / edited by Joshua M. Murray and Ross K. Tangedal.
Description: Clemson : Clemson University Press, 2021. | Series: African American literature series | Includes bibliographical references and index. | Summary: "Editing the Harlem Renaissance foregrounds an exhaustive approach to editing and editorial issues, exploring not only those figures who edited in professional capacities, but also those authors who employed editorial practices during the writing process and those texts that have been discovered or edited by others following the Harlem Renaissance"-- Provided by publisher.
Identifiers: LCCN 2020052126 (print) | LCCN 2020052127 (ebook) | ISBN 9781949979558 (hardback) | ISBN 9781949979565 (ebook)
Subjects: LCSH: American literature--African American authors--History and criticism. | American literature--20th century--History and criticism. | Editing--United States--History--20th century. | Literature publishing--United States--History--20th century. | Harlem Renaissance.
Classification: LCC PS153.N5 E35 2021 (print) | LCC PS153.N5 (ebook) | DDC 810.9/896073--dc23
LC record available at https://lccn.loc.gov/2020052126
LC ebook record available at https://lccn.loc.gov/2020052127

Typeset in Minion Pro by Carnegie Book Production.

To Babacar M'Baye and Robert W. Trogdon,
and in memory of Kevin Floyd.

Contents

List of Figures	ix
Acknowledgments	xi
Introduction: Editing the Harlem Renaissance	1
Joshua M. Murray and Ross K. Tangedal	

I Editing an Era

1	The Renaissance Happened in (Some of) the Magazines	15
	John K. Young	
2	The Pawn's Gambit: Black Writers, White Patrons, and the Harlem Renaissance	45
	Adam Nemmers	
3	Clad in the Beautiful Dress One Expects: Editing and Curating the Harlem Renaissance Text	63
	Ross K. Tangedal	

II Writers, Editors, Readers

4	The Two Gentlemen of Harlem: Wallace Thurman's *Infants of the Spring*, Richard Bruce Nugent's *Gentleman Jigger*, and Intellectual Property	87
	Darryl Dickson-Carr	

viii   EDITING THE HARLEM RENAISSANCE

5 Editorial Collaboration and Creative Conflict in *Outline for
   the Study of the Poetry of American Negroes*   109
     Shawn Anthony Christian

6 Jessie Fauset and Her Readership: The Social Role of
   The Brownies' Book   127
     Jayne E. Marek

7 Pure Essence without Pulp: Editing the Life of
   Langston Hughes   145
     Joshua M. Murray

III   Editorial Frameworks

8 Desegregating the Digital Turn in American Literary History   165
     Korey Garibaldi

9 (Re-)Framing Black Women's Liberation in the Classroom:
   Nella Larsen, Zora Neale Hurston, and Twenty-First-Century
   Editorial Frameworks   185
     Emanuela Kucik

10 Editing Edward Christopher Williams: From "The Letters of
   Davy Carr" to *When Washington Was in Vogue*   207
     Adam McKible

11 Editing Claude McKay's *Romance in Marseille*: A
   Groundbreaking Harlem Renaissance Novel Emerges from
   the Archive   223
     Gary Edward Holcomb

Coda: Editing as Infrastructural Care   241
     Brigitte Fielder and Jonathan Senchyne

Notes   249

Contributors   287

Index   293

Figures

1.1. Jean Toomer, "Song of the Son," *The Crisis*, 23, no. 6 (Apr. 1922): 261. The Modernist Journals Project. Brown University and The University of Tulsa. https://modjourn.org/issue/bdr514203/.

1.2. Advertisement for "Madam C. J. Walker's Beauty Aids," *The Crisis*, 23, no. 6 (Apr. 1922): back cover. The Modernist Journals Project. Brown University and The University of Tulsa. https://modjourn.org/issue/bdr514203/.

1.3. Bert Williams Obituary, *The Crisis Advertiser*, *The Crisis*, 23, no. 6 (Apr. 1922): 284. The Modernist Journals Project. Brown University and The University of Tulsa. https://modjourn.org/issue/bdr514203/.

1.4. "Overseas Secretaries of the Y.M.C.A.," "The Horizon," *The Crisis*, 23, no. 6 (Apr. 1922): 266. The Modernist Journals Project. Brown University and The University of Tulsa. https://modjourn.org/issue/bdr514203/.

Acknowledgments

An edited collection takes the hard work of many individuals to be successful. We are grateful for the overwhelming positive responses and encouragement we received from the selected contributors, as well as the scholars who could not participate in the volume for one reason or another. Your enthusiasm provided the impetus to get this project off the ground and out to the public. The contributors to this book deserve special mention for their time, expertise, and patience. Thank you to John K. Young, Adam Nemmers, Darryl Dickson-Carr, Shawn Anthony Christian, Jayne E. Marek, Korey Garibaldi, Emanuela Kucik, Adam McKible, Gary Edward Holcomb, Brigitte Fielder, and Jonathan Senchyne. We also wish to thank Dean Casale for his early contributions to the volume. This group of scholars was a joy to work with, and we are especially moved by their trust in us to collect their work here.

The team at Clemson University Press gave this book life. We wish to thank the following for their contributions to the book: John Morgenstern, director of the press, has been with the book from the beginning pitch to final production. He is a sterling example of what a press director should be: dynamic, enthusiastic, and an advocate of our work. Alison Mero, aside from her thoughtful editing, kept the business of this collection together, from contract to promotions and marketing. We are proud to publish an early volume in the press's new African American Literature series. Series editors Valerie Babb and Rhondda Robinson Thomas believed in the approach from the outset, and they offered insightful ways to expand the reach of the collection beyond the initial proposal. Finally, the anonymous reviewers and press editorial board helped shape the breadth of this collection with excellent early feedback.

Editing the Harlem Renaissance is a fusion of our particular scholarly interests, which were honed at Kent State University under the guidance of Babacar M'Baye and Robert W. Trogdon, and the late Kevin Floyd. We dedicate this volume to them for their tutelage, generosity, and friendship, and for helping us become the scholars we wanted to be. We also wish to thank our current institutions, Fayetteville State University and the University of Wisconsin–Stevens Point, for their support. Finally, thanks to Donavan Ramon and Clark Barwick for allowing us to present on this research at the 2020 South Atlantic Modern Language Association Conference.

We would be remiss if we did not acknowledge the people closest to us who make our work meaningful and possible—our wives and children. We thank them for their love and support: Joshua M. Murray to Kendra, Silas, and Zelda Murray; and Ross K. Tangedal to CJ, Adeline, and Hazel Tangedal.

Introduction: Editing the Harlem Renaissance

Joshua M. Murray and Ross K. Tangedal

Near the beginning of *The Big Sea* (1940), Langston Hughes recalls the moment when he first became conscious of language as a formal expression of identity. Lonely in his grandmother's house in Oklahoma, he discovers books: "then it was that books began to happen to me, and I began to believe in nothing but books and the wonderful world in books—where if people suffered, they suffered in beautiful language, not in monosyllables, as we did in Kansas."[1] While a key part of any *Künstlerroman* is the discovery of the artform and its transformative effect, Hughes recognizes shaping words to lift up a people beyond their trappings. Language elevates us. Hughes's friend Arna Bontemps underwent a similar transformation when met with a difficult choice while teaching at Oakwood College in Huntsville, Alabama, in the mid-1930s. Told to burn his collection of Harlem Renaissance books—their theme of social unrest proved too controversial for the school administration—Bontemps chose to resign and curate those texts, spending a career amplifying and remembering the work of his contemporaries. "Time," he wrote in a 1968 introduction to his novel *Black Thunder* (1936), "is not a river. Time is a pendulum."[2] Though his curatorial efforts no doubt kept alive dozens of texts, he is uncertain that readers in 1968, to whom his introduction is addressed, will read his work any differently than it was read in 1936.[3] Even in his cynicism, one recognizes the effort to keep a fire burning, a movement moving, and a

2   JOSHUA M. MURRAY AND ROSS K. TANGEDAL

history documented. Books need keepers and protectors to gauge the swing of that pendulum.

In the spirit of our title we ask the obvious question: How does one "edit" the Harlem Renaissance? In the decades following the proliferation of African American art and literature that has come to be called the Harlem Renaissance, numerous writers and scholars have attempted to delineate the trajectory of the New Negro Movement. Historical studies such as Nathan Irvin Huggins's *Harlem Renaissance*, David Levering Lewis's *When Harlem Was in Vogue*, and George Hutchinson's *The Harlem Renaissance in Black and White* have outlined the major events and contributors of the movement. Other critics have filled in the gaps with specialized studies such as Cheryl A. Wall's *Women of the Harlem Renaissance*, Michael Soto's edited collection, *Teaching the Harlem Renaissance*, and *Temples for Tomorrow: Looking Back at the Harlem Renaissance* edited by Geneviève Fabre and Michel Feith. And, perhaps most pivotally, several previously unpublished or undiscovered manuscripts have been brought into the public sphere, such as Edward Christopher Williams's "The Letters of Davy Carr" (retitled *When Washington Was in Vogue* upon first book publication), Zora Neale Hurston's *Barracoon*, and Claude McKay's *Amiable with Big Teeth* and *Romance in Marseille*. In each of these cases, scholars have attempted to frame and edit the Harlem Renaissance and its texts, creating both historical context and textual analysis. Generally lacking from these publications, however, has been a critical examination of the *process* by which the literature of the Harlem Renaissance was drafted, edited, revised, and produced. Yet, even during the Harlem Renaissance, many authors and careers were predicated on some form of editing, whether by way of magazine editors, publishing house editors, opinionated patrons, disagreeable collaborators, their own perfectionism, or some combination thereof.

During the 1920s, others played key roles in editing and publishing much of the literary output of up-and-coming artists. Jessie Redmon Fauset, labeled a "midwife" by Hughes, cultivated the literary careers of young writers in her role as editorial assistant alongside W.E.B. Du Bois at *The Crisis*.[4] Fauset published many eventual literary figures before they had achieved name recognition themselves, and, playing a similar role, Alain Locke guest edited the March 1925 issue of *Survey Graphic*,

INTRODUCTION   3

incorporating essays, poems, and short stories about the burgeoning movement. The issue was so successful that he expanded it into a stand-alone volume titled *The New Negro* in December of the same year. His editorial role placed him in a position of responding to a clear cultural shift, and he relished the opportunity to attempt to take the reins. In the eponymous introductory essay, Locke identified the "New Negro" as the "younger generation [that] is vibrant with a new psychology; the new spirit is awake in the masses, and under the very eyes of the professional observers is transforming what has been a perennial problem into the progressive phases of contemporary Negro life."[5] He contrasted this with "the Old Negro," which he described as "a creature of moral debate and historical controversy," necessitating a metamorphosis into a literary art that would embrace modernism and leave sentimentalism behind.[6] Speaking more practically, Locke expressed his belief in a later essay in the volume that young artists "take their material objectively with detached artistic vision; they have no thought of their racy folk types as typical of anything but themselves or of their being taken or mistaken as racially representative."[7] He continued:

> The newer motive, then, in being racial is to be so purely for the sake of art. Nowhere is this more apparent, or more justified than in the increasing tendency to evolve from the racial substance something technically distinctive, something that as an idiom of style may become a contribution to the general resources of art. In flavor of language, flow of phrase, accent of rhythm in prose, verse and music, color and tone of imagery, idiom and timbre of emotion and symbolism, it is the ambition and promise of Negro artists to make a distinctive contribution.[8]

In Locke's mind, then, the younger generation—i.e., Langston Hughes, Claude McKay, Zora Neale Hurston, and Wallace Thurman, among others—would deviate from the prior generation through a unique, individually crafted oeuvre. Instead of formulating a ubiquitous African American literature characterized by stereotypes and moral didacticism, Locke's prophesied canon of works would be as diverse as the writers themselves, in terms of both content and style. New Negro art, left to

Locke's idealistic guidance, would rival existing modernist movements in its reaction against unrealistic, Victorian depictions and its presentation of the unfiltered beauty and pain of life.

Not to be outdone, Du Bois acted upon a similar desire to seize the moment in his speech-turned-essay "Criteria of Negro Art" (1926) and to offer a counterpoint to Locke's liberal praise of literature's artistic potential. Though Du Bois also valued the aesthetics of art, he did so from a perspective of racial obligation:

> Thus it is the bounden duty of black Americans to begin this great work of the creation of Beauty, of the preservation of Beauty, of the realization of Beauty. ... The apostle of Beauty thus becomes the apostle of Truth and Right not by choice but by inner and outer compulsion. Free he is but his freedom is ever bounded by Truth and Justice; and slavery only dogs him when he is denied the right to tell the Truth or recognize an ideal of Justice.[9]

To this end, Du Bois claimed famously that

> all Art is propaganda and ever must be, despite the wailing of the purists. I stand in utter shamelessness and say that whatever art I have for writing has been used always for propaganda for gaining the right of black folk to love and enjoy. I do not care a damn for any art that is not used for propaganda. But I do care when propaganda is confined to one side while the other is stripped and silent.[10]

In his view, white cultural productions served as propaganda by reinforcing stereotypes and prejudices of the antebellum and Reconstruction periods. Du Bois's response dictated that African American art should remain cognizant of the competing propaganda. More important than conveying the diversity of individual experience, literature should take a stand by directly illustrating and advocating for racial progress.

Contemporaneously with the authors writing and the texts being produced, then, Locke and Du Bois attempted to mold and guide Harlem Renaissance authors, as well as control critical reception. Their roles as editors proved influential in the careers of many writers and in the movement itself, yet the reality is that the generation of writers who came of age in the 1920s and 1930s composed works that conveyed their personal ideas of art, race, community, and progress. As a whole, no pervasive quality unites what we now deem Harlem Renaissance literature outside of the era in which it developed. The inconsistency and varied nature of the works therefore place an even greater emphasis on the editorial processes that produced this canon. While the popular period has received much scholarly attention, the significance of editors and editing in the Harlem Renaissance—aside from the formative efforts of Du Bois and Locke—remains understudied. As a remedy, *Editing the Harlem Renaissance* foregrounds an in-depth approach to relevant editing and editorial issues, offering a variety of voices to become the first centralized authority on the subject. Rather than limiting the examination to a narrow understanding of editorial practices, this collection takes a broad and inclusive approach, exploring not only those figures of the Harlem Renaissance who edited in professional capacities but also those authors who employed editorial practices during the writing process, as well as those texts that have been discovered and/or edited by others in the decades following the Harlem Renaissance. To achieve this end, the collection comprises chapters in several areas, including professional editing, authorial editing, textual self-fashioning, textual editing, documentary editing, and bibliography.

Editing the Harlem Renaissance features eleven chapters divided into three parts. Part I, "Editing an Era," examines how the Harlem Renaissance was and is edited in various ways, with critical analyses of periodical culture, patronage, and textual editing and bibliography. Part II, "Writers, Editors, Readers," pays close attention to individual textual histories, with investigations into issues of composition and plagiarism, anthology building, magazine editing, and autobiography. Finally, Part III, "Editorial Frameworks," focuses on ways in which Harlem Renaissance texts have been shaped for the contemporary reader. Chapters on the digital humanities, framing narratives within reprinted work, and the discovery and publication of forgotten Harlem Renaissance texts provide a brief but necessary survey of the era's continued impact. While far from exhaustive, these eleven contributions, along with a critical coda by Brigitte Fielder and Jonathan Senchyne, showcase the potential of sustained study into editorial issues related to the Harlem Renaissance.

John K. Young opens the collection by posing a series of editorial questions arising from the intersection of periodical and African Americanist studies in "The Renaissance Happened in (Some of) the Magazines." How might we conceive of Harlem Renaissance "little" magazines along a spectrum of modernist magazine production? How should we edit the poems, stories, and essays of Harlem Renaissance figures within the run of a magazine, in such a way that editors can historicize that publishing context, in other words asking what it would have meant to encounter this text within its original publication history? Finally, how should editors of Harlem Renaissance works respond to the unique challenges posed by forms that are more ephemeral and diffuse than (many) books, especially when doing so often requires culling material from a wide range of archival sources? This kind of work, Young suggests, can position the works of the Renaissance within a more accurately historical framework, demonstrating both the extent of cross-racial textual production and circulation and the material constraints that often kept such cultural encounters temporary and contingent.

The mutually beneficial patron/artist relationship of the period is examined by Adam Nemmers in "The Pawn's Gambit: Black Writers, White Patrons, and the Harlem Renaissance." With a particular focus on Zora Neale Hurston, Nemmers analyzes literature of the Harlem Renaissance through both racial and postcolonial lenses, providing a necessary correction to narratives that portray African American authors as pawns in a white man's game, when the obverse was just as often true. As Nemmers argues, the interaction between white godparents and Black godchildren, as patron Charlotte Osgood Mason termed them, was a hidden yet powerful force in "editing" the written work of the Harlem Renaissance before it ever reached publishers, much less readers. In sum, as patronage was such an essential component of literary production during this period, analysis of its editorial impact on the works produced thereof enlightens our understanding of the movement and its writers.

Ross K. Tangedal interrogates a particular textual controversy that grew into an editorial controversy—the endings to Nella Larsen's 1929 novel *Passing*. In "Clad in the Beautiful Dress One Expects: Editing and

Curating the Harlem Renaissance Text," Tangedal surveys five editorial notes that accompanied five versions of Larsen's novel, spanning over twenty years, in order to show the urgent need for greater bibliographical and editorial attention when investigating the Harlem Renaissance. Working without a complete textual record, a sound bibliographical foundation, or within the confines of a scholarly edition, the scholars who edited these versions present a case study in editorial controversy by virtue of their personal choices. Though an editor does, and must, make choices when preparing a text for publication, these scholars (rather than editors) made choices without the benefit of sound bibliographical evidence—all the more reason to demand a more thorough textual examination of the Harlem Renaissance. At the heart of this essay are issues of audience, reception, market dynamics, and access, as Tangedal argues for a more rigorous investigation into the dynamic relationship between the textuality and the materiality of Harlem Renaissance texts and the writers who created them.

Darryl Dickson-Carr investigates the compositional history and issues of plagiarism and ownership in "The Two Gentlemen of Harlem: Wallace Thurman's *Infants of the Spring*, Richard Bruce Nugent's *Gentleman Jigger*, and Intellectual Property." Thurman and Nugent began writing drafts of novels with similar pseudonymous characters and events they had shared while they were roommates in 1928. However, since Thurman's novel was published first, Nugent's manuscript fell by the wayside until it was published posthumously in 2008. While some consider the episode a case of plagiarism, Dickson-Carr asks a more pertinent set of questions regarding the controversy: Who could claim ownership of the events both writers recount in their narratives? Do Nugent's more prodigious talents lend him more credibility as the first to write of these events? Do Thurman's editorial experience, critical eye, and reported production of a first draft make him more believable? Ultimately, Thurman and Nugent's shared efforts reveal how much the New Negroes disdained the expectations laid at their feet, and how sometimes editing takes the form of being the first on the scene.

The Harlem Renaissance saw the release of several anthologies of African American poetry, verse, folklore, and art, influential collections that showcased the flourishing of Black art and culture. In "Editorial

8   JOSHUA M. MURRAY AND ROSS K. TANGEDAL

Collaboration and Creative Conflict in *Outline for the Study of the Poetry of American Negroes*," Shawn Anthony Christian reads *Outline* as a compelling way to understand how creative conflict and artistic collaboration within anthology building shaped the period. In doing so, Christian employs editorial theory and methods from print culture studies to reflect on and then analyze *Outline*'s content in relation to letters, drafts, production notes, interviews, and the less visible creative labor and exchange between editor Sterling A. Brown and James Weldon Johnson—editor of the earlier *Book of American Negro Poetry* (1922)—that went into completing the study guide. As Christian argues, though Brown's aims predominate, especially in representing his and Johnson's (initially) different perspectives on dialect, *Outline* is a collaborative instance of how the impulse to better understand and ultimately validate varied conceptions of black identity in print functioned as an editorial imperative.

Jayne E. Marek addresses the contents and contexts of children's magazine *The Brownies' Book* under Jessie Redmon Fauset's guidance in "Jessie Fauset and Her Readership: The Social Role of *The Brownies' Book*." By its own account, *The Brownies' Book* was intended for "children of the sun" and included stories, letters, poems, songs, games, photographs, and illustrations. While the journal certainly addressed the era's need for a sensible, encouraging publication aimed at Black children and youth, the journal's real significance extends much further. Many items in its pages speak as directly to adult readers as to young ones. With her editorial experience, how much did Fauset truly shape the ideas of the Harlem Renaissance, above and beyond her perceived role as a "proper lady" novelist? How do her editorial decisions reflect the era's constraints in terms of gender, race, class, and literacy? How and why did *The Brownies' Book* extend the topics and ideas promoted by *The Crisis*? Marek examines what Fauset's editing strategies, at that crucial stage of American social history, meant to a public negotiating the complexities of African American identities in a changing and violent environment.

Taking a more nuanced approach to his famous subject, Joshua M. Murray examines Langston Hughes's editorial process for his two published autobiographies—*The Big Sea* (1940) and *I Wonder as I Wander* (1956)—as well as his plans for a third autobiography that never materialized, in "Pure Essence without Pulp: Editing the Life of Langston

Hughes." Murray unpacks Hughes's life writings from the perspective of literary construction and self-representation, two considerations Hughes attempted to balance. Murray extends editorial theory to incorporate the autobiographical process, taking into account Hughes's multifaceted identity and formulating a thorough explication of the self-fashioning of his protagonist persona. Additionally, other letters and archival materials from the 1930s, 1940s, and 1950s demonstrate Hughes's keen awareness of autobiographical editing, as he deliberately planned his life story and meticulously edited the texts with an eye to the finished products and their eventual public reception. Such an approach sheds light on the editorial nature of autobiography, while also granting an unusually candid glimpse at Hughes's understanding of the tension at play when self-identity, literary art, and public marketability intersect.

Dealing with early twentieth-century Black literature more broadly, Korey Garibaldi considers how racial segregation in twentieth-century American society and print culture has informed and undermined numerous achievements made possible by the digital turn in the humanities in "Desegregating the Digital Turn in American Literary History." As just one valuable yet under-examined historical example, literary interracialism in the early twentieth century could offer digital humanities (DH) practitioners countless generative case studies for considering when and where racial lines and related categories blur in the digitized past. Despite numerous problems and setbacks, there were countless experiments with literary pluralism in the forms of writing and working across racial divides in the first three decades of the twentieth century. By investigating the roots, dismantling, and re-emergence of segregation in literary culture—as well as shifts in how persons of Black African descent were racialized—Garibaldi offers a valuable case study for contextualizing the need for inclusive DH designs and professional collaborations.

Emanuela Kucik engages in a timely pedagogical study in "(Re-)Framing Black Women's Liberation in the Classroom: Nella Larsen, Zora Neale Hurston, and Twenty-First-Century Editorial Frameworks," wherein she uses Larsen's *Passing* and Hurston's *Their Eyes Were Watching God* as case studies for illuminating the editorial significance of the twenty-first-century frameworks that accompany recent printings of Harlem Renaissance literature and the transformative capabilities of analyzing said literature within the context of those frameworks. Kucik argues that today's students are performing expansive, emancipatory readings of these novels, as they enter these classic texts *after* reading introductions that urge them to think about the novels' protagonists and authors in the context of Black women's liberation. These introductions guide students to think about how Clare, Irene, and Janie challenge the categorizations and limitations society tries to impose upon them; guidance from Edwidge Danticat and Carla Kaplan produces a practice of reading in which students approach the novels focused on the emancipatory capabilities embedded within their pages. Additionally, Kucik contends that these guided readings provide students with an amplified understanding of the ways that Larsen and Hurston pushed for robust, flexible, and liberated imaginings of Black womanhood.

The final two chapters in the collection double as "on-the-ground" accounts of editing the Harlem Renaissance. In "Editing Edward Christopher Williams: From 'The Letters of Davy Carr' to *When Washington Was in Vogue*," Adam McKible provides a historical account of the novel's journey from the pages of *The Messenger*, through the multiple layers of publication and publicity, to the subsequent stewardship of the novel's reception and legacy. McKible recounts the innumerable decisions—and some significant compromises, including the retitling of the novel—that were made along the way as well as what transpired after the novel's release, including media appearances and the novel's reception in and out of academia. Similarly, Gary Edward Holcomb discusses in "Editing Claude McKay's *Romance in Marseille*: A Groundbreaking Harlem Renaissance Novel Emerges from the Archive" how he and co-editor William Maxwell edited the manuscript and composed the introduction on its provenance and history, with attention given to comparing the two extant manuscripts of the novel, the array of correspondence and additional materials that shed light on its progress and ultimate lack of publication, and the singular obstacles in the way of its publication over the past twenty years. These two essays serve as encouraging guideposts for scholars looking to turn their found archival discoveries into marketable texts.

Editing the Harlem Renaissance thereby offers a glimpse into the unedited history of the production of the Harlem Renaissance. The work in this volume, whether explicitly acknowledged in each chapter

INTRODUCTION 11

or not, builds upon the many previously "lost" texts that are available today through the diligence of tireless scholars. This textual archeology has required a concerted effort of recovery and reevaluation. Individual scholars and dedicated book series—such as the Library of Black Literature series published originally by Northeastern University Press and then by the University Press of New England (with general editor Richard A. Yarborough), the Multi-Ethnic Literatures of the Americas (MELA) series at Rutgers University Press (with series editors Amritjit Singh, Carla L. Peterson, and C. Lok Chua), the African-American Women Writers, 1910–1940 series from G.K. Hall (with general editor Henry Louis Gates, Jr.), and the American Women Writers series from Rutgers University Press (with series editors Joanne Dobson, Judith Fetterley, and Elaine Showalter)—have ensured the availability of textual artifacts through the republication of a number of formerly out-of-print Harlem Renaissance texts. We are indebted to the scholars who made accessible many of the works of James Weldon Johnson, Zora Neale Hurston, Nella Larsen, Claude McKay, George S. Schuyler, Jessie Redmon Fauset, Wallace Thurman, Langston Hughes, W.E.B. Du Bois, Sterling A. Brown, Rudolph Fisher, Walter White, and others, as well as those scholars who curated various anthologies and collections of essays, poetry, prose, and drama. We are likewise indebted to the work of several scholars, many of whom are cited throughout this volume, whose efforts—like those of Arna Bontemps—kept (and keep) the work of the Harlem Renaissance in a steady state of examination. The significance of this scholarly curation and the work of many others cannot be overstated; without such imperative reclamation work, *Editing the Harlem Renaissance* would not exist. And so, by pulling aside the curtain to witness the creation of the period, we can therefore gain the most candid insight into the minds of this pivotal era's key figures and the work that they felt was needed in an ever-changing America.

I Editing an Era

CHAPTER ONE

The Renaissance Happened in (Some of) the Magazines

John K. Young

Modernism happened, as the saying goes, in the magazines.[1] But because much—though by no means all—of the vibrant field of modernist magazine studies has focused on "high" modernist journals, such as *The Little Review*, *The Dial*, or *Broom*, the Harlem Renaissance often seems to have happened outside "the magazines," or in magazines associated with the Renaissance specifically and so not always understood as typically "modernist." Historically, however, magazines and newspapers presented vital publishing spaces for Harlem Renaissance writers, especially if we understand that term to refer not only to the confines of New York City in the late 1920s and early 1930s.[2] This is the case not only for important journals that were oriented around African American culture, such as *The Crisis*, *Opportunity*, the single-issue *Fire!!*, or the Chicago-based *Negro Story* in the mid-1940s, but also in various magazines aimed at "mainstream" American culture. James Weldon Johnson's "The Dilemma of the Negro Author," for example, originally appeared in H.L. Mencken's *American Mercury*. The famous debate between George Schuyler and Langston Hughes on Black aesthetics, resulting in Schuyler's essay "The Negro-Art Hokum" and Hughes's response, "The Negro Artist and the Racial Mountain," appeared not in *The Messenger* or *Opportunity*, to which those writers often contributed, but in *The Nation*. Zora Neale Hurston's "How It Feels to be Colored Me" ran in *World Tomorrow*,

15

16   JOHN K. YOUNG

a Christian socialist journal (where Wallace Thurman worked as an editor following the collapse of *Fire!!*).

The same is true for fiction and poetry in this period: the story that ended Nella Larsen's literary career, "Sanctuary," was published in *Forum Magazine*, a commercial enterprise that had never before published a Black writer. Jean Toomer published across a wide spectrum of magazines in the years before *Cane*, including in *Little Review* and *Broom*, but also in the Marxist *Liberator*, the Midwestern *Prairie* (which moved from Milwaukee to Chicago), and two journals from the deep South, the New Orleans-based *Double Dealer* and the short-lived *Nomad* in Birmingham, Alabama. Richard Wright's career began largely in the pages of *New Masses* and other Communist or left-leaning periodicals before his stories and essays came out in a wider range of periodicals in the 1940s. And, of course, the text that arguably was more influential than any other in this period, Alain Locke's *The New Negro: An Interpretation*, originated in *Survey Graphic*, with a primary audience of sociologists and popular readers interested in the field. As George Hutchinson notes, cross-advertising practices found ads for *The Crisis* and *Opportunity* circulating in such magazines as *Modern Quarterly*, *The Nation*, and *New Masses*, and vice versa, leading him to ask, "if there is as great a difference between 'white aesthetics' and 'black aesthetics' as we are often told, one has to wonder why such a high proportion of what the white magazines first published is generally agreed to be the best work of African American literary modernism."[3] Just as these publishing arrangements remain a largely underrepresented aspect of histories of the Renaissance, so too have they largely fallen into the margins in editorial representations of the writers, artists, publishers, and magazines constituting the literary networks through which African American art and literature were being produced and distributed.

An important task for editors working with authors and texts associated with the Harlem Renaissance, then, should be to engage with this aspect of their publishing history, which created a space for many important pieces to reach their first, often inter-racial, audiences. For the most part, editorial attention has focused, often admirably, not on magazines as distinct bibliographical environments in themselves, a position I will take here, but within editorial projects organized around a particular author's career, where periodical publications operate as part of the repository of historical documents in which a text has circulated. There, the relevant question would be how to position a magazine text in relation to an array of other material texts and versions, in order to situate the magazine text within the broader scope of an edition and the larger work (the novel, poetry volume, short story collection, book of essays) which the edition represents. William Maxwell's edition of Claude McKay's *Collected Poems*, for instance, notes original periodical publications where relevant, along with other versions extant in manuscript and/or typescript, in order to document the variants present across those published and unpublished versions.[4] Such comparisons have long been part and parcel of the editorial task, of course, for authors and texts across multiple periods and nationalities, but I argue that, for the particular case of periodical publication, this approach tells only part of the story. This blind spot develops because of the ways in which magazines function differently from books, resulting in fundamentally distinct reading performances, in Peter Shillingsburg's terms.[5] To read "How It Feels to be Colored Me" in the collection *I Love Myself When I am Laughing ... and Then Again When I Am Looking Mean and Impressive*, for instance, or to encounter Toomer's story "Carma" in an edition of *Cane*, is not the same experience as coming across those texts in an issue of *World Tomorrow* or *Liberator*, not only because of the distinct historical and material circumstances of those original publications but also because the process of reading magazines, versus that of reading books, is importantly and substantially different. "Only in the most extraordinary of circumstances will two readers ever share the same experience of a magazine, will they read it, in other words, in the same way," Sean Latham, a leading figure in the sphere of periodical studies, writes. "Again, this does not mean that they interpret it differently—but that they encounter the words, the articles, the ads, and even the paper in unique, disjunctive, and not easily anticipated ways."[6] To edit periodical texts *as* periodical texts, as parts of that distinct bibliographical environment, rather than only as nodes on an array of a text's history as conceived from the point of view of the author's career, would therefore require a different theoretical and practical orientation toward the scope of an edition—an edition, namely, of the magazine as its own kind of work, not of the work associated with a single one of the magazine's contributors and

18   JOHN K. YOUNG

ultimately published elsewhere, typically in a book to which the earlier periodical text takes up an ancillary relationship.

While a wide variety of modernist magazines have been edited and curated, most notably at the Modernist Journals Project (MJP), this activity has largely developed outside the purview of editorial theory. I seek to begin redressing that imbalance here by posing a series of editorial questions arising from the intersection of periodical and African Americanist studies. How might we conceive of Harlem Renaissance magazines, "little" or otherwise, along a spectrum of modernist magazine production? How should we edit the poems, stories, and essays of Harlem Renaissance figures within the run of a magazine, in such a way that editors can historicize that publishing context, in other words asking what it would have meant to encounter this text within its original publication history?[7] Finally, how should editors of Harlem Renaissance works respond to the unique challenges posed by forms that are more ephemeral and diffuse than (many) books, especially when doing so often requires culling material from a wide range of archival sources? This kind of work, I suggest, can position the works of the Renaissance (broadly construed) within a more accurately historical framework, demonstrating both the extent of cross-racial textual production and circulation and the material constraints that often kept such cultural encounters temporary and contingent.[8]

In order to ground that discussion in specific examples, I will consider here three magazine issues from the 1920s: the April 1922 *Crisis*, which featured Jean Toomer's poem "Song of the Son" (Figure 1.1) and Robert W. Bagnall's short story "Lex Talionis" alongside articles on "The Negro Bank" and "The Portuguese Negro"; the September 1926 *The Messenger*, where Zora Neale Hurston's "The Eatonville Anthology" ran with poetry from Georgia Douglas Johnson and Langston Hughes in addition to the magazine's by then usual coverage of the Pullman porters' union; and the December 1928 *American Mercury*, where Johnson's "Dilemma of the Negro Author" shared space with articles on "The Confusion of Prohibition," "Confusion Among the Liberals," and "The Writing of 'Moby-Dick.'" Expanding the geographical and temporal boundaries of the Harlem Renaissance with a brief final case, I close with a reading of the spring 1942 issue of *Accent*, edited by a University of Illinois professor, which published two excerpts from Wright's "The Man Who Lived Underground" along-side contributions from Katherine Anne Porter, R.P. Blackmur, Kenneth Burke, Jackson Mac Low, and Delmore Schwartz. My approach here is to consider these examples from a dual perspective, both in terms of the magazine text as one in an array of texts constituting the work of the story or poem in questions, and by conceiving of the totality of a magazine issue as itself a work, in the editorial sense, on its own.

The periodical text—a term by which I refer to both an individual entry within a magazine issue and to that issue as a whole—occupies a liminal position between typical conceptions of text and work within editorial theory, where those terms have largely been understood of late along an axis of immateriality (the work) to materiality (the text). To cite a representative recent example, Hans Walter Gabler maintains that "works in language can be instantiated both materially and immaterially. As instantiated, we perceive works as texts. Any one given text instantiates the work. What binds the instantiations together is 'the work'. The work exists immaterially, yet it is at the same time more than a mere notion."[9] Thus, any particular material instantiation (a text) comprises a representation of the work, yet the work is not reducible to a single text, adhering instead from a collective, immaterial perception of one or (almost always) more texts. In the same ways that the script for a play or the score for a composition might not seem to comprise the entirety of the work as performed in a variety of social and historical contexts, the literary work as produced (and "performed," perhaps, by readers) often figures in contemporary editorial theory in ways that yield various material artifacts, where a particular document functions in loosely analogous terms to a particular performance in a theatrical or musical context. We would thus say that Johnson's *The Autobiography of an Ex-Colored Man*, for example, was "instantiated," in Gabler's terms, by his drafts of the novel while an undergraduate at Columbia, again upon its anonymous 1912 publication (or for the first time then, from a materialist editorial perspective), and once more in its revised and authorially sanctioned 1927 version (along with other possible unpublished texts along the way).[10]

The situation is inherently more complicated when considering works that have existed in both periodical and book versions. When, for example, does *Cane* become a work as understood by editorial theorists? Certainly

20   JOHN K. YOUNG

at some point in the months leading up to its September 1923 publication in book form from Boni & Liveright, as Toomer was completing revisions and arrangements for the collection, but what might we make of the various pieces of *Cane* published in periodicals between January 1922 and September 1923? When *Broom* published two portions of the book's closing section, "Kabnis," in its September 1923 issue, the magazine noted: "One of a collection of stories and poems to be published this fall by Boni & Liveright (New York) under title of 'Cane.'"[11] Clearly the work as it would appear in its initial book form was in existence when this issue of *Broom* went to press, but this was not the case when, say, the January 1922 *Broom* included Toomer's story "Karintha." Six months later, Toomer wrote to Waldo Frank that he "had the impulse to collect my sketches and poems under the title perhaps of CANE."[12] From an editorial perspective, we would of course need to account for the earlier published versions of *Cane*'s stories and poems, in addition to their draft forms, in preparing an edition; such editorial work would operate under the rubric of *Cane* as a work instantiated among various texts.

But we might also understand each of these periodical publications as both its own text and work—in principle and in practice; after all, some readers of *Broom* or the various other modernist magazines distributing Toomer's work would not perceive them as parts of the larger whole called *Cane* and/or would perceive them differently within the context of their original magazine form, and, from an authorial perspective, Toomer only retroactively conceptualized these early publications as part of a larger whole. In perceiving the *Broom* "Karintha" as part of *Cane* as a work, then, editors would be following the same process as Toomer himself, allowing for the considerable extent to which authors' perceptions of a work may develop and change over the course of its composition and revision. As Daniel Ferrer notes, "the point of view of the writer constantly changes during the creative process, so that what is already written must be reinterpreted from a—marginally, in most cases, but sometimes radically, new—perspective."[13] An expansive enough view of authorial reinterpretation would certainly leave room for reconceiving of an earlier work as now part of a new work unimagined at the time of the original publication in question, a process that Toomer is hardly alone in having followed. Perceiving a magazine text *only* as a function of a work that becomes

THE RENAISSANCE HAPPENED   21

apparent retrospectively, however, expresses a kind of authorial idealism about the existence of the text (and the work), whereas also perceiving the magazine text on its own terms as part of the work that is constituted by the magazine would proceed from a more McGannian emphasis on the material conditions of initial publication, though perhaps traveling farther down that road than McGann himself would necessarily follow.

Along related lines, Paul Eggert has proposed a kind of nominalist view of the work, with a greater emphasis on the phenomenological experience of the work rather than on its ontology. "The name of the individual work," he writes, "is the container that we project from the document for the textual and other meanings we raise or extrapolate from our dealings with it."[14] In the case of the relationship between *Cane* as a work, projected from the document either first produced by Boni & Liveright or reprinted and edited since, and "Karintha" in the work produced by the document that is the January 1922 issue of *Broom*, we have, clearly, two very different documents and thus, I maintain, two entirely different works (though a part of the text of each is largely identical). The textual meanings extrapolated from *Cane* as a document have tended to obscure the periodical works in which parts of *Cane* were originally contained, I would argue, as is the case more generally for the relationship between books and magazines (or newspapers) as documents from which works are projected or perceived. Proceeding backwards, so to speak, from the point of view of the established, book-bound, version of a work (*Cane*, in this case) tends to presuppose at least a roughly linear, evolutionary, sequence of versions moving toward eventual publication in book form. This kind of teleological impulse, though, obscures both original texts (and works) and their readers, as they existed in and through periodicals.

Further, and perhaps more radically from within an editorial framework, we might well consider each of these magazine issues as a work, in the editorial sense, in its own right, at each of two levels, that of the issue and that of the magazine. For instance, the March–April 1923 issue of *Prairie* instantiates the periodical text of Toomer's "Blood-Burning Moon," as well as both the text and the work of that issue as a whole, and a text that makes up one element of *Prairie* (originally titled *The Milwaukee Arts Monthly*) as its own larger work. That is, I am arguing that the particular issue of *Prairie* where Toomer's story was published constitutes a work in the editorial sense, at least conceptually, but it also functions as a text in relation to the supervening work represented by the magazine's full run. (As it happens, Toomer's story appeared in what would be the magazine's fifth and final issue.)[15] In addition to including the text of Toomer's *Prairie* story within the editorial corpus serving as the documentary foundation for an edition of *Cane*, we could (and should, I would argue) approach the magazine story on its own terms, asking what it would have meant to have read this story in this magazine at this time, and, by extension, by then envisioning an edition of the magazine itself—not only a digital copy, like those available for other titles in the MJP, but as an edition on its own, in need of annotation and attention to textual history, even if, as is likely, a given magazine or given issue might only appear in a single printed run. While Toomer's story in this issue of *Prairie* would ordinarily be included among the repository of material texts from which a copy text would derive for an edition of *Cane*, we might also think of the entire issue as a copy text for an edition of the magazine.

This way of thinking about a magazine as a work may well seem counterintuitive, particularly at the level of a single issue, where the one–many or part–whole relationship between the immaterial work and the material collection of texts would not seem to apply. But precisely what makes a single issue of a magazine inhere as a kind of work, I would argue, is its immateriality as what Shillingsburg terms a "reception text." In "Text as Matter, Concept, and Action," Shillingsburg distinguishes among three types of performance: creative performance (the "primarily inventive" activity associated with an author); production performance (activity "associated with manufacture and publishing the material text"); and reception performance, the process of "'conceptualizing' the material text" or "what we do when reading and analyzing."[16] As Shillingsburg explains, the reception performance yields a reception text, which is itself an immaterial text based on a reader's performative reception of a material text: "the author's essayed conceptual text takes form as a material text that the reader uses to construct the reception conceptual text."[17] The key difference between the reception conceptual text for a book versus a magazine, however, derives from the immateriality of the magazine at the level of the work, though this immateriality is still generated by and instantiated in the existence of the magazine as a material text.

The material text of the magazine issue generates an immaterial work because the material text is designed to be read in a deeply non-linear, ergodic fashion, rendering it "a strange object whose codes exceed the ones we are equipped to see," as Patrick Collier writes.[18] Most magazines invite any number of possible sequences of reading, including those which will ignore one or more parts of the magazine. As Margaret Beetham notes, "Most readers will not only construct their own order, they will select and read only some of the text. The periodical, therefore, is a form which openly offers readers the chance to construct their own text."[19] Of course, there is nothing inherent in the form of the book that compels readers to start at the beginning and proceed forward from there. No doubt many readers encountering Charles Chesnutt's *The Conjure-Man Tales* or Georgia Douglas Johnson's *Bronze* have skipped among the stories and poems gathered there, and the hybrid contents of collections like Locke's *New Negro* or Nancy Cunard's *Negro* especially invite reading practices that are importantly similar to periodicals in ways that are broadly true of anthologies generally, as Rachel Farebrother and others have noted. But even in those cases, the material text of the book is resisting the form of the book: what makes *The New Negro* a "diverse and self-divided text," as Hutchinson puts it, is its divergence from the standard experience of the codex.[20] Yet there is still a clear sense of order in the volume as a whole. As Farebrother writes, "In spite of its diverse content, the volume is carefully structured."[21] While collections like *The New Negro* invite readings against their textual grain, then, such encounters proceed with the knowledge that there is an internal structure to read against. Magazines, in contrast, are designed for multiple readings and rereadings without a particular "right" or "wrong" order; they are, in a philosophical sense, emergent wholes that, despite a linear order of contents, are inherently open to, and designed for, readings that begin at multiple points and proceed in multiple directions; there is no "forward" or "backward" or "out-of-order" sequence for reading a magazine.

While editorial theorists have not typically focused on periodicals as distinct types of texts (or works), my discussion of them in such terms is broadly amenable to recent conceptualizations of the work nevertheless. Shillingsburg has more recently emphasized the performative aspect of the work in its reception (and production) by audiences responding to

24   JOHN K. YOUNG

particular material texts, concluding, "Each text of the work represents in some unique way the historical circumstances of its production as a social, political, economic, and literary event that might be significantly misrepresented by some other form of the text."[22] This McGannian sense of a text's historicity leads Shillingsburg to insist on ontological distinctions between types of texts in contrast to a phenomenological sense of the work: "I hold that a document is a document, not a work. A book is a book, a historical artifact, not the work of art that it only implies—sometimes imperfectly. The work, on the other hand, is performed into existence sequentially and ephemerally in the reading process." Thus, for Shillingsburg, "Works exist most immediately as performances in process."[23] I would add that a magazine is a magazine, also not the work that it necessarily implies imperfectly, as that work exists precisely as a myriad of possible readerly constructions grounded in encounters with the material text of the magazine issue, and so magazines understood as works exist at that level not only most immediately but *only* as "performances in process."

In his recent study of the work as an editorial concept and in practice, Eggert similarly shies away from positing the work as "figured" in the mind of the reader as a "transcendent ideal," instead understanding it as the result of a negative dialectic between documents as material objects and as the locus for readers' interactions at both a material and immaterial level.[24] Positioning the material text as the "stable thing" in readers' experience of the work, Eggert maintains that "it is not a matter of 'the work' somehow transcending the process: the work (broadly construed) *is* the process. It is also how we name it."[25] While different readers will, by definition, move through different versions of this "process," thus producing their own conceptions of the work in relation to a material document, this sense of process is, again, even more deeply entrenched in magazines, both in readers' perceptions of them as material documents and as an essential feature of those material documents themselves, which, despite their arrangement as a linear sequence of pages, are made for contingent constructions and reconstructions as readers move through, and return to, those pages across an array of alternative arrangements.

This conception of periodicals and their texts would be particularly rewarding, I would argue, for editorial approaches to the Harlem

Renaissance. Like many of the key works of the Harlem Renaissance, magazines are inherently mixed forms, combining multiple linguistic and visual registers in addition to an array of types of text and images, from the magazine "proper" to its advertisements and cover. As Beetham explains,

> Periodicals are heterogeneous in that they are made up of different kinds of material. Many mix text and pictures. Indeed the relation of blocks of text to visual materials is a crucial part of their meaning. Even where it does not use visual and literary material together, the periodical is still characteristically a mixed form.[26]

Farebrother, building on earlier work by Anne Elizabeth Carroll and Martha Jane Nadell, has similarly argued that "many Harlem Renaissance texts are characterized by the patching together of diverse sources, which can be identified and held in view by the reader."[27] This is the case, I would add, not only for the examples Farebrother cites, such as *Cane*, *The New Negro*, or Cunard's *Negro*, but for each magazine issue in which Harlem Renaissance texts found part of their published lives. Thus I will seek to outline here a program for reading—and editing—not only Toomer's poem in *The Crisis*, Hurston's story in *The Messenger*, Johnson's essay in *American Mercury*, or Wright's story in *Accent*, but also for conceptualizing those magazine issues as works in their entirety, and therefore as objects of editorial inquiry. The interpretive upshot of this approach, I hope, will be to suggest new lines of historizing the Harlem Renaissance through the particular routes its texts took to their multifarious publics. This entails an openness to a kind of historical lack of initial knowledge, to the kinds of connections that emerge when following the juxtapositions created by the shared space of the periodical text. If we conceive of race, as Kinohi Nishikawa has argued, not as "an a priori category to be read *into* literature, but a complex effect of distinct social, cultural, and textual mediations," the magazine modernism that helped to shape much African American literature of that period will offer fertile ground for this kind of scholarship, which is open to new questions and new discoveries about how these texts were actually produced, distributed, and consumed.[28] While the field of periodicals studies has offered numerous examples of how to read a magazine, both in a single issue or across a partial or

26   JOHN K. YOUNG

complete run of a title, what Mark W. Turner thinks of as the question of whether "to read horizontally or laterally," editorial theory (and practice) has not yet arrived at similar ways of representing magazines as editions.[29]

By examining the four magazine issues referenced above in terms of hypothetical editions centered on these titles as works, I hope to demonstrate two main outcomes of this approach. In keeping with Eggert's sense of an edition as an implied argument about how best to present the documents on which the edition is based, I am thinking here of editorial arguments designed to demonstrate to their readers how deeply and complexly Harlem Renaissance literature, as well as the surrounding sociopolitical environment, were implicated in the ostensibly wider arena of American modernism.[30] I aim also to model the kind of close engagement with the periodical text at the material level that would sustain this kind of edition and offer new directions for tracing the relationships among contributors, publishers, and readers constituting the original production and reception of what is now referred to as the Harlem Renaissance.

In reading these magazines as "ergodic and recursive" texts in Latham's sense, I focus especially on the interactions between an issue's, or a run of issues', textual contents and material forms. Peter Brooker and Andrew Thacker provide a useful model of this reading practice in what they term "periodical codes," an offshoot of Jerome McGann's sense of "bibliographic codes," as the kinds of non-verbal elements of any material text. Brooker and Thacker posit periodical codes as keys to both a magazine's internal dynamics and to its modes of production and distribution:

> We can also distinguish between periodical codes internal to the design of a magazine (paper, typeface, layout, etc.) and those that constitute its external relations (distribution in a bookshop, support from patrons). However, it is often the *relationship* between internal and external periodical codes that is most significant. Advertisements, for example, constitute both internal and external codes, indicating, on the one hand, an external relationship to an imagined readership and a relationship to the world of commerce and commodities, while operating, on the other hand, in their placement on the page or position in the magazine as a whole, as part of the magazine's internal code.[31]

Here I would point especially to Brooker and Thacker's emphasis on the relationship between internal and external codes.[32] The kinds of advertisements surrounding texts in modernist journals speak to the kinds of audience those magazines aimed to develop, and to the kinds of cultural networks into which they sought to insert themselves, both in the case of cross-advertising with other magazines and in more conventional promotions of commercial products. Ads are an especially useful lens into the types of readerships magazines attempt to construct for themselves, both in terms of the types of commercial goods being marketed and for the ways in which ads for other magazines suggest the kind of sphere in which the host magazine aims to be seen. (This is most directly the case, of course, for house ads, that is, ads in which a given magazine promotes itself.)

The Crisis and *The Messenger* both played key roles in establishing audiences, not only for their different projects of Black aesthetics but also for their political, social, and cultural coverage of the period. In 1922, Du Bois was beginning his second decade as the *Crisis* editor, with Jessie Redmon Fauset on board as fiction editor since 1919 as well. As several scholars have observed, the monthly magazine was instrumental in presenting visual and verbal portraits of Black life that self-consciously departed from stereotypically racist depictions of the time, combining a range of visual culture (photographs, illustrations, and advertisements) with its equally "diverse content, in which pan-Africanism, revisionist history, and anti-lynching campaigns sit alongside poetry, essays, short fiction, and pioneering children's literature, which targeted a specifically African American audience."[33] Priced at 15 cents (with an annual subscription rate of $1.50),[34] the April issue comprises forty-eight pages, with a cover illustration titled "Spring" from Du Bois's daughter, Yolande, then an undergraduate at Fisk University. In keeping with the magazine's standard practice at the time, a full-page ad from the Southern Aid Society of Virginia, the first Black-owned chartered insurance company in the United States, appears on the verso side of the cover, opposite the table of contents.[35] Following the contents are three pages of ads, all for secondary schools or colleges and universities, renewing the emphasis on Black professional life established by the insurance ad. No ads return until the issue's closing eight pages, a typical arrangement in many magazines of the early 1920s. There we find a wider array of businesses promoting themselves to *Crisis* readers, including various schools and colleges once again, but also a home builder, "Dr. Welters' Antiseptic Tooth Powder," music lessons, made-to-order pants, furs, regalia, real estate, and, on the back cover, Madam C.J. Walker's Beauty Aids, a variety of cosmetics designed to "whiten" African American women's hair and skin (Figure 1.2). Perhaps most striking from a literary viewpoint is a list of books "Dealing with the Negro Problem" and all for sale directly from the *Crisis* offices, including a mix of literary and historical titles, with several from Du Bois, Carter G. Woodson, Benjamin Brawley, and others, as well as a full-page ad from Black Swan Records (Figure 1.3) responding to the death of the vaudeville entertainer Bert Williams, which laments:

> Bert Williams was an Artist. He was a Great Actor. He might have been Known as a Great Tragedian had he Been Born White. But the World for a Long Time now Has Refused to Take Black Men Seriously. So the White World made Bert Williams the World's Greatest Comedian.[36]

The issue's contents open with Du Bois's editorial, "The World and Us," on a range of international events and the anti-lynching Dyer Bill then before the U.S. Senate (where it would ultimately be defeated by a filibuster from Southern Democrats). Following this editorial sequentially—though not necessarily for any given reader's practice—is a survey of "Negro banking," of which there were sixty according to the magazine's estimate, with a brief history of Black-owned banks and photographs of four bank presidents, three from the South and one from Chicago. "Lex Talionis," a work of speculative fiction by National Association for the Advancement of Colored People (NAACP) executive Robert W. Bagnall, in which an African American doctor invents a potion that turns white skin dark, offers "an imagining of an alternative reality as an act of political resistance."[37] As Eurie Dahn notes, a page-long collection of photographs from the preceding article on banking arrive in the middle of Bagnall's story, along with a photograph of the protagonist's sister (whose assault prompts the doctor to use his race-changing procedure on her attacker); combined with (fictional) clippings from white newspapers about the events of Bagnall's story, this mixture "adds to the sense of authenticity," as the cumulative effect of text and image "testifies to the worth of African Americans in virtue of their respectability."[38] Just as Bagnall's story overlaps with the survey of bankers, the end of "Lex Talionis" shares space with the following article, "The Portuguese Negro" by Nicolas Santos-Pinto, a speech he had delivered at the Second Pan-African Congress the previous September. This piece, too, runs directly into another, Fauset's review of Benjamin Brawley's *A Social History of the American Negro*, published in 1921.

This mix of emphases on African American business, transnational liberation movements, domestic anti-racist politics, and speculative fiction constitutes the bibliographical environment surrounding Toomer's "Song of the Son." The poem appears, unlike the previous magazine items, entirely on its own page, surrounded by a floral motif arranged to form a rectangular border around the poem, a notably unusual arrangement for poetry in *The Crisis* during this period, when the magazine typically published short poems filling a space at the bottom or top of a page.[39] Immediately following Toomer's poem is a report from the NAACP on the current status of the Dyer Bill (which had passed the House but not yet been taken up by the Senate); a report on "The Bullock Case," concerning an African American man who had fled from North Carolina to Canada after his brother had been lynched, and whom the NAACP had helped to defend, successfully, during an extradition hearing; the organization's financial report for 1921; and a report of a New York City lodge, the Knights of Pythias, that had paid for a membership in the NAACP; with a brief poem, "Pride" by Mortimer G. Mitchell, run in at the bottom of the page, extolling "Negro youth" to take pride in the United States because their fathers "fought / To give this country might."[40] The remainder of the issue, before reaching "The Crisis Advertiser," consists of two round-ups of news items of interest to the magazine's broad audience: "The Horizon," compiled by Madeline G. Allison (Figure 1.4), reports on various local political and financial accomplishments by African Americans, such as being elected hospital trustee or town constable, performing in musical concerts, or the fact that "The Negro race built 25 per cent." of the homes in Atlanta in 1921;[41] and "The Looking Glass," consisting of opening and closing brief poems (by Rabindranath Tagore and Mary Effie Lee Newsome) and longer reports on political and cultural events, including the Dyer Bill once more, an exhibit of "Negro art" at the New York Public

30   JOHN K. YOUNG

Library's 135th Street branch, and a discussion of lingering tensions from the Great War, among other topics. Both columns stretch across multiple pages, with several photographs included as part of "The Horizon," which was praised at the time as a valuable service to the community: "In monthly compiling the tremendous new store of varied and far-reaching data her department contains, Miss Allison is doing a grand and unique piece of literary writing the workmanship and quality of which any magazine of any race would be proud to carry."[42] These sections point to one of the multiple readerly paths through this or any issue of *The Crisis* in this period, as "The Horizon" and "The Looking Glass" were likely, for much of the magazine's audience, as or more important a part of *The Crisis* as any particular poem, story, or article. While the magazine clearly signals bibliographically that "Song of the Son" is a significant work meriting a special visual effect, or that the racial pride derived from the banking industry accords that article a prominent place within the issue's linear arrangement, individual readers will, of course, place greater or lesser emphasis on any particular item, generating their own idiosyncratic reception conceptual text, in Shillingsburg's terms. For scholars returning to this issue through a specific historical lens—excavating *Cane*'s publishing history, recovering largely forgotten works of Harlem Renaissance literature like Bagnall's story, tracing the historical development of Black banks, or others—this sense of the issue's readerly variability also gestures toward the different kinds of historicist narratives that might be constructed from any of those periodical texts' placement within this issue and within the larger work, in the editorial sense, of *The Crisis* in the early 1920s.[43]

Relative to *The Crisis*, *The Messenger* pursued a more radical political and aesthetic agenda in this decade. "More often than not," Hutchinson observes, "the magazine ridiculed notions that African American culture was fundamentally different from white American culture and supported an assimilationist as well as integrationist cultural politics."[44] By 1926, the magazine was at something of a crossroads in terms of its audience, both commercially and culturally. While *The Crisis* "had begun losing its influence" by the middle of the decade, thanks to the rise of *Opportunity* and the greater accessibility for Harlem Renaissance writers in "white" magazines, *The Messenger* had become the official publication of the Brotherhood of Sleeping Car Porters in 1925, resulting in its "politics becoming more

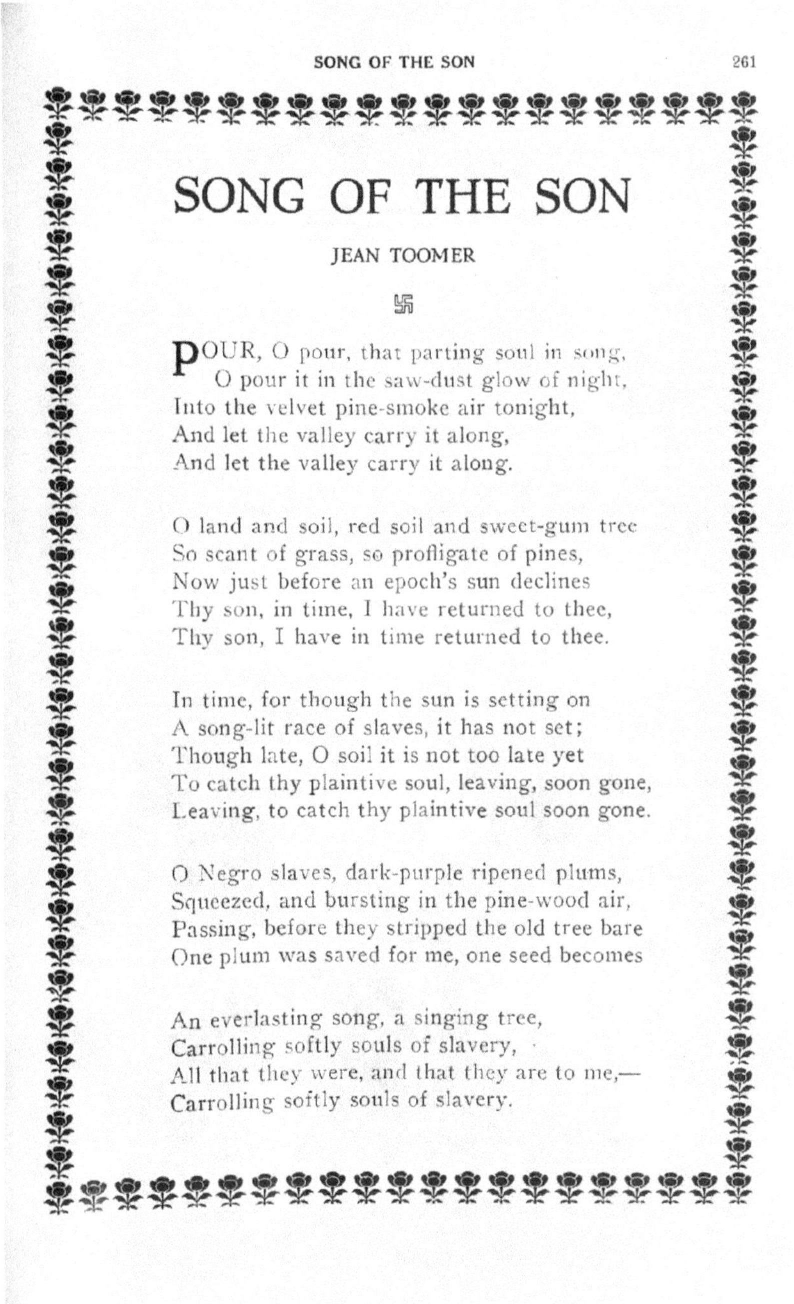

THE RENAISSANCE HAPPENED 31

SONG OF THE SON 261

SONG OF THE SON

JEAN TOOMER

POUR, O pour, that parting soul in song,
    O pour it in the saw-dust glow of night,
Into the velvet pine-smoke air tonight,
And let the valley carry it along,
And let the valley carry it along.

O land and soil, red soil and sweet-gum tree
So scant of grass, so profligate of pines,
Now just before an epoch's sun declines
Thy son, in time, I have returned to thee,
Thy son, I have in time returned to thee.

In time, for though the sun is setting on
A song-lit race of slaves, it has not set;
Though late, O soil it is not too late yet
To catch thy plaintive soul, leaving, soon gone,
Leaving, to catch thy plaintive soul soon gone.

O Negro slaves, dark-purple ripened plums,
Squeezed, and bursting in the pine-wood air,
Passing, before they stripped the old tree bare
One plum was saved for me, one seed becomes

An everlasting song, a singing tree,
Carrolling softly souls of slavery, ·
All that they were, and that they are to me,—
Carrolling softly souls of slavery.

Figure 1.1. *The Crisis*, May 1922, p. 261. The Modernist Journals Project.
Brown and Tulsa Universities. www. modjourn.org

The Horizon

COMPILED BY MADELINE G. ALLISON

MESSIAH Baptist Church in Yonkers, N. Y., and Mt. Olivet Baptist Church, in New York City, have appointed women as members of the Board of Trustees. The appointees are Mrs. Emily Brown at Messiah and Mrs. Richetta R. Wallace at Mt. Olivet.

❡ Bishop Brooks, formerly of Baltimore, Md., is now Chaplain for the Supreme Court of Liberia.

❡ A 10 percent dividend has been declared by the Sumter Investment Corporation, a Negro real estate enterprise in Sumter, S. C. Messrs. W. T. Andrews is president; R. M. Andrews, vice-president; and H. D. McNight, secretary-treasurer.

❡ Anita Patti Brown, the noted Negro singer of Chicago, Ill., is studying in Europe under Herr Victor Beigel. Miss Brown is attended by her accompanist, Miss Doxie. They will resume recitals in America in the fall of 1922.

❡ Messrs. James B. and Benjamin N. Duke have donated $75,000 toward a hospital for Negroes in Durham, N. C. A similar sum is now to be raised by colored and white citizens. The following persons have been elected members of the Board of Trustees for the hospital: Dr. S. L. Warren, president; W. G. Pearson, vice-president; I. M. Avery, treasurer; W. Gomez, secretary.

❡ During 1921, over 1,200 homes were constructed in Atlanta, Ga. The Negro race built 25 per cent. of thest homes.

❡ During the 20th National Conference of the Y. M. C. A., the overseas secretaries held a reunion. In the picture are Messrs. B. F. Lee, Jr.; J. E. Blanton, B. F. Hubert, Robert E. Parks, William Stevenson, George Thompson, John Hope, A. L. James and B. F. Seldon.

OVERSEAS SECRETARIES OF THE Y. M. C. A.

266

Figure 1.2. *The Crisis*, May 1922, p. 266. The Modernist Journals Project. Brown and Tulsa Universities. www.modjourn.org

THE RENAISSANCE HAPPENED   33

284   THE CRISIS ADVERTISER

BERT WILLIAMS

The Greatest Entertainer the World has Ever Known is Dead.

He brought Joy and Forgetfulness of Care to Millions. Many Men Learned to Laugh Because of Him. And Laughter is a Big Aid to Life.

Bert Williams was an Artist. He was a Great Actor. He might have been Known as a Great Tragedian had he Been Born White. But the World for a Long Time now Has Refused to Take Black Men Seriously. So the White World made Bert Williams the World's Greatest Comedian.

He Could say more with a Grunt than Most Men Can in a Monologue. His Gestures were Sentences and his Words Complete Stories.

Fortunately his Genius is Preserved to the World on Phonograph Records. He was under contract, made several years ago, to a White Company.

Had He Lived out this Contract He would have become, as he had promised, an Exclusive Black Swan Artist.

In the Early Months of this Undertaking, when Every Dollar Counted Double, He put Thousands of Dollars into the Making of Black Swan Records. He gave his Encouragement, his Advice, his Help, his Love to us. He Lightened our Burdens. He Assured us of Success.

Bert Williams is Dead. But the Joy that He Gave to the World will Live Forever and Multiply.

PACE PHONOGRAPH CORPORATION
Makers of
BLACK SWAN RECORDS
2289 Seventh Avenue, New York, N. Y.

Mention THE CRISIS.

Figure 1.3. *The Crisis*, May 1922, p. 284. The Modernist Journals Project. Brown and Tulsa Universities. www.modjourn.org

Figure 1.4. *The Crisis*, May 1922, back cover. The Modernist Journals Project. Brown and Tulsa Universities. www.modjourn.org

THE RENAISSANCE HAPPENED   35

eclectic but moderate overall."[45] By 1928, the magazine had gone under. A brief reading of the September 1926 issue's periodical codes demonstrates a structurally similar sense of mixed reception texts, as above, though here with a somewhat different route to that destination in terms of both textual and advertising contents and the relationships between them.

Subtitled "World's Greatest Negro Monthly" and retailing for 15 cents per copy or $1.75 per year, *The Messenger* of the mid-1920s typically featured a cover image of a woman's face or upper body (hair inevitably straightened), but the issue in question departs from that practice, with an overtly political illustration titled "Dawn of a New Day," in which a man and woman are both engaged in using sledgehammers to smash a large chain draped across a stone slab.[46] The issue's contents are a striking mix of literature, literary criticism, and union politics. In the first category, we find the opening installment of Hurston's "The Eatonville Anthology," Georgia Douglas Johnson's "Three Poems," and "A Group of Poems," including Langston Hughes's "Formula" and two other poems by Hughes, "Autumn Note" and "For Dead Mimes," published under the pseudonyms J. Crutchfield Thompson and Earl Dane.[47] Criticism here includes an essay on Coleridge, Wallace Thurman's review of Carl Van Vechten's *Nigger Heaven*, as well as George S. Schuyler's regular satirical column, "Snails and Darts," J.A. Rogers's cultural column "The Critic," and Theophilus Lewis's theater column. Political and union coverage begins with an open letter from the magazine's business manager, Roy Lancaster, at the front of the issue, with a later article from union president and *Messenger* editor A. Philip Randolph on the Brotherhood's one-year anniversary, an "exposé" of the Pullman Porters Benefits Association, which had been established by the Pullman company in 1921, and two closing pieces on the recent history of the Brotherhood and its incipient future. Finally, a brief essay on African American life in Arizona and New Mexico, "The Land of Esperanza" by Anita Scott Coleman, comes between Rogers's column and the three Hughes poems, and stands somewhat apart from the remainder of the issue's contents.[48] The issue's advertisements display a similar mixture, comprising both those related to the pullman porters' association and those focused on literature and education, with one for Howard University as "The Capstone of Negro Education" at the bottom of a back page, with, strikingly, adjacent smaller promotions in the page's

36   JOHN K. YOUNG

top half for Van Vechten's novel and the upcoming inaugural issue of *Fire* (without the exclamation marks), to "be issued around September 25," in addition to a standing ad for *Modern Quarterly* positioned next to the table of contents.

From an editorial perspective premised on "author-centricity," in Gabler's terms, Hurston's stories, Hughes's poems, and Thurman's review would presumably be the most interesting and significant texts included in this issue, while an editorial approach more grounded in the materiality of documents, the course which Gabler pursues, would (or at least should) emphasize the entirety of the magazine's contents in relation to the texts that stand out from a contemporary perspective.[49] An edition of *The Messenger* would thus allow readers (or users, in the case of a digital edition) to explore more fully the historical circumstances in which the magazine interacted with its original readers; while an edition of a single author's texts might well gesture toward that kind of historicist horizon, an edition oriented around the magazine itself would go much further in allowing its audience to reconstruct this important historical register on its own terms.

To be sure, this issue of *The Messenger* also offers much in the way of "author-centric" editorial pursuits. As Hurston biographer Robert E. Hemenway points out, there are kernels in several of the folk tales and vignettes collected in "The Eatonville Anthology" (two more installments appeared in the October and November issues of *The Messenger*) that resurface in her later work, including *Dust Tracks on a Road*, *Mules and Men*, *Seraph on the Sewanee*, and *Their Eyes Were Watching God*.[50] Hughes's poems would contribute to a completist sense of his career, including those published under other names, as Arnold Rampersad notes in his edition of the *Collected Poems*. Thurman's review, finally, would hold interest for reception studies of Van Vechten's novel, accounts of Thurman's career as an editor and critic in relation to his work as a novelist, and broader studies of debates from the period about the relationship between competing racialized views of aesthetics.[51] Like Toomer, upon the appearance of "Song of the Son" in *The Crisis*, Hurston was a relatively unknown new writer when *The Messenger* brought her Eatonville tales into print, while Hughes was, of course, a much more established figure, and Thurman would have been familiar to many readers of the magazine,

THE RENAISSANCE HAPPENED 37

where he regularly appeared as a reviewer. In the issues surrounding his review of Van Vechten, for instance, Thurman had written about *Black Harvest*, a story about a mixed-race Senegalese soldier by the popular Australian novelist I.A.R. Wylie; Walter White's *Flight*; W.C. Handy's collection *Blues: An Anthology*; the Irish writer George Moore's version of *Heloise and Abelard*; a portrait of rural Tennessee life, *Teeftallow* by Thomas Sigismund Stribling (who would win the Pulitzer Prize in 1933); and the lone issue of *Fire!!*, while also writing for "mainstream" journals like *The New Republic*, *The Bookman*, and *The Independent*.

But to return to Hurston's fiction, Hughes's poems, and Thurman's review (or any other single literary text in *The Messenger*) through a kind of editorial and interpretive silo would also mean reading those sections of the magazine apart from their political and economic contents, which equally shape *The Messenger* as a work. While *The Messenger* represents an important strand of Black aesthetics in the modern period, typically set apart from the views espoused in *The Crisis* and *Opportunity*, it is equally significant in a history of Black political activism, both before and after its iteration as the organ of the Brotherhood of Sleeping Car Porters. The most significant figures in this history of the magazine would not be Schuyler, Lewis, Rogers, or Thurman, but Randolph, Chandler Owen, and Frank Crosswaith, all union organizers and frequent contributors to the social activist movements of the 1920s and 1930s. While *The Messenger* was to the left, politically, of *The Crisis* in the late 1910s and early 1920s, by the middle of the decade the magazine's political orientation "mellowed into a more casual, less radical form of democratic socialism," as "Owen and Randolph discovered that theoretical dialectics did not sell magazines as well as simple platitudes," in the estimation of media historian Richard Digby-Junger.[52] This shift is reflected in the magazine's advertisements as well, which became increasingly friendly to capitalist ventures, even while the majority of ads came from labor unions.[53] Editorial representations of *The Messenger* or any magazine might well, then, need to develop ideas of editorial intention, in ways that would potentially both complement and sometimes compete with the intentionality ascribed to individual authors within one or more issues of the magazine.[54]

The magazine's political stance toward labor activism and civil rights similarly shifts during this decade, following the editors' opposition to the political leanings of both Du Bois and Marcus Garvey. As Cornelius L. Bynum notes, Randolph and Crosswaith gradually articulated a position emphasizing racial consciousness in class terms more strongly than Du Bois or Locke, while also challenging capitalism on the basis of an "egalitarian rationale," yielding "an independent strain of black radicalism in the war years that was not intellectually beholden to whites."[55] Thus, Randolph argued, as in his 1919 *Messenger* article "A New Negro—A New World," for interracial collaboration by political radicals in the service of both racial and class justice, with this "dual awareness of race and class to emphasize a vision of social justice rooted in the shared humanity of all races of people" continuing through the 1920s.[56] This political program aligns largely with the magazine's aesthetic outlook, which, as Hutchinson and others have noted, typically insists on a greater degree of inherent racial equality, and thus a decreased focus on the particularities of "Black" aesthetics, than the ideas advanced in *The Crisis*, *Opportunity*, or elsewhere. Thurman's praise for Van Vechten's novel, though somewhat muted, proceeds from this premise, finding that the white novelist has "beat the Negro litterateurs to a vibrant source pot of literary material which they for the most part have glossed over," and thus "laid himself liable to being referred to, in the provinces, as another Negro writer."[57] Hurston's stories, similarly, are as much about class as about race, but these texts take on at least a potentially different valence when read as subsumed under the magazine's political scope, or within its cautious embrace of capitalism and the role of union labor therein, rather than as part of *The Messenger's* aesthetic interests per se.

The conceptual editorial challenge for an edition of *The Messenger* (as for any edition of any magazine) would thus be how to represent the different possible audiences interacting with the magazine, both as a material object and as a work (in terms of an individual issue and/ or in relation to a broader conception of the work as manifested across multiple issues). The latter sense of a magazine as a work extends as well to Matthew Philpotts's sense of periodical "texture," a term for measuring formal and thematic patterns, comparatively across different magazines but also temporally, within the span of a particular title. Philpotts's Periodical Mapping Application (P-MApp) visualizes these kinds of textural patterns and could form a useful part of an editorial apparatus seeking to reconstruct the multiple kinds of audiences encountering a particular periodical, both on its own and in conjunction with other magazines of the period.[58]

This problem presents different implications in imagining an edition of the *American Mercury* issue containing Johnson's "Dilemma of the Negro Author" (or an edition of the magazine at a larger scale), in order to enable readings of the essay on its own terms but also within the circumstances of its initial publication, and there for multiple possible audiences (including those readers who would ignore the piece altogether). This would be both a question for the editorial apparatus, in order to account for the variety of intersecting historical contexts informing various possible reconstructions of the magazine texts, and for the material presentation of the edition itself, whether in print or digital form (or even as part of a hybrid edition).[59] This example serves, I hope, to demonstrate the ways in which a magazine like *American Mercury*, while not ordinarily understood as a part of or contributing to the Harlem Renaissance, might well be read in those terms, something an edition of the magazine could bring into sharper focus. While Johnson's essay constitutes the only author and text typically associated with the Harlem Renaissance to appear in the December 1928 issue, the magazine as a whole in this period was importantly connected to that movement, or at least to the political and aesthetic debates emanating from it. Editor H.L. Mencken was fiercely committed to exposing the stupidity and venality of anti-Black racism. George Schuyler was one of the *American Mercury*'s most frequent contributors during the Harlem Renaissance period, and the magazine also published important work by Countee Cullen, Du Bois, and Hughes, among others.[60] As Hutchinson points out, the magazine's audience in the 1920s and early 1930s surely comprised both white and Black readers, not as distinct groups but as mutually aware ones, offering "the beginnings of a 'transracial' yet 'national' discursive formation."[61] Given this background, we might profitably think of *American Mercury* and others like it not as "white" or "mainstream" magazines tangentially connected to the Harlem Renaissance but as themselves engaged in that movement, even if not at its center.

Such a redirection would entail a move away from the usual way of reading "Dilemma of the Negro Author" as a periodical text—that is, as an

40   JOHN K. YOUNG

entry within the wider field constituted by the magazine in the late 1920s. Instead, we might ask how the magazine's other contents, those with no apparent connection to the Harlem Renaissance, might be thought of as peripheral figures within that conceptual orbit. As Faye Hammill and Karen Leick demonstrate, Mencken and his editors aimed the magazine at what they "imagined as an educated audience, open to new ideas, aligned with a metropolitan perspective, and prepared to pay the relatively high price of 50¢."[62] Such a readership would certainly overlap with the demographic targets of Alfred and Blanche Knopf, Boni & Liveright, and B.W. Huebsch in their publishing of various important Harlem Renaissance books, as well as, to varying degrees, the readers constructed by *The Crisis* and other magazines of the movement. From this kind of perspective, we might see pieces like Schuyler's "Our White Folks" (December 1927) and "Keeping the Negro in His Place" (August 1929); Johnson's "A Negro Looks at Politics" (September 1929); Eugene Gordon's "The Negro's Inhibitions" (February 1928); an anonymous review of Nella Larsen's *Quicksand* (April 1928); and ads for "Harper's Books of the Month," including Cullen's *The Ballad of the Brown Girl* alongside several titles by white writers (August 1928) and for Claude McKay's *Home to Harlem* (August 1928), alongside such contributions as John McClure's "The Domination of Literature" (July 1925), Waldo Frank's "Mid-America Revisited" (July 1926), and Jim Tully's story "Jungle Justice" (April 1928) as part of a larger fabric of writers and texts variously committed to anti-racist agendas—not to mention the frequent skewering of the Klan and other racist agents in the magazine's "Americana" column, which carefully curated short news segments from around the country. Of course, such a view of *American Mercury* would necessarily overlook the magazine's other abiding topics, including acerbic criticisms of "organized religion, Coolidge Prosperity, Prohibition ... false assumptions, and sentimentality," but that would be the case for any historical or critical perspective emphasizing a particular aspect of a work, or arguing implicitly for that emphasis as the groundwork for an edition.[63]

This kind of editorial and conceptual reorientation leads me to my final example, the place of Wright's "The Man Who Lived Underground" in *Accent*, a literary journal launched in 1940 by University of Illinois professor J. Kerker Quinn.[64] *Accent* featured only advertising focused on other literary and artistic journals and publishers or bookstores, such as *Poetry*, *Chimera*, *View* (an arts magazine based in New York), *Kenyon Review*, *The Explicator*, *Sewanee Review*, New Directions, Random House, Charles Scribner's Sons, J.B. Lippincott, Harcourt Brace, Reynal & Hitchcock, Gotham Book Mart, and local book retailers in Urbana–Champaign. In addition, the magazine frequently ran ads for new books recently published, such as the *New Poems* anthology (offered for a special combination price of $3.00 with a one-year subscription to *Accent*), Sterling Brown's collection *The Negro Caravan*, Lilian Smith's *Strange Fruit* (a bestseller from a white novelist on interracial romance), H.R. Hays's *Lie Down in Darkness* ("A psychological novel of terrifying suspense"), William Carlos Williams's *The Wedge* and Robert Lowell's *Land of Unlikeness* (offered together from the Cummington Press), Robert Frost's *A Masque of Reason*, as well as titles by Marguerite Young, Karl Shapiro, and even a brief ad from Henry Miller promoting his water colors: "If you know anyone who would like to own one of my water colors, please refer him to me at the address below." The quarterly sold for $1.00 for a year or $1.75 for two years (the latter price at $2.00 outside the United States), with each issue's front and back cover printed in a solid color. In the mid-1940s alone, Quinn published a wide array of modernist and late modernist novelists, poets, and critics. That list includes: Eric Bentley, R.P. Blackmur, Bertolt Brecht, John Malcolm Brinnin, Cleanth Brooks, Kenneth Burke, E.E. Cummings, Alfred Kreymborg, Mina Loy, Henry Miller, Flannery O'Connor, Katherine Anne Porter, Rainer Maria Rilke, Muriel Rukeyser, Wallace Stevens, Genevieve Taggard, Robert Penn Warren, Richard Wilbur, Oscar Williams, and Marguerite Young, in addition to many other figures who have lapsed into obscurity.

Much recent scholarship on the Harlem Renaissance has pushed the field's chronological and geographical boundaries. As Adam McKible and Suzanne Churchill note in their introduction to a 2013 special issue of *Modernism/modernity* on the Harlem Renaissance and the new modernist studies (though several contributors there question the efficacy of the term "Harlem Renaissance," doubts I largely share), "The constellation of cultural activities—artistic, musical, theatrical, political, and sociological—not only began much earlier but also extended well beyond the decade 'when Harlem was in vogue,'" with a "subsequent, continuous

42   JOHN K. YOUNG

contribution to American and global literatures."[65] But such expansions of the field's scope might not make room for a small college literary magazine, even one attracting as many major figures as *Accent*. However, that is nevertheless where we find two brief excerpts from Wright's novella, more substantial portions of which appeared in Edwin Seaver's collection *Cross Section* in 1944, after the manuscript had been rejected by Wright's publisher, Harper & Brothers.[66] The spring 1942 *Accent* locates the excerpts from Wright's fiction, designated as "Two Excerpts from a Novel," between a Kenneth Burke essay, "Motives and Motifs in the Poetry of Marianne Moore," and a poem by Jackson Mac Low, "The Odyssey of Despair," which is run in on the bottom of the page below the conclusion of Wright's story, facing the opening page of a Delmore Schwartz essay on Edmund Wilson. The issue opens with Katherine Anne Porter's "Affectation of Praehiminincies," an excerpt from her (ultimately unfinished) biography of Cotton Mather, and concludes with reviews of new books by Thomas Wolfe (*The Hills Beyond*), Irwin Shaw (*Welcome to the City*), Eudora Welty (*A Curtain of Green*), Harry Levin (*James Joyce*), and Allen Tate (*The Language of Poetry*), among others. The list of contributors, on the verso page facing Porter's essay, notes: "RICHARD WRIGHT'S highly successful novel, *Native Son*, has been followed by an enlarged edition of his earlier story collection, *Uncle Tom's Children*, as well as by his ambitious narrative of the Southern Negro, *12 Million Black Voices*." At this stage of his career, with the considerable success of *Native Son* established, Wright was one of the best-known authors in this issue, along with Blackmur, Burke, and Porter. The contributors' notes list Burke's "reputation as one of America's most important students of literature and society," as well as Porter's being "widely known" for her first two books (*Pale Horse, Pale Rider* appeared in 1939). Mac Low, meanwhile, was an undergraduate at the University of Chicago at this point, and Schwartz was in the midst of a teaching fellowship at Harvard (*In Dreams Begin Responsibilities* was published in 1938).

A scholarly edition of "The Man Who Lived Underground" would, of course, compare these two published versions with the much longer manuscript in Wright's papers at the Beinecke Library.[67] Such an edition, while no doubt a valuable contribution to Wright scholarship, African American studies, and textual scholarship, would be unlikely to capture the richness and complexity of the story's original publications, both in *Accent* and in Seaver's collection,[68] where it was joined by Ellison's "Flying Home" and three Hughes poems, along with writings from Shirley Jackson, Norman Mailer, Stanley Edgar Hyman, Norman Macleod, and Arthur Miller, among a large number of more obscure figures. Imagining an edition of *Accent*, either the spring 1942 issue on its own or a larger run of the magazine, would yield an editorial argument for adjusting still largely received notions of African American modernism in relation to the historical and geographical boundaries of the "Harlem Renaissance," especially if we were to exchange that rubric for an alternative like "New Negro movement," as Barbara Foley proposes.[69] This context would entail reading the excerpts from Wright's fiction in the context of a much more broadly modernist periodical environment, even a nascent postmodernist impulse in such entries as Mac Low's poem. But a full rendering of the magazine *as* a magazine, both interpretively and editorially, would also reverse this cultural flow and perhaps even dissipate it altogether; not only would such an orientation make possible hitherto unthought connections among Wright and Porter or Burke or Mac Low or Schwartz (not to mention the other authors circulating in other issues during this period), but would also redirect our perceptions of those texts and works in dialogue with Wright's, as part of a larger constellation of texts making up *Accent* as a work.

Returning to the broad questions I posed toward the beginning of this essay, I will conclude by emphasizing the inherent sociality of the magazine, both as a form and as a site of textual production. If we think of a magazine as a node in a cultural network, through which various agents and objects are passing and encountering each other, including texts, images, and advertisements, among other entities, an edition of a magazine should reflect its deeply social nature. This goal would entail an editorial rendering of the entirety of the magazine, of course, very much including the ads that Robert Scholes and Clifford Wulfman have famously called the "hole in the archive" of modernist magazines.[70] A magazine edition might also provide readers or users with access to drafts and alternative versions of the texts published periodically, as well as annotations filling in the historical background of the magazine's production, an area that obviously might be construed fairly narrowly or quite widely. In the

44 JOHN K. YOUNG

case of African American literary history in particular, editions of magazines and newspapers would offer a unique lens into the extent to which Black writers, artists, editors, and publishers were acting with and against a wide variety of agents connected directly or indirectly to the field that is still often cordoned off as a movement produced and consumed only by African Americans. Such an approach could, I believe, contribute to the ongoing revisions to histories of (African) American modernism.

CHAPTER TWO

The Pawn's Gambit

Black Writers, White Patrons, and the Harlem Renaissance

Adam Nemmers

The system of artistic patronage is so ancient that Cicero believed "it must have been brought to Rome by Romulus himself."[1] During an era in which most of the population was impoverished and illiterate, artists depended upon direct funding from wealthy families (like the Roman *clientelae*), the Church, and local royalty to finance stupendous works that took years to produce. Though original to medieval Italy, in time patronage became the predominant system of artistic production around the world, spanning Africa and Asia, art, architecture, and literature. During the European Renaissance, patrons and artists began competing within a loose system of alliances whereby luminaries including Michelangelo, Leonardo, and Galileo, and later Shakespeare, Mozart, and Beethoven negotiated long-term contracts to devote themselves exclusively to a patron's request. As Jeffrey C. Stewart outlines, patrons could be quite demanding, dictating the composition, quality, and timeline of work to be performed.[2] After a long growth arc, patronage underwent a swift decline with the emergence of capitalism and market-based systems of publishing, which required an infrastructure of agents, editors, and booksellers to bring writers' works before the remunerative public. Patronage of the Italian sort is rarely practiced today.

45

46   ADAM NEMMERS

During the Harlem Renaissance, however, patronage staged a short-lived revival, when a massive wealth disparity prompted many African American writers to engage white benefactors to support their work. This outreach coincided with a decade-long fad wherein whites attended Negro plays and concerts, frequented Negro nightclubs, and read works of Negro literature—in other words, as Langston Hughes put it, an era "when the Negro was in vogue."[3] He and his compatriots entered into relationships—whether informal, intimate, or contractual—that, as in the past, occasionally lent patrons considerable influence on the subject, composition, and delivery of an agreed-upon work.[4] In this way patrons and benefactors served as unofficial editors and intermediaries between writers and presses, as well as between writers and their largely white readership. So profound was patrons' influence that, as Ralph D. Story declares, "it is impossible to say that the art produced by black Americans between 1920 and 1932 would have ever made it into print without the support of rich whites."[5] In sum, as patronage was such an essential component of literary production during this period, analysis of its editorial impact on the works produced thereof enlightens our understanding of the movement itself.

Scholarly discussions of Harlem Renaissance patronage have often characterized patron–writer arrangements as coercive and manipulative, as just another "one-sided and unequal relationship between blacks and whites [that] has obliged blacks to serve as the eternal footmen holding the identity coats for whites."[6] David Levering Lewis details Aaron Douglas's "being ordered down from his scaffolding after his repeated refusals to appear at 399 Park Avenue" and Alain Locke's condition of "bondage," in which he was subject to "patronizing lectures and occasional acts of rank tyranny."[7] Rodney Trapp holds that "the artists of the Harlem Renaissance found themselves indentured to this atmosphere of patronage"[8] while Hughes's biographer, Arnold Rampersad, devotes much of *The Life of Langston Hughes* to discussion of the writer's "pathetic enslavement by Mrs. [Charlotte Osgood] Mason."[9] Stewart uses the same metaphor several times in his volume, referring to Hughes, after his departure from Mason, as "a slave freed from the plantation."[10]

Critics also promote the general narrative that the strings attached to patron arrangements corrupted writers' work. Story writes that once writers and painters "agreed to a patron-artist relationship—especially a financial one—it seemed to obligate them to produce a certain kind of product that would meet the patron(s)' approval."[11] Sharon L. Jones asserts that "Mason controlled Hurston financially through the stipends she allocated the author and artistically by designating when, where, and how Hurston would disseminate her findings."[12] "The problem with Mrs. Mason, as perhaps with all patrons," Robert E. Hemenway sweepingly proclaims, "was that she expected some return on her money,"[13] and Robert C. Hart stipulates that, in general, "the white patronage situation meant that black writing suffered distortions to meet white expectations."[14] In all, especially when using terms like "bondage," "indentured," "enslavement," and "slave," existing scholarship on these relationships characterizes literary patronage as an echo of (though assuredly not equivalent to) the antebellum system of chattel slavery. In this metaphor, Black writers are merely field hands laboring to produce literature to the satisfaction of their white owners and overseers, who in turn play the role of puppet-master or ventriloquist, pulling strings behind the scenes to promulgate their own views. White message, Black envelope: an inversion of John Sekora's famous formulation.[15]

This portrayal is surely worth revisiting. Indeed, the last thirty years have brought about a sea change in our understanding of the American system of chattel slavery itself, which is much more complicated than the binary which holds enslaved persons as either Uncle Toms or Nat Turners. As Stephanie M. H. Camp explains:

> Some scholars of slavery now consciously explore the contradictory and paradoxical qualities in bondpeople's lives: for instance, the ways in which they were both agents and subjects, persons and property, and people who resisted and who accommodated— sometimes in one and the same act. Enslaved people were many things at once, and they were many things at different moments and in various places.[16]

In this chapter I wish to extend this sort of revisionist analysis to the study of Harlem Renaissance patronage—claiming, as Camp does, that Black writers might be both agents and subjects, resistors and

48   ADAM NEMMERS

accommodationists, contradictory and paradoxical. In other words, I assert, African American writers were not simply the Black pawns in a white man's game but instead employed a host of clever strategies of resistance and subversion: employing subterfuge and satire, inserting cryptic allusions and in-group jokes, and even withholding publication until and unless they could deliver the work they wanted. Furthermore, in navigating the complex system of patronage African American writers utilized Signifying and other "trickster" tactics to appease and manipulate their patrons while disguising their true meaning and beliefs—in many cases, it was the writers pulling the strings and not the other way around. Revisiting these patron/writer relationships offers an important corrective to the essentially negative view of patronage and white influence, in the process shedding new light on the literature of Black writers whose work had been assumed corrupted by the influence of white patrons.

The "Negrotarians"

Despite the outsized reputation earned by a notorious few, the majority of white patrons were unobtrusive benefactors or institutions, and many were silent or even anonymous to the Black writers they supported. As Cary D. Wintz details, "White patronage of the Black arts took several forms, but generally it consisted of providing money for prizes, grants, scholarships, and the support of individual writers."[17] Within the first flowering of the New Negro Renaissance a number of financial wellsprings had opened: The Spingarn Medal, the Van Vechten Award, the W.E.B. Du Bois Literary Prize, the Guggenheim Foundation, the Julius Rosenwald Fund, the Garland Fund, and a thousand-dollar award for the "best novel on 'Negro life' written by a Black author," sponsored by the publishing firm Boni & Liveright.[18] Most prizes were offered without conditions and, like those of the William E. Harmon Foundation, simply intended to recognize "distinguished achievement among Negroes in creative endeavors."[19] Langston Hughes, for example, received several of these awards in concurrence, garnering not only a significant side income but also the sort of public fame that could only be granted by wide-scale institutional patronage.

BLACK WRITERS, WHITE PATRONS   49

Many Black writers also were sponsored through less official arrangements. For instance, after reading Nella Larsen's *Passing* manuscript "in one sitting," Carl Van Vechten "marched straight to the Knopf office" and demanded they publish it, even promoting the book "relentlessly" at the Knopfs' anniversary party.[20] In December 1923, Countee Cullen was sponsored directly by a less powerful patron when he received

> a five-dollar check from an unknown benefactor who identified himself as Jedidiah Tingle. Tingle, the pseudonym for an unidentified person who sent contributions to individuals for something they said, did, or wrote, mailed Cullen the check because he was impressed with a poem and story about the young poet he had read in the *New York Times*.[21]

Even more incredibly, some writers apparently had earned a global reputation among the unlikeliest of sources, as in 1931 when Englishman Thomas Clarke died and left £40,000 to Locke, whom he had never met.[22] While such instances of unexpected patronage were rare, they speak to the genuine admiration many white benefactors had for New Negro writing, which they wished to support with no strings attached. In most instances, Wintz summarizes, "black writers received these benefits while surrendering little of their artistic freedom."[23]

Though financial assistance from various awards, grants, fellowships, and gifts was a welcome bonus, many Black writers sought a steadier stream of income, which necessitated selecting an individual patron and entering into a more personal arrangement. Thankfully, there existed a pool of what Zora Neale Hurston termed "Negrotarians"—wealthy white people who specialized in African American uplift. As David Levering Lewis explains, "The motives of WASP philanthropy were an amalgam of inherited abolitionism, Christian charity and guilt, social manipulation, political eccentricity, and a certain amount of persiflage."[24] Whatever the reason for patrons to loosen their purse strings, Black writers were eager to take advantage, and employed ad hoc matchmaking services akin to an adolescent dating game. Arna Bontemps writes that he spent considerable time arranging for the "'debut' of the younger Negro writers" in order to drum up a market of patronage for their work.[25] One such

50   ADAM NEMMERS

"coming out party," thrown by Charles S. Johnson in 1924, was attended by a who's who of Black Harlem literati, including Cullen, Locke, Walter White, Eric Walrond, Jessie Fauset, and Gwendolyn Bennett, as well as prominent white New York literary personages such as Carl Van Doren, Frederick Allen, Walter Bartlett, Devere Allen, Freda Kirchwey, Paul Kellogg, and Horace Liveright. Arriving auspiciously on the upswing of the Renaissance, the meeting was a resounding success: several writers obtained patrons who supported them with modest but steady stipends.[26] This common mode of patronage was a voluntary agreement between two parties—usually an older, established, white benefactor and a promising young Black writer—who entered into their relationship willingly and for mutual benefit.

To continue the metaphor, like all employment and romantic relationships some patron–writer arrangements were lasting partnerships and others had a limited shelf life. Hurston was peripatetic in her patronage, beginning under Johnson's wing, then proceeding to Annie Nathan Meyer, and finally working as the secretary, driver, and travelling companion of Fannie Hurst.[27] Yet Hurston eventually tired of Hurst and transferred her allegiance to Mason, for whom she wrote between 1928 and 1932. On the other hand, Aaron Douglas transitioned from the patronage of Mason to a Barnes Foundation fellowship,[28] and Langston Hughes similarly left Mason and took up with Noël Sullivan, in whose Carmel, California cottage he lived and wrote from 1933 to 1934.[29] Far from the established narrative of "tyranny," "obligation," and "enslavement," this freedom of movement reveals that Harlem Renaissance writers were not "bound" to a particular "owner," but instead shopped around when their current situation was not to their liking, or terminated the arrangement outright if they felt they were being exploited. Wintz, for instance, documents a prominent "misunderstanding" between Claude McKay and one of his benefactors, the shipping heiress Nancy Cunard.[30] As the story goes, Cunard, who fancied herself a muse, poet, and publisher, asked McKay to contribute a piece to her anthology of African American writing, *Negro*. But "when McKay finally sent his manuscript to Cunard and asked when he might anticipate payment ... Cunard responded that she had expected the contributors to write without compensation, out of a shared commitment to the project's goals."[31] McKay blanched at the expectation that he

BLACK WRITERS, WHITE PATRONS   51

provide uncompensated labor for the pet project of a millionaire, firing off a letter that proclaimed, "Writing is my means of livelihood. ... I have not the slightest wish now to appear in your anthology, and I hope you will respect that wish."[32] Cunard complied with his request, and McKay instead sought to place the piece where he might receive proper payment for it. The episode (among others) demonstrates that Black writers were not indentured to their patrons, but rather independent agents who valued their artistic integrity and the worth of their work.

Although many Black writers did rely upon patrons for financial support, the fact that many chose not to, or solicited patronage intermittently, or moved between patrons, or worked alongside patrons, speaks to the agency Black writers possessed. For example, though pursued with generous offers of monthly retainers, prominent Black artists including Paul Robeson, Roland Hayes, Jean Toomer, and Cullen "steadily resisted receiving any assistance from Mason" and opted instead to sponsor their own work.[33] At other times, writers collaborated directly with patrons as fellow artists and equals. Meyer courted Hurston with promises of "full acknowledgement" as well as "one half (½) of all royalty" if Hurston would undertake novelization of Meyer's controversial drama *Black Souls*.[34] In advance, Meyer "sent Hurston money, recommended [Hurston] to a friend who was a *Vanity Fair* editor," and "used her pull to persuade Barnard to accept Hurston on a scholarship."[35] The women even began to collaborate on the project, swapping drafts and working together on plotting and characterization. But after Hurston expressed doubt about the efficacy of an interracial love scene, Meyer changed course and produced the play herself: the sort of falling out common to artistic partnerships between peers, as later occurred between Hurston and Hughes.

Far from a system of "control" or "bondage," patronage provided African Americans an opportunity to capitalize upon white fascination with "Negro writing" while it lasted. Locke, Lewis reports, "walked a tightrope between obsequious accommodation to [Mason] ... and nervous fidelity to his own beliefs, dissembling masterfully and taking the cash."[36] He and Hughes conspired to exploit their patron's largesse through feigned obeisance, as evinced by their shared saying "Masque in one pocket and thick white envelope in another."[37] Warrington Hudlin notes that Hurston, for her part, "suspected the interest was a fad and decided to play it for

52 ADAM NEMMERS

whatever it was worth" and other "hustlers in the group" similarly "made some extra money."[38] In this light, it is hard not to see patrons as "marks," "whales," or "touches" being pursued by Black writers, rather than the common capitalist model whereby an employer profits from a contracted employee, much less the master/slave dynamic suggested by some critics. Given the power and financial deficiencies they faced, operating within a system of entrenched income inequality and white supremacy, Black writers were savvy to engage with patrons, produce the work both parties desired, and accrue their rightful compensation accordingly.

Writing for Godmother

By far the most infamous Harlem Renaissance patron was Charlotte Osgood Mason, the wealthy white widow who came to have a "collection" of writers and artists including Hughes, Locke, Douglas, Hurston, McKay, and Louise Thompson. Born Charlotte Louise Van der Veer Quick in 1854, Mason was a scion whose fortune almost doubled through marriage to a physician and parapsychologist nearly twenty-five years her senior. When he passed away in 1903, she was left with millions of dollars to invest in causes dear to her heart—first the study of Native Americans in the Great Plains and Southwest, then the art and literature of promising "Negro" writers in Harlem. By and large, critical opprobrium directed at Mason is twofold: the first strand condemns what Melinda Booth calls "her essentialist fascination with a primitiveness unspoiled by Western society."[39] The second criticism is lodged against the "heavy-handed" manner in which she "controlled" her collection of writers. Trapp writes that "Mason's style of patronage consisted of dominance and control. She required strict obedience and was quick to cut off those who did not obey her wishes."[40] Bruce Kellner similarly argues that Mason "got [her way] most of the time, because the purse strings she controlled were like tentacles."[41] And Steve Watson asserts that "her patronage exacted the more debilitating tolls of dependency, control, and infantilization."[42] To some extent all of these charges are true. Mason did have an obsession with so-called "primitive peoples," whom she felt had a more direct relationship with the natural and unspoiled world (what we would now term essentializing), though to be fair these views were somewhat common during the era and embraced by Locke and other African Americans.[43] On the count of her domineering nature, Mason did request that her writers share intimate details of their lives with her, and also made a sustained effort to influence their artistic output. In caricature, however, Mason has earned a reputation as the villain of the Harlem Renaissance, a conniving white witch who forced her Black writers to promulgate her essentialist racial views through their writing.

A survey of Mason's patronage reveals a fascinating and more complicated creature than caricature would suggest. To begin, the nature of Mason's arrangements with her writers was much closer to personal relationship than employment—perhaps to their eventual detriment. As the intimate nomenclature suggests, "Godmother" wished her "Godchildren" to act as such, with all the trappings of love, responsibility, and gratitude owed to the one who provided for them. Her interventions into their lives were largely conducted on an informal basis, as a kind of maternalism predicated upon good will and mutual affection. The basic arrangement was simple: as long as they would share themselves and comply with her wishes, Mason agreed to provide generous monthly stipends so that her writers could focus exclusively on their work. On occasion it went beyond this; much notoriety has been given to Hurston's "signed, witnessed, and notarized" contract that "spelled out exactly what [Mason] was offering and what she expected to receive."[44] On its face, the notion that a wealthy white woman might exercise ownership over a writer's life and material certainly seems troubling. And yet, the fact that a Black writer might enter into a personal agreement with her employer demonstrates that the power dynamics at play were more balanced than supposed: comparing their situations to enslavement, even metaphorically, is mistaken. Put another way, patron/writer contractual agreements established the two parties on equitable legal ground and differ little from the contract a present-day author might sign with a press stipulating terms and payment for producing a work of literature.

Whether informal or on paper, these arrangements were resisted and subverted in a number of ways, proving that Black writers did not feel unduly "bound" to any contract or patron. For example, in an effort to keep her affairs private Mason asked her stable of writers and artists to refer to her by the pseudonym "Godmother" when speaking in public.

54   ADAM NEMMERS

Where others held their tongues, even after her death, Hurston named her in correspondence and, more brazenly, in her autobiography, *Dust Tracks on a Road*. Yet even those who followed the letter of her request violated its spirit by portraying her in fiction, including appearances as Agatha Cramp in Rudolph Fisher's *Walls of Jericho* and Dora Ellsworth in Langston Hughes's *The Ways of White Folks*.[45] These renderings were not always pleasant or positive, and they offered other patrons and the public a glimpse into Mason's reclusive persona without technically violating the terms of their arrangement. Though a queen in her penthouse palace, outside the apartment she exercised little control over the lives of her godchildren, or for that matter their work.

In this vein, there is little evidence that Black writers compromised their artistic integrity in any meaningful way under Mason's thumb. Though her own views and preferences were clear and well known, and she occasionally offered editorial input on their works, the writers had final authority over the content they put to paper. Put another way, while she (and other patrons) might exercise influence over the format, medium, and venue in which writers' words were produced, they could not force those words onto the page. In the spring of 1929, for instance, Hughes composed a preamble to an assigned study of Lincoln University, where he was enrolled as an undergraduate, on the topic of student attitudes towards its current all-white faculty. As a brief foreword he appended a flowery paragraph with references to "harmony," "tribal lore," and the "earth" and "stars," and concluded, "The strength of the surest dream is the strength of the primitive world."[46] When he realized that it "was really Godmother's Credo," however, Hughes promptly excised the paragraph, demonstrating that he did not wish to parrot Mason's views or serve as her mouthpiece.[47] In fact, rather than submit to their directives, writers would often quit when patrons' demands became onerous, as when Hughes "terminated the 'godmother–protégé' relationship abruptly ... when she made it clear that she expected him to be guided in his writing by her philosophy."[48]

More often the writers were happy to accede when Mason's interest aligned with their own and departed from her when it did not. When Hurston discovered that both she and Mason had abiding interest in Negro folklore, they came to an agreement: Mason would provide Hurston

BLACK WRITERS, WHITE PATRONS 55

a monthly stipend and a vehicle for her work, while Hurston relinquished legal control over the material she gathered. Rather than working strictly for Mason, however, Hurston used her funding as a bulk research grant, traveling throughout the South and gathering folktales for her own purposes. Against Godmother's wishes, she also began collaborating with Hughes on a play entitled *Mule Bone*, based on one of the stories she had gathered and "dangerously close in focus to what Mason had specifically told [Hughes and Hurston] not to work on."[49] Mason flexed her contractual muscle in response, reminding her that she was barred from pursuing publication in that form. But Hughes had only received an admonition from Mason, not signed an agreement with her, and, realizing this, Hurston proposed to Hughes "that the whole be done in his name since she knew Mason would never allow her to do it herself."[50]

Mule Bone went belly-up in a famous contretemps too lengthy and lurid to explore here. Yet Mason's interference and Hughes's withdrawal did not prevent Hurston from disseminating the folk material she had uncovered. In this instance, she reasoned that though Mason might control the written word she produced for publication, the knowledge she gathered could not be another's property; in other words, no one, no matter how wealthy or powerful, could own a people's folklore. Per her contract she could not publish her findings in print, so she found a different outlet and produced a series of "concerts" in a theater tour that took her from New York to Chicago to Florida. Including folk songs, a Bahamian Fire Dance, and a performance by Hurston herself, plays such as *The Great Day*, *From Sun to Sun*, and *Singing Steel* offered the dramatization of a working day on a Florida railroad camp. Kaplan reports that *The Great Day*, in particular, "made ample use of the wealth of material on black spiritual practices—conjure especially—that [Hurston] had collected in the South from 1928 on, under Mason's contract. That was precisely the material Mason did not want used."[51] Even more brazenly, when Mason nevertheless authorized funding for the play, Hurston countermanded her direct stipulation that Locke write an explanatory preface and appear during an intermission to help "interpret" what was occurring onstage to the white audience. During the premiere, "in a surprise move, Hurston took the stage in the middle of the show" and "did her own explaining."[52] Afterward, though Mason considered the play a failure, Hurston excised Locke's preface and put *The*

56   ADAM NEMMERS

Great Day on tour, unmediated, for audiences throughout the South. As Wall details, "Hurston's goal in these productions was not simply to turn a profit ... [i]t was rather to offer her version of 'the real voice' of her people" in a "far more intimate way than academic publication allowed."[53] Hurston had cleverly devised a workaround to share her knowledge with her audience, just one of the methods by which Black writers produced their desired art in contradiction of patrons' wishes.

On a basic level, much of the communication between Mason and her "Godchildren" would have been conducted in the African American tradition of "Signifyin," a concept delineated by Henry Louis Gates, Jr. that can be traced back to the Yoruba trickster Esu Elegbara. Roger D. Abrahams writes that Signifying, in brief, "refers to the trickster's ability to talk with great innuendo, to carp, cajole, needle, and lie. It can mean in other instances the propensity to talk around a subject, never quite coming to the point ... [or] making fun of a person or situation."[54] In the United States, as Winifred Morgan observes, enslaved persons "needed to use all their skills at manipulation and chicanery while they appeared to act with decorum and apparent politeness toward those who might devour them."[55] William Faux wrote in 1819 that enslaved persons commonly used lyrics to Signify, "abounding either in praise or satire intended for kind and unkind masters."[56] And Wash Wilson, a previously enslaved man, reported: "When de niggers go round singin' 'Steal Away to Jesus,' dat mean dere gwine be a 'ligious meetin' dat night. Dat de *sig'fication* of a meetin.'"[57] Signifying spanned Emancipation and was widely known and practiced into the twentieth century, when prominent Black writers including Cullen, Hughes, and Hurston utilized Signifying in their own writing, featuring traditional African American tricksters and slippery storytellers.[58] As an African American and anthropologist of the Deep South, Hurston was particularly well versed in the practice and included a gloss in her *Mules and Men* explaining "that to signify is to 'show off'"[59]—a tactic she employed frequently in both her personal and professional lives.

Given this background, Black writers naturally employed Signifying in their correspondence and conversation with Mason and other patrons, as well as to triangulate with each other to maneuver around her.[60] Of course her Godchildren were careful to eschew criticism or ridicule of Mason directly tête-à-tête, but each also devised multiple rhetorical strategies to artfully manipulate the prideful woman. In one instance, when Mason fell ill, Locke composed a letter "ostensibly expressing concern for her health, but ending with the hope that in her current illness she had regained full control of her mind," a barb that "infuriated her."[61] Hurston would often mock Mason behind her back. According to Yuval Taylor, "Mason would send Zora exotic dresses to wear and Zora would call her to tell her how stunning they looked. After hanging up she would tell Louise [Thompson], laughingly, that she wouldn't dream of wearing such a thing."[62] And what are we to make of Hughes and his fawning correspondence with Mason? His letters to her offer extravagant, purple declarations of praise and sentiment: "I know that all you have ever given me came on the wings of the spirit. Only my hands have been clay—unworthy to receive the beauty—and I have not known how to keep the flight."[63] Hughes assuredly had genuine admiration and even love for Mason, but his abundance of sycophantic prose, in conjunction with his insubordinate actions behind her back, suggests that he intermittently utilized Signifying in an attempt to placate, flatter, and cajole his Godmother, a tactic that he thought might keep him in her good graces and patronage.

Though perhaps the most compelling, Signifying was just one of the many methods used by Black writers engaged in complex and sophisticated patronage relationships. Their struggle over money and work included a host of strategies common to parties locked in negotiation: duplicity, obfuscation, language play, editorial tug-of-war, and other internecine maneuvers. This is to say that African American writers were not dupes, pawns, or marionettes controlled by Mason or anyone else. Rather they engaged in a series of relationships more akin to friendships, romances, or employment, and accordingly profited and were harmed on a case-by-case basis.

Barracoon: A Case Study

In order to chart the influence of patronage on a notable work of the Harlem Renaissance, I wish to trace Zora Neale Hurston's *Barracoon* all the way from its genesis in 1926 to its publication in 2018. *Barracoon* is the oral biography of Cudjoe Lewis (or Kossola), one of the last enslaved African Americans to have survived the Middle Passage, as told to

58   ADAM NEMMERS

Hurston in a series of interviews in his home north of Mobile, Alabama. Her mission had begun under the direction of the legendary anthropologist Franz Boas, who supervised her as a student at Barnard College, where she was not only the first Black woman to earn a degree but one of the first to study anthropology anywhere. Through Boas and Carter G. Woodson, Hurston received a fellowship for postgraduate fieldwork, funded jointly by the Association for the Study of Negro Life and History and the American Folklore Society. Deborah G. Plant explains that, as part of their arrangement, "Hurston was to collect black folk materials for Boas and scout around for undiscovered black folk artists" and eventually to publish her research in the *Journal of Negro History*.[64] Her tour of the Deep South brought her to Africatown, where she encountered Lewis, then in his late 80s.

Rebecca Panovka reports that, even with this considerable support, "Hurston's first stab at interviewing Lewis had not gone well. ... [S]he seems to have had so much trouble getting material from Lewis that she plagiarized much of her report on the encounter."[65] Indeed, the article Hurston published in 1927, "Cudjoe's Own Story of the Last African Slaver," borrowed heavily from Emma Langdon Roche's *Historic Sketches of the South* (1914), perhaps an indication of the immense pressure Hurston felt to satisfy her patrons, the list of whom was now growing. In December of that year Hurston had signed her formal contract with Mason and agreed to undertake another trip to the Deep South, gathering folklore from a number of previously un- or underexplored sources, including Lewis. As Frank Salamone notes, during the subsequent period Hurston was torn between patrons, striving to complete her dissertation under Boas while making progress on her research for Mason. In a May 1929 letter, for instance, Boas offered Hurston $150 to help "develop a test of music in which the special ability of the Negroes ... might play an important role";[66] at the same time, Mason was "cold toward Hurston's getting the PhD but will put up money for further research not leading to her degree."[67] To complicate things, Mason had a personal dislike for Boas, as she did for Van Vechten, and would not hear of a collaboration among all parties.

On the surface, Mason's steady stipend won out and, aided by Godmother's continued involvement, Hurston's prospects with Lewis improved as well. Whether from a desire to facilitate the project or sincere interest in Lewis's welfare, Mason provided him monthly stipends, and he in turn "would come to consider Mason a 'dear friend.'"[68] Mason supported Lewis and Hurston not only to ensure their continued production but also to withhold their contact from others. When word spread of Lewis's status as one of the last enslaved African Americans, his account became a hot commodity; indeed, Panovka reports, "Over a period of months, [Mason] and Locke conspired to prevent Paul Radin, a prominent anthropologist who had read Hurston's article, from interviewing Lewis," instituting a "plan to 'blocade [sic]'" and "seal" Lewis's lips by reminding him where "the money to buy his fruit and tobacco every month" came from.[69] Incredibly, Lewis had himself sold off portions of Hurston's manuscript to local newspapers, a betrayal that must have made Mason furious. Thereafter she increased her stipends, a maneuver that proved effectual, for he wrote an apologetic letter to her promising to comply henceforth. That Lewis would establish a close personal (if only epistolary) relationship with Mason testifies to Godmother's charm, intertwined with the potency of her pocketbook. Mason had funded the research, her hand had shepherded the project to fruition, and she eagerly looked forward to its publication.

But Mason was not in control of the situation. Though Hurston was serving as Mason's contracted proxy in the South, Hurston began to commandeer agency over her work and the information she had gathered. Sensing this, Mason appointed Locke to monitor Hurston's progress and ensure she would receive an appropriate return on her investment. But Hurston distrusted Locke and, Stewart writes, "began to put her findings before Hughes, who became her confidant and often the real middleman between Mason and her."[70] Hurston additionally squirreled away the best morsels and sources, as when she wrote Hughes, "I found another one of the original Africans, older than Cudjoe. ... She is most delightful, but no one will ever know about her but us."[71] This sort of conspiracy between Godchildren would surely have rankled Mason had she known about it, but their clandestine communication made enforcement of the contract impossible. At the same time, Hurston was scheming to use the material to complete her dissertation, regularly consulting with Boas on the anthropological angle and "promis[ing] to show him her material in secret" even though she "accepted the money on the condition that [she] should write

60   ADAM NEMMERS

no one."[72] Hurston may have traveled to the Deep South under the employ of Mason, but she worked there for her own purposes and planned to use what she found for her own benefit.

After nearly a year of firsthand research, Hurston emerged from the South with a wealth of material that could be formed into a manuscript, a process that Godmother sought to expedite. Yet the research was still in Hurston's hands and Hurston's name, and, despite their contract, Hurston controlled the production of that material. Hurston could not publish without Mason's approval, but neither could Mason publish without Hurston's initiative. The manuscript was eventually shopped around prominent houses in New York but repeatedly declined on account of Hurston's and Lewis's extensive use of dialect, which was unusual for the time and considered an impediment for public readership. Mason again employed Alain Locke to smooth things over, and he reported that an editor at Viking was still "particularly anxious to see her manuscript."[73] She summarily instructed Locke to send a copy directly to the editor, only to discover that Hurston had dispatched her personal literary agent to retrieve the manuscript before it could be evaluated. Mason assumed that Hurston had done so in order to make revisions for her next draft, and made a point to follow up repeatedly, writing to Locke, "Remember I would like to succeed in my ideal in this matter, depressed times or no."[74] But, as Hurston continued to delay, "Mason slowly came to the realization that Hurston had no intention of making the 'extensive revision' her agent had promised," partially due to intransigence and partially because "she was working on stories and theatrical projects instead."[75] The final word in the matter belonged to the editor at Viking, who told Locke that despite the patronage contract neither he nor Mason could publish against Hurston's wishes. Despite her prodigious funding and considerable effort over a number of years, Mason had not, in fact, gotten what she paid for.

Apparently, Hurston never revisited the manuscript, and it languished in storage until its critical recovery and 2018 publication by HarperCollins. According to Plant, the editor of that volume, other than minor edits in typography, "the text remains as Hurston left it,"[76] telling Lewis's story in his own dialect and ultimately according with Hurston's design. Curiously, the volume begins with a dedication from Hurston to "Charlotte Mason" that was not a part of the original typed manuscript, but may have been

BLACK WRITERS, WHITE PATRONS 61

developed in concordance: "My Godmother, and the one Mother of all the primitives, who with the Gods in Space is concerned about the hearts of the untaught."[77] Hurston's allusions to "primitives" and the "hearts of the untaught" carry tone of irony well in line with her other Signifying. Is Cudjoe Lewis a primitive? Is Hurston herself, or Mason's other Godchildren? What does it mean that Mason is their "Mother," or to compare her to the "Gods of Space"? Regardless of the undercurrent, Hurston's act of naming Mason countermands Godmother's express order of anonymity and serves as declaration that Hurston was unbound by the gag order Mason had insisted upon. And yet Hurston does express gratitude and pay Mason tribute and employs exactly the sort of mystical language with which Godmother would have been most pleased.

The ambivalence of Hurston's dedication must be tied to the complex and drawn-out relationship between the writer and her patron. Panovka documents that "After Mason had terminated their relationship, Hurston wrote to a friend: 'I have kicked loose from the Park Avenue dragon,' but later, in her memoir, fondly recalled their 'psychic bond.'"[78] Hurston surely could not have written *Barracoon* without Mason's extensive support, and yet she elected not to publish the book through her, even going so far as to shelve the volume without explanation, a decision that violated Godmother's direct wishes. Those in the know offer speculation that in this, as well as other instances, Hurston may have withheld publication for her individual benefit.[79] After all, material gathered on her research trip could eventually be incorporated into the theatrical show that she controlled and profited from, or, in disguise, as part of the plays and novels she eventually published. Even while the *Barracoon* manuscript languished, Hurston's star was rising, and during the 1930s she produced a number of works incorporating her research, including *Jonah's Gourd Vine* (1934), *Mules and Men* (1935), and her masterpiece *Their Eyes Were Watching God* (1938), for which she is now canonically famous.

In contrast, for all her wealth and power in her heyday, Mason did not even merit a printed *New York Times* obituary upon her 1946 death. Little, as well, is remembered of the men behind the Spingarn Medal, Barnes Fellowship, and Rosenwald Fund, and even the illustrious Carl Van Vechten is now best known for his photographs of others. And yet these patrons' influence lives on, for without such "Negrotarians" to provide steady stipends, fellowships, and cash prizes, many African American writers would have lacked the time and resources to produce their best work. Of course, Harlem Renaissance patronage was not an unmitigated good, either. Even if well-intentioned and characteristic of their era, patron–writer relationships were rife with "refined racism" and essentialism, paternalism and maternalism, and the concomitant abuses of power inherent to all employer/employee relationships. Writ large, however, the *Barracoon* affair reveals the complex web of interaction that undergirded production of a single Harlem Renaissance text and offers yet another example of how Black writers adroitly utilized the system of patronage for their own ends.

CHAPTER THREE

Clad in the Beautiful Dress One Expects

Editing and Curating the Harlem Renaissance Text

Ross K. Tangedal

A people may become great through many means, but there is only one measure by which its greatness is recognized and acknowledged. The final measure of the greatness of all peoples is the amount and standard of the literature and art they have produced.

James Weldon Johnson, preface to
The Book of American Negro Poetry (New York: Harcourt, Brace & Company, 1922), vii.

Upon the 1927 republication of James Weldon Johnson's *The Autobiography of an Ex-Colored Man*, the *New York Times* ran a review heralding the new version, carrying Johnson's name for the first time (the first edition having been published anonymously in 1912). In it, the reviewer adds that the book is now "clad in the beautiful dress one expects"[1] from powerful publisher Alfred A. Knopf, who published a number of African American texts throughout the early twentieth century.

63

A reader's expectations are heightened, generally, when a book is released by a major publisher. The cover needs to be polished, professional, and attractive. The blurbs on the back cover must come from major critics or writers of the moment. The novel, once released without an author's name printed on the cover, now has a name with its title. Knopf most famously published various works by Harlem laureate Langston Hughes, and the firm employed the innovative cover designer Aaron Douglas, whose sharp colors and vivid silhouettes helped define a generation of book designers. Alfred A. Knopf dressed its books well, with the expectation that a wide and popular readership would snap up the brightly colored book about Black life in the new America. The review mentioned previously goes so far as to suggest that there was demand for the book due to its being out of print, and now that Johnson had gained a foothold as a more public writer, his book demanded reemergence with his name on the cover.

The first edition was met with very little fanfare upon release by the publishing house Sherman, French & Company out of Boston, and it quickly went out of print. By 1927, Knopf had just published Langston Hughes's *The Weary Blues* to great acclaim, and Johnson had helped kick-start the Harlem Renaissance with anthologies from major presses: *The Book of American Negro Poetry* (Harcourt, 1922) and two volumes of African American spirituals (Viking, 1925; 1926); but his reputation as a writer had centered almost exclusively on his poetry. His choice to publish *The Autobiography of an Ex-Colored Man* with Knopf was no accident, and the firm made the most of their opportunity. The reissue was met with critical praise, with an Aaron Douglas cover design and an author's name appended to the title (which was changed to the UK spelling of "Coloured Man"). While African American writing up to the time of the release of the first edition had played a major role in antebellum abolitionism and Reconstruction, it was to go through a major stylistic shift by the early twentieth century. Johnson, having spent five years publishing African American verse and song, laid the groundwork for his emergence (or re-emergence?) as a prose writer. The void of anonymity can only be filled by the maker coming back to his or her work and assuring the reading public that the book was written not by phantasms or spirits but by a person of flesh and blood. In 1927, James Weldon Johnson came back to *The Autobiography of an Ex-Colored Man*, and he has never left.

Editing and Curating the Harlem Renaissance Text   65

Power dynamics, such as Johnson's choice to put his name on his book, are at the heart of textual presentation, especially when the text requires re-introduction into the literary marketplace. Harlem Renaissance texts have long been available in a number of versions, ranging from university press editions (Rutgers University Press in particular) to casebook trade editions (Norton Critical Editions) to trade paperbacks (Penguin Random House). Most popular versions of texts like Jean Toomer's *Cane*, Johnson's *Autobiography of an Ex-Colored Man*, and Nella Larson's *Passing* have been prepared for publication by scholars and published in trade editions for Norton and Penguin, primarily, as well as in university press editions more sparingly. Editions of classic texts like Claude McKay's *Home to Harlem*, Jessie Redmon Fauset's *Plum Bun*, Walter White's *The Fire in the Flint*, and Hughes's *The Ways of White Folks* include paratextual materials by scholars, not editors. In recent years, two complete manuscripts by McKay were unearthed and brought out by Penguin with notes and introductions by prominent Harlem Renaissance scholars: *Amiable with Big Teeth* (2018) (edited by Jean-Christophe Cloutier and Brent Hayes Edwards) and *Romance in Marseille* (2020) (edited by Gary Edward Holcomb and William Maxwell). These texts have been critical in rediscovering and reinvigorating Harlem Renaissance writers, especially in the classroom, and almost all include textual essays that discuss, in one way or another, how the scholars came about putting together the edition. Penguin editions are priced affordably, as are Norton Critical editions, and university professors seek out these versions regularly, due partly to there being no other academic alternative.

But while there are several popular editions of Harlem Renaissance texts to choose from, the era is lacking in comprehensive textual and bibliographical materials. To date, there are no descriptive bibliographies[2] of Harlem Renaissance texts, which would aid in cataloguing the vast number of reprints, reissues, and rebirths the era has undergone since 1920. Nor are there are any scholarly textual editions of any Harlem Renaissance texts, complete with apparatuses, critical introductions, collations, and notes, as well as a clear rationale explaining how and why editorial decisions were made.[3] In fact, most Harlem Renaissance texts are presented to a popular audience rather than a scholarly one. Rafia Zafar's nine-volume Library of America (LOA) editions of Harlem Renaissance novels from

66   ROSS K. TANGEDAL

the 1920s and 1930s come closest to resembling a textual treatment of the period.[4] However, LOA's model, while cognizant of textual preparation and history (G. Thomas Tanselle is the primary textual adviser), does not require editors to create critical apparatuses, collations, or rationales for editorial choices. Those items are the domain of the scholarly textual edition, an academic exercise whose purpose is to present a corrected text to the public. Consequently, these volumes are more than just the author's text; they include critical pieces of editorial process, including collations of various textual witnesses (which can run to several pages, depending on the disparity between versions of a text), critical notes and appendices, exhaustive critical introductions, and editorial rationales for why choices were made in preparing the edition. Tanselle discerns that "lists of variants present the raw material" of a scholarly edition, while textual essays "offer interpretations of that material," though they are "not substitutes for lists of variants."[5] Most editions of Harlem Renaissance texts provide the interpretation but not the raw material; and some editions leave the reader wondering if any raw material was, at any point, consulted in the making of the edition in their hands. This is not to say that popular editions of Harlem Renaissance texts are lacking or are inadequate; rather this shows us where scholarly attention is aimed when preparing those texts for the public. We want, instead, to understand historical and literary contexts without the foresight of textual integrity, which could alter the former drastically.

But work like descriptive bibliography, and to the same degree textual editions, are what G. Thomas Tanselle calls "a crucial cultural activity."[6] He argues:

> All artifacts are important as the principal class of evidence for reconstructing what human beings were doing and thinking in the past. Descriptive bibliography is a quintessential humanistic discipline because it rests on that irreducible fact. It begins— where all must begin if we wish to approach the past—with the objects that have come down to us.[7]

The responsibility of curating the voices of the past has never been more urgent than now. Black voices, in particular, are in great need of restoration

EDITING AND CURATING THE HARLEM RENAISSANCE TEXT   67

and proper care by editors, bibliographers, and textual scholars. We have descriptive bibliographies (and, for some, a number of scholarly textual editions) of twentieth-century American writers like Willa Cather, Ernest Hemingway, F. Scott Fitzgerald, Wallace Stevens, Eugene O'Neill, Edith Wharton, Frank Norris, Marianne Moore, Joseph Heller, Tennessee Williams, Robert Penn Warren, Raymond Chandler, Dashiell Hammett, Ring Lardner, James Gould Cozzens, John O'Hara, Ross McDonald, John Berryman, Thomas Wolfe, Arthur Miller, and James Dickey.[8] The lack of diversity among bibliographical subjects is alarming, and the problem spreads to scholarly textual editions of work by Black writers as well. In short, the work being done to predominantly white, male writers of the twentieth century is not being done to Black writers of the Harlem Renaissance (and beyond) such as Langston Hughes, Claude McKay, Jessie Redmon Fauset, James Weldon Johnson, Walter White, Countee Cullen, Arna Bontemps, Jean Toomer, Zora Neale Hurston, W.E.B. Du Bois, Marita Bonner, Alain Locke, and Nella Larsen. Omitting from "a crucial cultural activity" the works of Black writers leads to their books becoming less and less likely to be preserved (or historicized) with anything resembling an authorial text. This is not to say that publishers defaulted to compromising their Black writers' texts, but scholars like John K. Young have shown just how far white publishers went to assure the success of a particular book (and writer) during a time when Black voices were, finally, being made more public.[9] Several editions of Harlem Renaissance texts exist, though none has been created with a scholarly, authoritative, editorial rationale as the starting point. In my estimation, a great disservice is being done to Black writers of the United States.

And what is the Black voice? Are Harlem Renaissance texts somehow immune from the attention of textual and bibliographical study? Is this an issue of cataloguing and curation? Have too many texts been lost to history, and therefore unrecoverable by even the most intrepid of bibliographers? I hardly believe that this is so. Instead, scholars have unwittingly (and sometimes willfully) ignored the textual histories of landmark texts of the Harlem Renaissance by refusing to do the work of crafting bibliographical documents crucial to the survival of texts beyond the confines of the present. For Tanselle, "It seems natural that human beings should pore over the objects they inherit, noting down their measurements, colors,

68   Ross K. Tangedal

and designs and attempting to read in them the story of their production and the meanings they held for their producers."[10] Material detail provides the scholar with the opportunity to see book and writer in economic, artistic, and historical terms, aiding in the analyses we are accustomed to receiving from literary scholars. These material texts need attention, and while the work of Henry Louis Gates, Jr., George Hutchinson, Thadious Davis, Carla Kaplan, Brent Hayes Edwards, and others has been vital in getting some form of these texts before a reading public, their work can only bring their subjects so far when it comes to textual and material study. Poring over the authorial intention of writers has been, to some, a key exercise in textual restoration since the nineteenth century, while others have pronounced the author "dead," their intentions meaningless when brought before readers and history.[11] Be that as it may, the work of curating the Harlem Renaissance is not finished; as long as the era remains devoid of careful, patient, bibliographical investigation and documentation, then how can scholars and historians say they have done everything they can to curate the work of Black writers? We must do better, and we must do more.

In this chapter, I interrogate a particular textual controversy that grew into an editorial controversy—the endings to Nella Larsen's 1929 novel *Passing*—in order to show the urgent need for greater bibliographical and editorial attention when investigating the Harlem Renaissance. Building on the work of John K. Young, I survey five editorial notes that accompanied five versions of Larsen's novel, spanning over twenty years. Working without a complete textual record, a sound bibliographical foundation, or within the confines of a scholarly edition, the scholars who edited these versions present a case study in editorial controversy by virtue of their personal choices. Though an editor does, and must, make choices when preparing a text for publication, these scholars (rather than editors) made choices without the benefit of sound bibliographical evidence; all the more reason to demand a more thorough textual examination of the Harlem Renaissance. Had these five scholars been able to develop their editions with a descriptive bibliography of the works of Nella Larsen (which, to date, does not exist), rather than with speculation and guesswork, these editions would most certainly have been better suited for an academic, as well as popular, readership. In their current state, each edition plays a role in the mystery of *Passing*, whose ending, to this day, is in dispute—and, more importantly, whose textual history is incomplete and unclear.

What we do with these various versions is ultimately up to us (and the many readers who have purchased and read them), questionable editing aside. However, a novel like Larsen's (and the works of many other Harlem Renaissance writers) would benefit greatly from a rigorous textual and bibliographical treatment. A simple question builds upon the complexity at the center of textual darkness: How did Nella Larsen want her novel to end? A question like this one should be the starting point for a scholarly edition, and surely a descriptive bibliography. Through no fault of their own, the five scholars under examination have been unable to address the paramount textual controversy with anything resembling authority; readers take their words at face value, and why would they not? Every one of these scholars is respected, well-established, and capable of speaking about Larsen's work with confidence. Their work results in editorial uncertainty cloaked in confident presentation and anchored to popular editions of a work that calls out for more than the standard (and light) textual treatment given so many Harlem Renaissance texts.

Endings

Centuries after, she heard the strange man saying: "Death by misadventure, I'm inclined to believe. Let's go up and have another look at that window."
—final paragraph to the first two printings of Passing

Her quaking knees gave way under her. She moaned and sank down, moaned again. Through the great heaviness that submerged and drowned her she was dimly conscious of strong arms lifting her up. Then everything was dark.
—final paragraph to the third printing of *Passing*

In 1989, Mark J. Madigan recommended that the third printing ending, "Then everything was dark," should end a "definitive" edition of *Passing*, "since there is no evidence that Larsen opposed the substantive change of dropping the final paragraph." He suggested that editors "discuss the

70   ROSS K. TANGEDAL

final paragraph in a textual note recounting its enigmatic history, a history which underscores the difficulty of establishing authorial intention."[12] By accepting the third printing ending, Madigan indirectly establishes Larsen's authorial intention; since she did not oppose the removal of a key final paragraph to her novel, she must have preferred it. If Larsen did not oppose the change, then the amended ending exists not under protest, but under acquiescence. The textual record suggests that we have no way of knowing whether Larsen accepted or rejected the change. No letters exist between her and her editor or publisher; no manuscript material exists with emendations in Larsen's hand. We are unable to determine Larsen's authority or intention. Though we witness, for instance, the authority of James Weldon Johnson when he republished *The Autobiography* with his name attached, we are left wanting with Larsen. Madigan wishes for Larsen to break through from the past and clarify her intentions so we can accept her legacy. But she does not. And she never will.

At the conclusion of *Passing*, once Clare Kendry falls to her death, Irene Redfield "never afterwards allowed herself to remember. Never clearly."[13] When editing Larsen, it is the unknowing and lack of clarity that haunts us. Fredson Bowers believed that "it is important that a reader trust the text he is using, that he should feel a symbiotic relationship with its editor."[14] Editors want to be able to present a case for stability amidst chaos, hence their reason for "correcting" or "reconstructing" a text. Elizabeth Eisenstein argues that we must acknowledge the "acceptance of discontinuity" imbedded in textual history, a discontinuity that frees us from understanding literature, literary history, and print culture as chronological or inevitable.[15] Tanselle describes the uncertainty inherent in literary works, much like Eisenstein's acknowledgement of discontinuity. We appreciate the uncertainty and textual questions rather than deny them a place at the textual table. Some texts exist as artifacts, while others "can survive only through the instructions for their reconstitution."[16] Instruction is key here, for textual editions are created, with the Greg-Bowers-Tanselle model, by using a careful process of determining authority and intention. Certain versions of the same text, or witnesses, help in the reconstruction of a text from one fraught with errors to one more closely resembling what the author intended. Tanselle expects us to recognize textual instability and uncertainty in order to reconstruct (and properly edit) a text

EDITING AND CURATING THE HARLEM RENAISSANCE TEXT   71

for publication. Uncertainty helps us appreciate the complexity of texts, and the reason we are drawn to them is because of their unique ability to be multivalent rather than fixed. However, save for the ending, Larsen's *Passing* appears today in mostly the same state as it did on 26 April 1929. She left no direction on how to reconstitute the text for future generations because the text was in its final state, until the final paragraph disappeared. Without evidence to support the excision, editors are left with uncertainty, and, since 1986, several scholars have rationalized their editorial decisions despite gaps in the historical, textual record. The trouble with the endings is that we read them as we read the book as we read Nella Larsen: mysteries on top of enigmas wrapped in unknowing.

John K. Young suggests that "whatever practical decisions might be made, the most accurate edition of the novel would, ironically, gesture only to the insolubility of its closing crux, because the most ethical editorial strategy would be the preservation of our lack of knowledge."[17] Since we do not have, nor does it seem we will ever have, a definitive answer regarding the missing paragraph in the third printing of *Passing*, the best we can do is allow the unknowable history of the novel's materiality to live on in a constant state of flux. Young is right when he posits: "Editing Larsen's novel in terms of that material history would bring readers face to face with questions we cannot answer, and with a history we cannot write, thus directing them to confront such gaps in the literary past and to address them directly in the future" (56). The endings to Nella Larsen's *Passing* mean more as mysteries than they do as finite certainties—all the more reason to encourage uncertainty as a driving narrative in editorial decisions. By casting Larsen, her book, and her endings as the products of unknowable intentions, we likewise cast the editor as a chronicler of compositional instability without the satisfaction of arriving at a fixed, intended conclusion. Yet the scholars who edited the editions under examination choose certainty over instability, even when certainty does not present itself.

Nevertheless, scholars have had difficulty pinning down which version of *Passing* is "correct," given the lack of material evidence to suggest a firm choice. Madigan was the first scholar to publish an article dealing with the disparity, noting that the original ending "gives no indication as to whether the death was in fact accidental, but it does give the

72   Ross K. Tangedal

impression—albeit one based on what the officer is 'inclined to believe'—that Clare's husband and Irene will be absolved of responsibility by the police," while the amended ending provides "no indication as to the legal consequences facing Clare's husband and Irene in this version, and the sense of conclusion to the novel is more 'open.'"[18] For Young, the point is not whether a version is correct. Rather, what can readers do with multiple versions of the same text? If readers knew the history of the missing final paragraph, what would they come to understand about the novel? He examines most available edited editions of Larsen's book, discussing the inconsistencies between editions. He argues that "to read *Passing*'s narrative instabilities while ignoring its textual instability transfers the narrative dynamics out of their original context of production and therefore passes off the text as a stable document, even while a productive ambiguity operates at both the narrative and material levels."[19] To see textual ambiguity as productive both agrees with and grates against scholarly editorial practice. Editors of this school expect textual uncertainty, though the hoped-for endgame of any edition is a more stable text constructed with clarity, not more ambiguity. However, Young's conclusions are sound: "The problem lies, of course, in not being able to know whether the omitted paragraph represented any intention at all, authorial or otherwise. The lack of either a relevant author's or publisher's archive makes it impossible to prefer one printing versus the other on the basis of intentionality." Without stable evidence, a stable conclusion is futile, even impossible. "What is important theoretically about this problem," concludes Young, "is, instead, the larger cultural lesson borne out by this bottom-line textual instability."[20] As a text without a fixed body, *Passing* as a material text offers much more as an unstable work. The instability teaches us about marginalized voices and their intentions, the commodification of Black writers, and how Harlem Renaissance texts were treated even at their most popular point. The only way to edit *Passing* is to inform readers that authorial intention (as it relates to the endings) is impossible to determine given the textual, historical record. Therefore, the book may, after all, live on with two endings, neither of which can be disputed with editorial certainty.

For many scholars, the acceptance (or recognition) of Clare's ambiguity results in the acceptance of ambiguity in the textual history and authorial intention behind the novel. Martha J. Cutter concludes that "for

Clare, 'passing' becomes a mechanism to get what she wants—which is not a singular identity, an identity that corresponds to a theoretical inner self, but an identity that can escape the enclosures of race, class, and sexuality."[21] Does Larsen's text (and Larsen herself) subscribe to the same kind of escape, outside the "enclosures" of textual definition? Deborah McDowell—whose 1986 Rutgers University Press publication of *Quicksand* and *Passing* remains a popular edition of both texts—also accepts the ambiguity of the novel. She concludes that the endings to both of Larsen's novels "show her grappling with the conflicting demands of her racial and sexual identities and the contradictions of a black and feminine aesthetic." The virtues of McDowell's "conflicting demands" result from endings that are "much more radical and original ... to acknowledge a female sexual experience most often repressed in both literary and social realms."[22] In reading Clare as an uncertain identity, thanks in large part to Larsen's decision to filter the novel through Irene's perspective, the text itself becomes uncertain, and readers accept this uncertainty as they accept Clare.

Judi Roller, in discussing the endings to feminist novels of the twentieth century, argues that "to an extent, many of the heroines are not so much fleeing or escaping as being driven away."[23] After being accused of plagiarism with her story "Sanctuary," Larsen was driven away by an industry that refused to absolve her of her alleged indiscretions, regardless of their merit. In *Quicksand*, protagonist Helga Crane moves from place to place (six locations in total) in an attempt to find acceptance. Joshua M. Murray argues that Helga "chooses to mobilize in an attempt to locate an accepting community," her dissatisfaction with each locale driving her from place to place. However, the novel ends with Helga marrying a Southern preacher and birthing five children, the opposite of the freedom of movement she once enacted. "Helga feels that marriage becomes the only way she can conclusively terminate her mobility," Murray claims, so she "resigns herself to a life of passivity, subjugation, and motherhood."[24] Helga feels driven to stasis not out of preference, but out of necessity, even though her choice leads to more, rather than less, dissatisfaction. Larsen's own transition from literary celebrity to forgotten writer followed a similar trajectory, with little to trace her choices other than speculation. The binary of movement/stasis and the need for disappearance both play significant parts in Larsen's depiction of (and experience with) racial

74   ROSS K. TANGEDAL

identity. Much like Helga's decision to settle into subjugation, *Passing* and Nella Larsen remain unknowable.

Biographies of the author feature Larsen's enigmatic character and disappearance from literary life, chiefly because that narrative draws our attention.[25] Charles R. Larson suggests that Larsen "inched along her own lonely pathway toward obscurity and oblivion," and "invisibility is often one's only guarantee of survival."[26] Thadious M. Davis concludes that Larsen

> stopped in place and remained there long enough to allow the problem to dissolve, to disappear as she herself had. When she began to move again, she concentrated on the smallest possible amount of space and motion so as to attract no notice to the self that had been Nella Larsen, novelist.[27]

George Hutchinson visited the Garden of Memory of Brooklyn's Cypress Hills Cemetery—the graveyard where Larsen (under Nella Imes) was buried—though he could not locate a marker for the author. After an unsuccessful search, he recalls the following:

> While I was washing my hands in the outside lavatory, Valerie Swan Young, a member of the staff, brought out the record for me to see. The card bore only the name "Nella Imes"—no date of birth or death, no record of a headstone. She was there all right, in that gap at the center of the Garden of Memory, but the grave had never been marked.[28]

Clearly, biographers read Larsen as a mystery, an ambiguous specter of literary history, and a destabilized personality. Our understanding of her work relies on the legend of disappearance, on her invisibility, and on her retreat into obscurity being amplified rather than explained. Though Larsen characterizes Clare's re-entry into Irene's life as "the menace of impermanence,"[29] we justify our understanding of Larsen and her book through it. The menace of impermanence is our refuge.

However, when editing a text for publication, or recreating a text for an edition, editors make choices. According to Young, given this editorial undecidability, the proliferation of both versions [of *Passing*] in print is an effective, if unintentional solution to the problem of which version of *Passing* to prefer: neither is the "correct" edition (even if the standards by which they are edited vary substantially), and so both versions should be available.[30]

Young fuses the discontinuity and uncertainty espoused by Eisenstein and Tanselle with his notion of editorial "undecidability." He seeks not to establish an ideal text of *Passing* but rather to promote the book as "a materially queer text—that is, in addition to its thematic resonances along those lines, the book refuses to settle into one edition or the other."[31] Tanselle, Bowers, and others argue fervently for the restoration of texts by attending to authorial intention; the uncertainty of texts allows us to aid in their restoration rather than leave them disparate, if only our evidence is sound. But Young cautions against stabilizing terms in reference to Larsen: "In works like *Passing*, the textual instabilities encourage discussions about *race* in America as an unstable term, one that has been premised not only on misreadings of bodies as physical texts but also on a social construction that often has inescapably real consequences."[32] The interweaving of Larsen, her narrative, and her endings results in the ultimate complication: to read Larsen is to bear witness to the subjugation of authorial intention in the face of uncertainty; we revel in the acceptance of discontinuity not out of ignorance or malice but out of necessity. For Young, *Passing* leads us toward "discussions that illuminate and historicize the specific terms through which culturally dominant images of blackness have been produced, marketed, and resisted."[33] Without this uncertainty, and without the mystery surrounding the endings, would the text as object matter? We link ambiguity from text to author and back to text freely, making a mystery out of undefinable authorial intention. However, those scholars who have edited reprints of *Passing* have attempted to deduce Larsen's authorial intention while still promoting (and therefore editing out) some level of uncertainty, providing readers with confusion rather than clarity. Whether suggesting subtly or prescribing outwardly Larsen's motives, the five scholars that follow choose between the endings to *Passing*, and they show us how far we are from clarity.

76   Ross K. Tangedal

Editors' Notes

Below are five editorial textual notes from various editors discussing their decisions regarding the ending to *Passing*. In each, we see the respective editors attempting to position the ending based on what evidence they appear to have at hand. My goal in discussing these notes is to continue and extend Young's narrative of textual unknowing that permeates editorial decisions regarding the novel. If we are to dictate editorial decisions upon a work, then we must be prepared to justify those decisions.

The first is Deborah E. McDowell's opening note on the text and her note regarding the ending in the Rutgers University Press reprint (1986):

> This edition of Nella Larsen's two novels has been reset, based on original editions. *Quicksand* was originally published by Alfred A. Knopf in 1928, and *Passing*, also issued by Knopf, appeared in 1929. The only significant editorial emendation occurs on p. 182 of *Passing*, where the word "sardony" in all likelihood is a mistake for "irony" and has been changed accordingly.[34]
>
> [Note 10] In 1971 Macmillan issued an edition of *Passing* that ended with the following final paragraph, which was not included in the 1929 Knopf edition: [reprints "Centuries after ..." paragraph]. This paragraph does not seem to alter the spirit of the original in any way.[35]

The second is Thadious M. Davis's note on the text from the Penguin Books reprint (1997):

> The text of this edition is based on the first edition, first printing of *Passing*, which was published by Alfred A. Knopf in 1929. The first printing of the first edition included a brief final paragraph that was dropped in the third printing of the novel: [reprints "Centuries after ..." paragraph]. Although it is possible that the revised ending conformed to the author's sense of her novel, there is no indication that Nella Larsen herself recommended, sought, or approved the excision of the final paragraph. The text of this edition, therefore, follows the original Knopf first printing.

EDITING AND CURATING THE HARLEM RENAISSANCE TEXT 77

With the exception of a few minor typographical errors, which have been silently corrected, the original punctuation, spelling, and division of words, such as "kerb," "favourite," "for ever," and "week end," have been retained throughout the text.[36]

The third is Charles R. Larson's note on the text from the Anchor Books edition of *The Complete Fiction of Nella Larsen* (2001):

This is the only complete edition of Nella Larsen's fiction, including her three published stories and the correct ending for *Passing*. Deborah E. McDowell argues erroneously for omitting the final paragraph of *Passing* because the second printing of the 1929 Knopf edition inadvertently omitted it. McDowell argues that Larsen was a perfectionist and decided to change the ending of her novel. Perfectionist she may have been, but there is no evidence for this conjecture. Rather, the missing final paragraph of the second printing would appear to be the result of a dropped printer's plate.[37]

The fourth is Mae Henderson's explanatory note regarding the ending from the Modern Library reprint (2002):

Two different endings to the novel were published by Alfred A. Knopf in 1929. The first and second printing concluded with the following paragraph: [reprints "Centuries after ..." paragraph]. The third printing, however, omits this passage, concluding with "Then everything was dark." Later editions, including those published by The Arno Press (1969), Negro Universities Press (1969), Ayer Publishing Company (1985), and Rutgers University Press (1986), close with the abridged version. In contrast, the 1971 Collier Books edition (Macmillan) and the 1997 Penguin Books edition conclude with the extended ending. The Modern Library edition also contains the original extended ending. Interestingly, editor Deborah E. McDowell states in her introduction to the Rutgers edition that "this closing paragraph does not seem to alter the spirit of the original in any way." I am inclined to believe that the ending

78   Ross K. Tangedal

does make a difference, in that the amended conclusion enhances its status as a "writerly" text—in the sense that French critic Roland Barthes defines as "writerly" an open-ended text that requires the reader to collaborate in producing its meaning.[38]

The fifth, and final, is Carla Kaplan's note on the text from the Norton Critical edition (2007):

Originally titled "Nig," the novel's title was changed to *Passing* prior to publication. It is unknown whether this change was made at the publisher's behest or Larsen's. Knopf printed three editions of the novel, which sold some 3,000–4,000 copies in 1929. The text of this edition is based on the first printing, which included the final paragraph. The third printing of the novel omitted this paragraph and it has, consequently, been omitted in many subsequent reprintings of the novel. However, since it is unknown whether the paragraph was dropped at Larsen's request or as a printer's error, the paragraph is included here, as it originally appeared. Larsen's original spelling and punctuation have been retained throughout this text.[39]

One immediately recognizes the problem: which printing of *Passing* saw the final paragraph disappear? McDowell (1986) does not acknowledge that multiple printings of the first edition exist; since she operates under the assumption that the third printing of the first edition is the only printing of the first edition, she gives very little weight to a paragraph that she believes was added forty-two years after the fact. Her conclusion that the paragraph "does not seem to alter the spirit of the original in any way" firmly establishes "Then everything was dark" as the "original" final line in the novel. Several scholars have corrected McDowell's error, but her edition was the first major reprint of Larsen's work in decades; its impact is still felt today, as various scholars continue to cite her edition of *Quicksand* and *Passing* in their work. Regardless of the incomplete textual history of her edition, McDowell's reprint brought forth—inadvertently—the oddity of Larsen's complicated ending. Conversely, Davis (1997) properly identifies the three printings of the first edition, though she leaves space

EDITING AND CURATING THE HARLEM RENAISSANCE TEXT 79

for interpretation when she presupposes that the "revised" ending may have "conformed to the author's sense of her novel." In titling the excised paragraph a revision, Davis trusts that the paragraph was removed intentionally (so as to be "revised"), rather than accidentally or flippantly. She notes in her biography that Larsen was "not satisfied with the ending of her novel" and "may well have been responsible for dropping the final paragraph in the second printing."[40] Though she corrects her biography's textual error in the note, she still suggests that the "revised" ending may be closer to what the author wanted, though "there is no indication that Nella Larsen herself recommended, sought, or approved the excision of the final paragraph." The first printing ending appears in Davis's edition, but she implies that the third printing ending may be closer to Larsen's aesthetic. We can deduce which ending Davis prefers.

Mae Henderson (2002) provides more textual information regarding the ending in her note, and she even lists which versions were published with the third printing "abridged" ending and which were published with the "original extended" ending. Phrases like "abridged" and "extended" imply active intentionality, much like Davis's use of "revised." The first printing ending was not an extended ending; it was simply the ending. The third printing ending was not an "abridged" ending since no one has taken credit for abridging it. If anything, the third printing produced an alternative version of the ending rather than an abridgement. However, Henderson is right to question McDowell, something Davis did not do, in order to connect the most popular versions of the book for scholars and readers. The "amended" conclusion—which I take to mean the third printing ending—while not textually correct to Henderson, performs a more Barthian "writerly" function, making the book a collaboration. It strikes me as odd that Henderson would conclude her note with this analysis, chiefly because she tips her hand in favor of the "amended" conclusion, much like Davis does in her note. She also alludes to Roland Barthes, who famously denied the existence of authorial intention when it comes to literary texts. If this is a note about Larsen's intentions, then Henderson effectively disregards her subject's agency. Perhaps it helps us understand why Henderson does not offer a justification for why she chose the "original extended ending" for the Modern Library reprint. She too prefers the third printing ending. The power of "Then everything was

80   ROSS K. TANGEDAL

dark" is palpable; the third printing ending is memorable, haunting, and satisfying. McDowell (though she lacks context, evidence, or an accurate record) supports the third printing ending, while Davis and Henderson offer their own silent support of the third printing ending through subtle misdirection under the guise of editorial propriety. In doing so, any notion of textual clarity is further muddied, rather than cleared up by editors whom readers trust to do so.

Charles R. Larson (2001) and Carla Kaplan (2007) side in favor of the first printing ending, yet both come at their conclusions for different reasons. Larson dubs the first ending "correct" from the outset, assuming an aggressive, authoritative persona lacking from McDowell, Davis, and Henderson, yet his authority is contentious: (1) He confuses the second and third printings of the novel, since McDowell did not acknowledge the existence of more than one printing in her note; (2) Larson takes McDowell to task for most of his note, but his editorial predecessor offers very little explanation in her short note regarding the ending; and (3) nowhere does McDowell mention "perfectionist" or assume that Larsen "decided to change the ending of her novel." Remember, McDowell was operating under the assumption that "Then everything was dark" *was* the original ending, and the "Centuries after …" paragraph was added forty-two years later from an extraneous source. Further, to McDowell's credit, she does not argue for omission; she simply states that a stray paragraph appeared in 1971, and, in her estimation, the paragraph does not alter the work she had come to know as the first edition of *Passing*. Rather than omit the final paragraph, McDowell merely disregards it.

However, nowhere is Larson more debatable than in the conclusion to his note, where he claims (without substantiation, definition, or evidence) that the third printing ending "appeared to be the result of a dropped printer's plate." Anyone with experience in the book printing process knows that a dropped plate would create more than a single missing paragraph, unless that paragraph were the only text on the plate. Further, that plate would hold several other pages, not just the page with the final paragraphs. Young agrees, having examined the first edition printings of the novel and deducing that it is not only improbable but impossible for a dropped plate to have caused the final paragraph to go missing.[41] The only way that the first printing final paragraph could have been dropped was as a result of direct textual intervention, the same intervention that Davis and Henderson suggest strengthens the ending. To suggest correctness with almost no proper evidence throws the endings into even more confusion, though Larson senses that the dubious editing done by previous scholars required a definite decision. Unfortunately, he was not in a position to provide an accurate, definite conclusion, though he obviously attempted one. But imagine a reader looking over Larson's rationale; to a layperson, his explanation may make perfect sense, since the printing of books is, to most readers, a mysterious and unknown process. Confusion borne from ignorance of the printing process only strengthens the need for a more robust bibliographical treatment of Harlem Renaissance texts.

Carla Kaplan also chooses to conclude her edition with the first printing ending. She provides readers with an accurate history of the muddled printing timeline carefully (and correctly). She also includes information about number of copies sold and a justification for her decision to end the edition with the "Centuries after ..." paragraph. However, Kaplan, much like Davis and Henderson, leaves room for questioning by beginning her note (the only editor to do so) with a mini-history regarding the novel's original manuscript title, "Nig." Biographers Davis and Hutchinson both mention the change; Davis argues that "someone at Knopf had suggested the change of its title because 'Nig' might be too inflammatory for a novel by an unproven writer, while 'Passing,' and the phenomenon's connection to miscegenation, would incite interest without giving offense. Larsen did not object."[42] George Hutchinson concludes that the title may have been shed "at Knopf's urging after the flak over the title *Nigger Heaven*."[43] One way to read the note is that since we cannot know whether Larsen requested the change or not, we can assume that there is the potential for publisher strong-arming or unauthorized retitling at the expense of Larsen's vision. However, disputed titling between authors and publishers is not new, nor does it necessarily suggest that an author's agency was questioned or denied in the process. Kaplan allows readers to believe that Larsen's autonomy may have been questioned in retitling her novel *Passing*, and the same questioning filters through the remainder of her note. If readers believe that Larsen may not have approved of the decision to retitle her work, then they may believe that the first printing ending was not Larsen's preferred ending. Kaplan lists only "Larsen's

82   Ross K. Tangedal

request" and "a printer's error" as potential reasons for the dropped paragraph; knowing now that the dropped paragraph could not have been the result of a printer's error, a dropped plate, or any other printing process malfunction, that leaves only one possible conclusion: Larsen requested the change. Kaplan is right (as was Charles R. Larson) to select the first printing ending for her edition, and (unlike Larson) she provides an accurate accounting of the textual history of the book. However, by refraining from including "publisher's error" or "publisher's decision" as a reason for the dropped paragraph, Kaplan suggests that unless a mechanical error caused the change, Larsen herself must have had something to do with the removal of the first printing final paragraph.

In her introduction to the Norton edition, Kaplan claims, "The novel reminds us of the (sometimes tragic) gap between what we think we believe in and what in fact we want."[44] Her sentiment sums up the questionable history that has guided the existing textual notes concerning the endings to *Passing*. Each editor, in their own way, knew what they thought they believed in, but each wanted something else to be true—a dropped plate, a requested change, a defiant slash, a more "writerly" text. In the end, everything is still dark.

Centuries After

James Weldon Johnson was right when he claimed in his preface to *The Book of American Negro Poetry* that "the final measure of the greatness of all peoples is the amount and standard of the literature and art they have produced."[45] Stories of Black lives in America only sixty years removed from the Civil War, in the middle of the Jazz Age and Jim Crow eras, and well into the Great Migration that had begun at the turn of the century, serve as the cultural touchstones of a generation of Black Americans. The Harlem Renaissance was a time of change, but that change was the result of professional writers working hard at their craft. We forget, more regularly than we like to admit, that writers *wrote*, first and foremost. Langston Hughes's poetry has not always been here, nor have the novels of Claude McKay or Jessie Redmon Fauset. They were created by writers willing to see beyond the confines of their servitude to American values and expectations; the Harlem Renaissance is a period of great textual output, yet we

EDITING AND CURATING THE HARLEM RENAISSANCE TEXT   83

are quick to deny the history of those texts' composition, development, and production. To get at the amount and standard of what the period produced we must be willing to do the work to unearth, present, and maintain those documents and histories that tell the story of the period. To paraphrase Tanselle, we must be concerned with history.[46]

Larsen's novel, and the controversy surrounding its endings, serves as a fertile testing ground for any bibliographer and textual editor were they to address the work as they have so many others. Were we to have in our possession, say, a complete descriptive bibliography of Larsen's (albeit constricted) canon, then each of the five notes in this chapter would be the better for the information such a volume would provide. Speculation would lessen, and confidence in the textual record would not be reserved for a small group of book historians waiting to call out non-editors for their shortcomings. The information would be there for all to examine and use, with "use" being the operative word. Instead of applying a scatter-shot approach to editing Harlem Renaissance texts, scholars should insist on the creation of eclectic scholarly editions of as many works as possible, as well as comprehensive descriptive bibliographies of major and minor Harlem Renaissance writers. Popular editions of books like Johnson's *Auto-biography*, Hughes's *The Ways of White Folks*, and Zora Neale Hurston's *Their Eyes Were Watching God* should be generated using strong, scholarly editions prepared by textual editors dedicated to the period. Doing so will lead to a textual equalizing long overdue in the academy. By showing that the work of scholarly editing and bibliography belongs to all writers, all scholars, and all readers, not just the predominantly white, male scions of the Western canon, we come one step closer to properly curating the crucial cultural activities of a wider and more diverse America.

II   Writers, Editors, Readers

CHAPTER FOUR

The Two Gentlemen of Harlem

Wallace Thurman's *Infants of the Spring,*
Richard Bruce Nugent's
Gentleman Jigger, and Intellectual Property

Darryl Dickson-Carr

The plagiarism controversy surrounding two of the New Negro or Harlem Renaissance's most storied novels, Wallace Thurman's *Infants of the Spring* (1932) and Richard Bruce Nugent's *Gentleman Jigger* (composed ca. 1928–33; published 2008), begins with an improbable friendship between two intellectual equals. The authors' novels, begun and composed largely when they were roommates in Harlem's storied "Niggeratti Manor"—the apartment building at 267 West 136th Street that housed many young Black artists—narrate some of the same events, a few in remarkably similar ways. The controversy, put simply, is whether Thurman copied Nugent's text, or vice versa. Since Thurman's novel was published two years before his death, and Nugent's posthumously, it appears that by beating Nugent into print with a similar narrative, Thurman stole Nugent's thunder and destroyed his chances of publishing his work, regardless of its quality. Since Nugent made no attempt to publish, Thurman's actions appear damning.

Yet this quite logical reading ignores what marked Thurman and Nugent's *ethoi.* It presumes that each was equally ambitious to get his work into print or felt sole ownership of the events that ground each novel. Those events—at least those that attract the most attention—are fabled

87

88   DARRYL DICKSON-CARR

incidents that took place during the New Negro Renaissance's most outrageous period, centered primarily in Niggeratti Manor. They involve nearly every major African American artist of the time and a number of patrons and "midwives" who brought one phase of the New Negro movement into being with their financial and moral support. They include salons, exhibitions, lunches, banquets, balls, and outlandish parties. But several of those events found their way into other narratives as well, including Rudolph Fisher's *The Walls of Jericho* (1928), Thurman's first novel, *The Blacker the Berry ...* (1929), and Countee Cullen's *One Way to Heaven* (1932). Thurman himself wrote numerous essays in 1929 that examine the Harlem literary scene and became part of his novel's narrative. In other words, he had an archive of experiences from which a novel could easily have been written by any reasonably skilled writer. For all of his frequent self-criticism, Thurman certainly possessed that skill. In short, he certainly could have written his second novel based entirely on his own notes.

Nevertheless, it is difficult to imagine that Thurman and Nugent's relationship, which comprised innumerable conversations about art, culture, and politics, did not feed into both authors' works. The events that they and the other writers mentioned previously recounted clearly made a strong impression on more than two brilliant roommates. Who, then, owns the events of the Harlem Renaissance, especially those of the younger literati? Who has greater claim on Niggeratti Manor's legacy? The Thurman–Nugent controversy speaks more to the power and agency that we believe Thurman might have as one with greater experience in the publishing world, but that still does not answer our questions. It might be best, however, to pause for a look at each author's background to understand what they brought to Harlem in the 1920s.

Thurman and Nugent

Wallace Henry Thurman (1902–34) was born and raised in Salt Lake City, Utah, where the African American population was and is meager, comprising only several thousand people in his lifetime. In contrast, Richard Bruce Nugent (1906–87) was born into a prominent Washington, DC family whose ancestors have been free since the early eighteenth century.[1] African Americans comprised the overwhelming majority of

THE TWO GENTLEMEN OF HARLEM   89

Washington, DC's population and stood as one of the most storied Black communities in the country, with a long tradition of abolitionism, Civil Rights activism, and appreciation for education and the arts defining its character. The Black middle class whence Nugent came was highly influential in the nation's capital and beyond. Thurman was dark-skinned and suffered the prejudice and scorn that color-struck African Americans heaped upon those of darker hue; Nugent was lighter-skinned, a characteristic associated not only with the miscegenation that defines American culture but also bourgeois status.

When these young men met in late 1925, it was a shock to both, but especially to Nugent. In *Gentleman Jigger*, the protagonist Stuartt—based largely on Nugent—narrates the encounter in precisely the same terms that the author would to interviewers later. Accompanying Langston Hughes to lunch to meet Thurman, Nugent discovered that the intellect he had admired belonged to a dark-skinned African American who could match his companions for wit and charm. He felt nauseated and excused himself. After apologizing to his new acquaintance, Nugent and Thurman soon became close friends, and a year later, roommates, at Niggeratti Manor for two years.[2] The pair's initial friendship and time as roommates coincided with some of the Harlem Renaissance's most notable moments, from the landmark publication of *The New Negro* (1925), edited by Alain Locke; Langston Hughes's first poetry collections *The Weary Blues* (1926) and *Fine Clothes to the Jew* (1927); Eric Walrond's short story collection *Tropic Death* (1926); Carl Van Vechten's *Nigger Heaven* (1926); James Weldon Johnson's *The Book of American Negro Spirituals* (1926) and *God's Trombones* (1927); *Fire!!* (edited by Thurman) in November 1926; *Ebony and Topaz* (1927), edited by Charles S. Johnson; Rudolph Fisher's *The Walls of Jericho* (1928); Nella Larsen's *Quicksand* (1928); and Claude McKay's *Home to Harlem* (1928).

At the same time, Thurman served as interim editor of A. Philip Randolph and Chandler Owens's socialist *The Messenger* magazine (1917–28) for most of 1926, when George S. Schuyler took a hiatus to pursue journalistic assignments for the Pittsburgh *Courier*, where he wrote for the next forty years. In November, Thurman became publication manager at *The World Tomorrow*, another magazine with a socialist outlook, allowing him to hold a steady job and write and edit on a

90   DARRYL DICKSON-CARR

regular basis. Thurman's immersion in the magazine publishing world and the various connections it produced allowed him to have not only a solid, if modest, income but also to gain extensive experience that few of his peers managed. Although Thurman's published output during his lifetime was relatively limited, his time working as an editor at both magazines made it easier for him to organize *Fire!!*—for which he was virtually the de facto sole editor—and later *Harlem* (1928), which, like its predecessor, lasted only one issue.

Thurman's ambitions, however, were clear: to create iconoclastic outlets for the cultural movement, especially its younger voices. In early 1928, Thurman sent a letter introducing himself to McKay, thanking him for admiring his contributions to *Fire!!* and intimating that McKay "must either think me a highly conceited ass or just a plain damn fool" for attempting to challenge the dominant course of African American literature and art.[3] His self-criticism is facetious at best; Thurman made clear in such essays as "This Negro Literary Renaissance" that *Fire!!* was "not interested in sociological problems or propaganda. It was purely artistic in intent and conception" and intended to "introduce a truly Negroid note into American literature" by going to "the proletariat rather than to the bourgeoisie for characters and material."[4] That proletariat comprised not only his fellow younger artists but also their alternately vicarious or immediate experiences of African American working-class life. Thurman certainly saw himself in those masses, indulging liberally in many of the Renaissance's sensual, sexual, and artistic excesses, even as he publicly decried these same problems in scathing essays and novels, and professed his lack of faith in the idea of the New Negro privately. Thurman directed no small amount of his antipathy toward himself, whether through coded terms in his published critiques or in haunting unpublished essays that reveal a writer desirous of fame and success simultaneously yet utterly convinced that such lofty goals were beyond his powers and native abilities.

In his 1927 *Bookman* essay "Nephews of Uncle Remus," Thurman stresses that African American writers have an equal chance to produce great work, but only if they transcend their immediate surroundings to achieve the universal. In echoes of both George S. Schuyler's "The Negro-Art Hokum" (1926) and T. S. Eliot's "Tradition and the Individual Talent" (1919), Thurman argues that

THE TWO GENTLEMEN OF HARLEM   91

> every facet of life can be found among Negroes, who being
> human beings, have all the natural emotional and psychological
> reactions of other human beings. They live, die, hate, love, and
> procreate. They dance and sing, play and fight. And if art is the
> universal expressed in terms of the particular, there is, if he has
> the talent, just as much chance of the Negro author to produce
> great literature by writing of his own people as if he were to write
> of Chinese or Laplanders.[5]

Thurman goes on to write that African American artists will be circumscribed as "*Negro* artist[s]" only if they fail "to rise above the province of petty propaganda, or [fail] to find a means of escape" from themselves and their environments.[6]

Like his peers, though, Thurman centered much of his writing on African America and its cultural products, with special attention to the movement he supported. He wrote many times about Harlem itself, whether by publishing a guide to the storied community for newcomers, editing a magazine that took Harlem as its namesake and inspiration in 1928, or co-authoring (with William Jourdan Rapp) a play that did the same in 1929. Thurman was both an outsider to this environment and deeply ensconced in it. But save for the possible limitations of one too many gin parties, the environment didn't hold back Thurman's ambitions. Eleonore van Notten's biography reveals that other motivations drove Thurman to bring *Infants of the Spring* to publication. In 1929, long after both *Fire!!* and *Harlem* had folded, Thurman traveled to Detroit, his native Salt Lake City, and Los Angeles to not only make a first attempt at screen-writing but also to get away from Harlem for the sake of focusing on his various writing projects. Thurman remained ambivalent about Harlem and its artists; despite his criticisms of the movement in numerous essays, in May 1929 he wrote that he "would never live permanently in any other American city" and praised several of his friends in the movement, with special attention to Nugent, "who has more diversified talent than anyone I know."[7] Nevertheless, Thurman benefited from leaving Harlem; between March and September 1929, he finished his essay collection, *Aunt Hagar's Children*, made great progress on a few plays, and wrote the first draft of *Infants of the Spring*.[8]

92   DARRYL DICKSON-CARR

The dates here are crucial. Thurman's time living and socializing with Nugent undoubtedly made a strong impression, but a great deal of time passed between their living arrangement and Thurman's first draft of *Infants*. We have no evidence that Thurman took any of Nugent's manuscripts on his sojourn in the West. If he did plagiarize any material that Nugent had completed between 1928 and 1929, we can only speculate how he would have done so. We know for certain that Nugent started writing in 1928, which means that Thurman was sure to have read and critiqued some material before Nugent went on tour with the play *Porgy* ca. March 1928, while Thurman departed for Detroit on April 9. Whatever Nugent wrote of what would eventually become *Gentleman Jigger* had to be scant and short. In all likelihood, it would have been the passages that even the most casual reader would find similar: accounts of parties, salons, and major figures of the New Negro movement. Thurman and Nugent generally shared a common outlook on the events that occurred in and around Niggeratti Manor between their first encounter and 1928. Thurman wrote to William Jourdan Rapp that the "varied manifestations of the decadent Harlem milieu—sweetbacks, numbers, rent-party etc— have been done to death," including in his and Rapp's own play.[9] Yet those were the elements that seemed to come most easily and quickly to both Thurman and Nugent for material. After Niggeratti Manor's notorious high living came crashing down, one or both of the authors may have captured its history before it faded.

Eleonore van Notten notes that when Thurman returned to Harlem after his sojourn in the American West, he was eager to end a "phase of his life" defined by hanging out with the largely Black bohemian crowd. Significantly, he reunited with Richard Bruce Nugent for a brief time and tried to resume indulging in the gin-soaked life that dominated the scene earlier. But Nugent "not only found Thurman 'sillier and more shallow,' but also suggest[ed] that their friendship had changed."[10] Thurman moved in with *Messenger* magazine drama critic Theophilus Lewis in a Jamaica, Queens home to write and tutor part-time, making a distinct physical break from Harlem's milieu. In summer 1930, he wrote to Harold Jackman: "Most of the people I know and used to enjoy bore me so that I would be most happy never to see them again in my life. And that goes for all my former associates," Nugent not excepted; he and

THE TWO GENTLEMEN OF HARLEM 93

Thurman saw less of each other from that point.[11] And while Thurman finished a first draft of *Infants* during this time, it took two years for it to see publication.

Intellectual Property and Claiming Ownership

The events outlined in the previous section, along with Thurman's earlier assessment of his own limited writing skills, offer additional, albeit limited insight to the controversy before us. We have a young, prolific, and ambitious author (Thurman), albeit one more likely to write than to publish, rooming with the bohemian (Nugent) who is seemingly uninterested in publishing. In 1928, both began writing drafts of novels with similar thinly veiled characters—often with the same or similar pseudonyms and events based on experiences they'd shared while rooming together. It adds to circumstantial evidence that Thurman would be apt to rely on his friend as a source for his second novel. But this narrative reveals a number of biases and assumptions about originality. Again, who could claim ownership of these events? Do Nugent's more prodigious talents lend him more credibility as the first to write of these events? Do Thurman's editorial experience, critical eye, and reported production of a first draft make him more believable? Does either of these arguments need to eclipse the other?

The true question here is about intellectual property, but beyond any sort of simplistic legal sense. As Peter Stallybrass writes in his essay "Against Thinking," the rise of the database in modern literary study has allowed us to "separate knowledge from academic prestige and from its attendant regime of intellectual property."[12] Stallybrass maps out how William Shakespeare constructed *Hamlet*'s most famous monologue from an archive of phrases and ideas in circulation in contemporary texts that an educated, well-read, and prodigious playwright would have known— and used. Shakespeare, in short, wasn't original in the standard sense of the term: *sui generis* creation. "It is only in a regime of originality," Stallybrass writes, "that such techniques become secretive and shameful."[13] Within the African American literary tradition, this sort of borrowing—what we would be apt to call plagiarism—may be found at many points. Multiple scholars have studied the extent to which abolitionist, editor, scholar, and novelist William Wells Brown frequently expropriated and repurposed

94   DARRYL DICKSON-CARR

other texts into his own books, including his most famous work, *Clotel, or the President's Daughter* (1853).[14]

This is not meant illogically to excuse plagiarism or to pretend that it is meaningless. Rather, it is to suggest that between Thurman and Nugent, it is unclear where one artist's mind ended and the other's began in recounting certain events. Consider the case of Nugent's and Thurman's friends and peers, Langston Hughes and Zora Neale Hurston, whose friendship came to a bitter end, for all intents and purposes, over the play *Mule Bone*. Hurston and Hughes argued strenuously over questions regarding who originated the idea at the play's heart as well as the plot, characters, and dialogue, with Hurston asserting that her greater experience and knowledge of Black Southern folk culture and language settled the question of provenance; she had no use for Hughes's suggestions and contributions.[15] Yet Hughes insisted that he played a crucial role in creating the play, and that Hurston effectively stole it and erased his role out of personal and artistic jealousy.[16]

I cite this example not to argue that the other cases explain fully what happened between Thurman and Nugent, of course. Instead, I suggest this: Both Thurman and Nugent—especially the former—may have considered the core events in their respective novels to be in the equivalent of the public domain and therefore free to use. And, in Thurman's case, after the tumultuous events of the preceding years, especially Thurman's assumption of most editorial work for *Fire!!*, he may have felt entitled to his claim, even at Nugent's expense.

Thurman and Nugent's immersion in all that the New Negro Renaissance in Harlem had to offer, whether in intellectual, artistic, or sexual terms, illustrates instead their steadfast belief in democratic expression of their individual selves. Little space stands between Langston Hughes's arguments for free artistic expression for Negro artists in "The Negro Artist and the Racial Mountain" (June 23, 1926) and those that Thurman and Nugent expressed in their own writings. The philosophical connection between these three writers underscores a common thread among satirists of the Harlem Renaissance: total artistic freedom, not a race-based pragmatism, is the ideal. As Amritjit Singh and Daniel Scott claim, Thurman "developed the critical vocabulary and theoretical frameworks that would make him an indispensable part of the African American critical tradition," but that part has remained largely that of the understudy waiting in the wings, eclipsed by the enormous reputation of the star players, even if those players admired him most of all during the New Negro movement. As Langston Hughes stressed in his first memoir, *The Big Sea* (1940), Thurman was "a strangely brilliant black boy" who could read eleven lines at a time, criticize anything and everything he read, and display his encyclopedic knowledge of American and continental literature.[17] Hughes goes on to detail Thurman's deep angst over his abilities as a novelist and poet, difficult history as an editor, simultaneous affinity and antipathy for gin, and demise in the charity ward at Bellevue. Though Hughes's portrait of Thurman has become iconic, it has less nuance than Nugent's; the latter revealed that their mutual intellectual admiration and shared passions for art, literature, and Harlem's sexual atmosphere created a strong bond, even if they were not themselves lovers. As Nugent's friend and biographer Thomas Wirth has documented, both men indulged in the fluid sexual atmosphere in Harlem and other sites in New York City, even as they cultivated the circle of artists that Thurman and Zora Neale Hurston later dubbed the "Niggeratti."[18]

Launching *Fire!!*

Thurman's *Infants of the Spring* and Nugent's *Gentleman Jigger* offer the most detailed, complex, and luxuriantly colored portraits of an artistic movement in the making. Yet the two *romans-à-clef* arguably retire the most common derisive view of the younger generation of Harlem Renaissance artists (one that Thurman bitterly supported himself), replacing it with a perspective that fully acknowledges the group's flaws, revealing their seriousness in creating a new space for their own aesthetic ambitions, as well those of subsequent generations. As Abby Arthur Johnson and Ronald Maberry Johnson have argued, *Fire!!*, the younger artists' voice, "deserves a place in surveys of American cultural history," as "the first black magazine that was both independent and essentially literary."[19]

A moment in Thurman and Nugent's early relationship as artists—and as editors—serves as a metaphor for the controversy surrounding their respective novels. *Fire!!*, as mentioned earlier, gained notoriety for the younger artists' willingness to break taboos within the African

96   DARRYL DICKSON-CARR

American community by writing about subjects that undermined the Black middle class's desire for "respectable" images: heteronormative; morally unambiguous; free from even the slightest hint of scandal, criminality, or transgression. *Fire!!* was intended to burn the middle class with glee and free Black art. As the Niggeratti plotted to *épater la bourgeoisie*, Thurman and Nugent consciously made a pact on a coin toss, according to Nugent: "Wally and I sat around figuring out what two things just will not take. Well, we'll write about a street walker or a whore, and we'll write a homosexual story. ... So we flipped a coin to see which one of us would do which."[20] Thurman's contribution, "Cordelia the Crude" centered upon a prostitute, while "Smoke, Lilies, and Jade," the first explicitly queer story by an African American, fulfilled Nugent's end of the bargain.

Fire!!, while ambitious, didn't last long enough to fulfill its contributors' dreams other than declaring their artistic independence. At a total cost of $1,000, with only $150 coming from the contributors and the rest being kited from Thurman's paychecks, it impoverished its chief editor financially and spiritually, adding to his skepticism toward the New Negro movement as a movement and toward his peers as serious artists. His experiences revealed that few movements survive intact the transition from exuberance to pragmatism. Realizing this problem, Thurman began planning *Fire!!*'s successor soon after its demise. The result, *Harlem*, was less ambitious artistically but more catholic in format. As he wrote Alain Locke in the fall of 1928,

> Harlem is to be a general magazine, containing verse, fiction, essays, articles on current events and debates on racial and non racial issues. We are not confining ourselves to [a]ny group either of age or race. I think that is best. The Crisis and The Messenger [a]re dead. Opportunity is dying. Voila here comes Harlem, independent, fearless and general, trying to appeal to all.[21]

Harlem, like *Fire!!* lasted one issue. If Thurman hoped to generate greater interest than the explicitly bohemian *Fire!!*, he hadn't the formula. Without links to national organizations or steady interest from philanthropists, Thurman's independent editorial projects couldn't gather momentum.

THE TWO GENTLEMEN OF HARLEM   97

Thurman nearly lost his position at *The World Tomorrow*, as the personal and financial strain of *Fire!!* affected his work.[22]

So why did Thurman go to such lengths to see to completion a publication that placed him in debt for years and severely strained his relationships with peers who seldom made good on their financial commitment to an African American literary and artistic magazine? To take Thurman at his word, it could not have been due to race loyalty; he expressed his antipathy towards group identity and politics on numerous occasions. It could not have been because of the promise his fellow editors exhibited as supporters; as Thurman wrote Langston Hughes in the midst of the editorial process, after staying up all night dummying the proofs, "Zora [Neale Hurston] had a date. Jeanette [Randolph] was in South Norwalk. Bunny [Jan Harold Stephansson] could not be found. Neither could [Richard] Bruce [Nugent]. Aaron [Douglas] eluded [Thurman]." His conclusion? "God damn Fire and all the editors."[23] With such nominal supporters, no detractors could do any more harm, though they tried.

Thurman's motivation resided in his desire to see a magazine devoted strictly to the arts that would make no pretense to social propriety and respectability, much less propagandistic purposes. Thurman's position regarding his own membership in a "race" must be separated from his recognition that no precedent for *Fire!!*—that is, an artistic magazine by and for a younger, modern set of artists—could be found in American literary history. As Thurman told Granville Hicks the following year, "we've done more for the race in five or six years than [the old guard of writers] have accomplished in a generation. We have shown people that the negro can do something instead of telling him that he can."[24] Although Thurman remained skeptical of the New Negro movement he helped to lead, the true spirit of the movement could be found in efforts like *Fire!!*.

Infants of the Spring (1932)

Thurman and the other *Fire!!* contributors' ultimate goal was to get Black artists beyond both mimicry of the various literary predecessors under which they operated and the ideological caretakers that were attempting to keep these artists under their wings. Thurman, however, did not know what lay beyond these limitations. When he illustrates his own artistic

DARRYL DICKSON-CARR

frustrations and anxieties in the following well-quoted passage from *Infants of the Spring*, Thurman could be talking about the Harlem Renaissance as a whole:

> He wanted to do something memorable in literature, something that could stay afloat on the contemporary sea of weighted ballast, something which could transcend and survive the transitional age in which he was living. ... He did not doubt that he had a modicum of talent, but talent was not a sufficient spring board to guarantee his being catapulted into the literary halls of Valhalla; talent was not a sufficient prerequisite for immortality. He needed genius and there was no assurance that he had it, no assurance that he had done anything more "than learned his lessons well."[25]

Infants of the Spring poses numerous seemingly irresolvable questions about the directions African Americans, especially African American intellectuals, should take in view of their political and social ties to other racial and ethnic groups in the United States. Thurman's primary question revolves around the possibility of the formation of group and individual identities for African Americans that will simultaneously avoid being essentialist, even as those identities carry the vast majority of African Americans forward. In that sense, it is but an extension of Thurman's deep-seated concerns about the construction of "race" and color-caste distinctions that dominated much of his journalistic work; African American culture's growth depends precariously on its ability to investigate and question itself, recognizing when, precisely, its greatest leaders and ideas are at hand, and devising institutions that support action rather than abstract culture building.

This view later informs Thurman stand-in Raymond Taylor's reaction to a meeting of Harlem's Black writers called by one Dr. A.L. Parkes, Thurman's pseudonym for Alain Locke. This meeting draws together most of the major Black voices of the Harlem Renaissance, as well as some of the minor ones, "for the purpose of exchanging ideas and expressing and criticizing individual theories," with the possibility of bringing "into active being a concerted movement which would establish the younger Negro talent once and for all as a vital artistic force."[26] This meeting is based upon

THE TWO GENTLEMEN OF HARLEM   99

salons that various Harlem Renaissance writers had with Locke, as well as Thurman's (and Nugent's) general attitude toward the sort of political mission that Locke, as editor of *The New Negro*, represented. Each of the characters present at Parkes's meeting represents a major artistic or intellectual figure of the Harlem Renaissance hidden beneath a pseudonym that plays on either the initials, rhythm, or other characteristics of the historical figure's name. "Sweetie May Carr," for example, is Zora Neale Hurston; "Doris Westmore" is Dorothy West; "Tony Crews" is Langston Hughes; "Dr. Manfred Trout" is Rudolph Fisher; and so on.

Unfortunately, neither Parkes's verbiage nor his agenda at the actual meeting effectively matches his noble purpose; he "perorate[s]" numerous disapproving allusions to the "decadent strain" running through the artists' work and cajoles them to cultivate "a healthy paganism based on African traditions."[27] Given Parkes's purported openness to the artists' ideas, Raymond and others find Parkes's exhortations patronizing, if they can comprehend them at all. When "DeWitt Clinton" (a pseudonym for Countee Cullen, who attended De Witt Clinton High School)[28] agrees with Parkes, Raymond imagines "that poet's creative hours—eyes on a page of Keats, fingers on a typewriter, mind frantically conjuring African scenes. And there would of course be a Bible nearby."[29] Raymond and Paul Arbian (a pseudonym for Nugent) then ask Parkes and Clinton if "there really [is] any reason why all Negro artists should consciously and deliberately dig into African soil for inspiration and material unless they actually wish to do so," and "[h]ow can I go back to African ancestors when their blood is so diluted and their country and times so far away," respectively.[30] Raymond and Paul thus consider the idea of a syncretic Black culture and literature as, at best, a myth. The discussion goes on heatedly until "Sweetie May Carr"/Zora Neale Hurston calls Cedric Williams (a pseudonym for writer Eric Walrond) "a polysyllabic expletive," and the room devolves into a carnivalesque state of "pandemonium," thus erasing the gathering's intellectual discourse, which is never fully regained. The meeting's attendants subsequently disperse, with no consensus attained as to what the responsibilities, goals, and obligations of Black artists might be.[31]

Parkes's literary summit thus becomes a metaphor for the state of Black art in the Renaissance. Raymond reflects soon thereafter that "[i]t

100   DARRYL DICKSON-CARR

was amazing how in such a short time his group of friends had become separate entities, wrenched apart, scattered" by its interest in matters both within and outside of Niggeratti Manor. Not unlike the pragmatic endings found in much satire, the latter portion of *Infants* finds the various Niggeratti pursuing careers that put their talents to more profitable uses than those found within the Manor's confines. The Manor itself follows this rubric, inasmuch as its landlady, Euphoria Blake, decides to convert it from, in Thurman's euphemisms, "a congenial home for Negro artists to a congenial dormitory for bachelor girls."[32] Soon thereafter, Paul, the novel's quintessential symbol of flamboyant bohemianism, commits suicide, prompting Raymond to ask, "Had Paul the debonair, Paul the poseur, Paul the irresponsible romanticist, finally faced reality and seen himself and the world as they actually were? Or was this merely another act, the final stanza in his drama of beautiful gestures," his final means "to make himself stand out from the mob."[33] Raymond's ponderings frame Paul's death as a synecdoche for the disintegration of Niggeratti Manor; in life, he "[w]ooed the unusual, cultivated artificiality, defied all conventions of dress and conduct" and consequently had "nothing left to do except execute self-murder in some bizarre manner," not unlike the Niggeratti's heavy flirtation with the flamboyant and subsequent dissolution in the cascade of economic necessity that overwhelmed any aspirations to a unique society within both Harlem and American culture in general.[34]

More important, Paul leaves behind the manuscript for a novel, but it is accidentally destroyed in the process of his suicide, except for one page that includes a drawing of

> a distorted, inky black skyscraper, modeled after Niggeratti Manor, and on which were focused an array of blindingly white beams of light. The foundation of this building was composed of crumbling stone. At first glance it could be ascertained that the skyscraper would soon crumple and fall, leaving the dominating white lights in full possession of the sky.[35]

Herein lies a final irony. In lived history, Paul/Nugent's destroyed manuscript was never destroyed but made untenable by *Infants of the*

Spring's publication. The alleged failure of one of the Harlem Renaissance's greatest artistic minds had more to do with others' ambitions rather than bohemian ennui. Publication of *Infants of the Spring* precluded *Gentleman Jigger*; Alain Locke's supplanting Nugent's art with Aaron Douglas's compromised both Locke's integrity and Nugent's artistic vision no less than Locke's alteration of the title of Claude McKay's "White House" to "White Houses," thereby undermining both the artist and the fire to be found in Black expressions. *Fire!!* emerged to correct this imbalance but could not compete in the cultural marketplace without the support of the artists, patrons, and other "midwives" of the movement. The high aspirations of the Niggeratti and, by extension, Black Harlem in general, are built upon a foundation of bohemian, carnal desires and excess that, while amusing in and of themselves, will contribute little or nothing toward solving African American problems without an increasingly exploitative, or at least unreliable, system of patronage from different quarters. Under the pressure of white racism and Black middle-class aspirations, which respectively seek to destroy African Americans and their culture and fail to patronize it without ideological or other restrictions, Black bohemians will end up consuming themselves, leaving no structure upon which to ensure the future of African America. A possible solution may be a group identity based upon respect for individuality, which offers a way out of an unacceptable dilemma.

At least this is Thurman's reading, which offers a convenient way to dismiss Nugent, arguably the most bohemian member of the younger group and a de facto intellectual rival and friend. Nugent later dismissed Thurman's ending as a half-hearted attempt to draw his novel to a neat conclusion, even as it reflected Thurman's own pessimism regarding the younger New Negro's artistic achievements.[36] If Paul Arbian were Nugent, then his demise is ironic in multiple ways. Nugent, of course, outlived his friend Thurman by more than five decades and evinced very little of the tragic nihilism that marks Paul's life. The Stuartt/Nugent of *Gentleman Jigger* not only survives, as his real-life counterpart did, but thrives, despite the bohemianism of both Stuartt and Nugent. The crux for Stuartt/Nugent is the decoupling of his art and life from commercial concerns altogether, as well as from the uplift narrative that the Black bourgeoisie comprises.

102   DARRYL DICKSON-CARR

Gentleman Jigger (2008)

Richard Bruce Nugent's *Gentleman Jigger* remains one of the New Negro Renaissance's few significant lost novels despite finally being published in 2008 by Thomas Wirth, Nugent's friend and most thorough amanuensis. Composed concurrently with Wallace Thurman's *Infants of the Spring*, Nugent never completed a final draft; Wirth notes that he found several partial manuscripts in Nugent's papers and assembled the published text from the latest versions of the novel's various sections and chapters. Despite this status, the novel generally coheres, at least to the extent that its quasi-autobiographical protagonist, Stuartt Brennan, anchors the plot.

Ultimately, though, Thurman and Nugent's shared efforts in *Infants of the Spring* and *Gentleman Jigger* reveal how much the New Negroes disdained the expectations laid at their feet. Each novel's conclusion reveals not only a failed enterprise but also an edifice constructed with a decidedly contingent aesthetic foundation. When the Manor's denizens go their separate ways in *Gentleman Jigger*, their dispersal results directly from the only prodigious issue of their associations and salons: talk. "In a moment of clarity," Stuartt muses,

> [Rusty] had summed up the great doings of the Niggeratti, and discovered that they mostly existed in talk. Rusty had written four articles that had been published and paid for. Nona had written any number of short stories, one of which had been published. She then had disappeared—gone South to further her studies in anthropology. Theresa had written one story since the appearance of the *Current*, had been kicked out of her position, and then had married. She was now somewhere in Georgia, either having a child a year or abortions.[37]

Stuartt wishes for Rusty (Thurman) to write the great book to which he has always aspired, but what finally emerges is the quasi-plagiarized manuscript analogous to *Infants*, "a play that had been produced on Broadway"—analogous to Thurman and William Jourdan Rapp's *Harlem* (no relation to the magazine)—that "was not a particularly good play."[38] Meanwhile, "all of the [other] promising young Negroes wrote. Bad books, but books. Stuartt

THE TWO GENTLEMEN OF HARLEM   103

himself had done one or two illustrations for magazine articles. That was all. Paul had gone back to Harvard, where he studied law." Worst of all, Stuartt's brother Aeon—equivalent to Jean Toomer—dies, leaving the movement without a truly great, modern poet.[39] Toomer had renounced his identity as an African American for the sake of being an American, despite his earlier inclusion in the movement's publications, and soon disappeared, for all intents and purposes, from the literary scene in Harlem and elsewhere.

As any reader will notice, however, *Gentleman Jigger* comprises two books. The first follows a basic plot nearly identical to *Infants of the Spring*, depicting many of the same events during the most crucial period for the young Harlem Literati ca. 1925–27. These include the first encounters between and among Thurman, Nugent, Langston Hughes, Rudolph Fisher, Eric Walrond, Aaron Douglas, Zora Neale Hurston, Louise Thompson, Helene Johnson, Jessie Redmon Fauset, Nella Larsen, Carl Van Vechten, Alain Locke, and W.E.B. Du Bois as they sought to invent, cement, and define the New Negro Renaissance as a foundation for Black artistic expression for the twentieth century.

Detailing Stuartt's evolving queer sexuality and exploits as a lover and companion both to Italian gangsters and to an actress/singer, the second half departs from the first plot almost entirely, with the Harlem group virtually absent. If *Gentleman Jigger* had been published in the early 1930s in its current form, this portion would have guaranteed both controversy and innovation. In nearly every respect an example of erotica—albeit not an explicit one—it extends Nugent's innovations from his story "Smoke, Lilies, and Jade" (1926) by analyzing sexuality, race, gender, and ethnicity in overlapping relationships. Nugent's earlier story stands as the first work by an African American to feature an openly bisexual character; *Gentleman Jigger* would have been the first novel to do the same if it had beaten *Infants* into print. It certainly merits analysis under a Queer Studies or Lesbian/Gay/Bisexual/Transgender aegis, to say nothing of Nugent's probably unique analyses of New York's organized crime underworld.

Turning almost completely away from Harlem, the second half of *Gentleman Jigger* focuses almost entirely on protagonist Stuartt's interest in recreating himself as a sexual being and artist, one with an abiding interest in "rough trade," or sex with heterosexual men.[40] This shift removes the second half to an entirely different genre and mode and lends credence to

104 DARRYL DICKSON-CARR

the argument that Nugent put the original manuscript that he shared with Thurman away for a time and returned at a different phase of his personal and artistic growth. No longer does the novel—and in this case, Nugent as author—seem interested in understanding the New Negro movement's flaws. Having thoroughly made the case that the New Negro fell victim to a lopsided ratio of loquaciousness over action and artistic integrity, Nugent has other topics to unpack.

As does *Infants of the Spring*, *Gentleman Jigger* details the New Negro movement's inherent flaws that led to its dissolution as a coherent and consciously purposeful cultural statement. Dwelling on the artists' personalities, Nugent blames their own egotism and apparent dearth of coherent definition amongst themselves rather than any external influences from powerful patrons or midwives. Unlike *Infants of the Spring*'s severe criticism of Raymond Taylor/Wallace Thurman's own failings, *Gentleman Jigger* offers a slightly more generous view of Nugent's close friend and erstwhile roommate, casting him explicitly as the movement's intellectual center. In effect, this counters common narratives that the movement's purported "midwives"—Du Bois, Van Vechten, Locke, Charlotte Osgood Mason, Charles S. Johnson, and Fauset—possessed as much agency in defining that center as scholars have commonly credited. In the novel, Nugent identifies seven young artists as the movement's true nexus, the "Niggeratti," "New Sepia Literati," and the "Negrotesque":

1. Henry Raymond "Rusty" Pelman (Wallace Henry Thurman), the brilliant, dark-skinned writer, intellectual, editor pro tem of the *Porter* magazine (aka the *Messenger*), and devotee of H.L. Mencken;

2. Stuartt Brennan (Nugent), the color-conscious, "queer," bohemian graphic artist, writer, and "vagabond poet" from Washington, DC's elite Black bourgeoisie;

3. Anthony "Tony" Brewer (Langston Hughes), celebrated poet and Rusty's close friend;

4. Nona (Zora Neale Hurston), the "student of anthropology" working with Columbia University's Franz Boas and

purveyor of "loquacious dialect witticisms" from her native Southern background;

5. Howard (Aaron Douglas), an "excellent artist" who draws heavily upon west African figures and Pablo Picasso's African-influenced modernism to become the movement's "Race Artist";

6. Paul (John P. Davis), another Menckenite writer and Harvard Law student who writes occasional short stories;

7. Theresa (Gwendolyn Bennett), native Harlemite and short story author.

Although many other figures from the New Negro movement appear in *Gentleman Jigger*, we can argue that Nugent identifies these seven as its center not only because they were somewhat simpatico as creative spirits, but they also stood as contributing editors to *Currents*, the novel's analogue for *Fire!!*.

Gentleman Jigger lampoons these artists for the same reasons that preoccupy Thurman in *Infants of the Spring*. Here we see how the line dividing Thurman's authorship of *Infants of the Spring* from Nugent's composition of *Gentleman Jigger* becomes fluid. As Thomas Wirth notes in his introduction to *Gentleman Jigger*:

> Nugent and Thurman were working on their novels at the same time; Thurman finished his first. Its appearance in 1932 effectively blocked whatever prospects for publication *Gentleman Jigger* may have had. ... The fact that Thurman's novel was published first does not necessarily mean that Nugent imitated Thurman. Indeed ... Nugent alleged the opposite: that Thurman copied from him to create a superficially similar *roman-à-clef*, but one with a different tenor and emphasis.[41]

For his part, Nugent allowed that he bore no ill will towards Thurman and any unacknowledged use of his work; according to David Levering

106   DARRYL DICKSON-CARR

Lewis's notes from his 1974 interview with Nugent, both "were borrowing from one another and knew it … [Nugent] in fact suggests that [Thurman] appropriated much of his novel—but it was ok."[42] Nugent would have to accept Thurman's borrowing, as he freely took some of Thurman's personal family history—already recounted in more oblique form in *The Blacker the Berry* …—to create Salt Lake City native Rusty Pelman's scandalous background, replete with a mother with questionable morals and a grandmother who owned a saloon.[43]

Conclusion

The novels' common origin and overlapping plot points corroborate and reify other accounts of the movement's history fictionalized in Rudolph Fisher's *The Walls of Jericho*, Countee Cullen's *One Way to Heaven*, and Thurman's *The Blacker the Berry* …, not to mention Hughes's nonfictional account in *The Big Sea*. Nugent and Thurman frequently charged their fellow Niggeratti with failing to care sufficiently about their own art or each other's work to the extent that the former roommates once had. Both Thurman and his avatar Rusty in *Gentleman Jigger* consider themselves intellectual leaders for the younger New Negro set precisely because they think and care deeply about African American literature and literary history far more than for the gin-infused atmosphere that fueled the New Negroes' salons. In one crucial scene from *Jigger*, Rusty expounds on Negro art and his place in the movement:

> He was the leader of the Niggeratti, and the Niggeratti led the New Negro. But except for Rusty, they were all rather apathetic leaders. Rusty was the only one of them who had the initiative to push things to the fore—anything, everything—and shade them with black. He was the superb showman—the black Barnum, the opportunist par excellence. He was also vain and had decided that the group was to be recognized as important, and that he was to be recognized as the most important of the group. He was.[44]

It might seem odd that Nugent would elevate Rusty/Thurman as the "most important of the group" after Thurman's alleged plagiarism. We

THE TWO GENTLEMEN OF HARLEM   107

know again from Wirth's interviews with Nugent that he fully appreciated Thurman's primacy as an intellectual leader.[45] Even stranger is Stuartt/Nugent as a necessary complement to the brilliant young writer. As we have already seen, though, Thurman's centrality had virtually nothing to do with chronological primacy or whoever made the first mark upon the New Negro Renaissance, much less published the first remarkable poem, story, or novel. Thurman's willingness to define unflinchingly where he and his peers had succeeded and failed *artistically* made him a prime mover, one that Nugent, Hughes, and other authors praised. Unlike Jean Toomer—analogous here to messianic Aeon, the "greatest of living American poets"—Thurman never eschewed his identity *as* a Negro artist, even if he could not accept easy definitions for the term.[46]

Infants of the Spring and *Gentleman Jigger* ask us to reconcile an individualistic group consciousness, normally considered an oxymoron in the context of the United States' traditional antipathy toward group cohesion, when it stands in the way of assimilation. In Thurman and Nugent's highly contingent shared sense of modernity, with its deep debt to the pragmatism of William James, this dilemma finds a complex pair of voices struggling with its implications. Through Raymond, Thurman tempts us to dismiss his ideological underpinnings as inherently unrealistic in view of the nationalism that Richard Wright argues is a natural, if problematic step toward the liberation of African American art and culture. If a nationalist consciousness requires at least a minimal degree of subsumption of the individual will to that of the loosely unified polity, how could the individual and his art *not* be conscripted into the forces of propaganda? As Thurman's complement, Nugent demands that these dueling imperatives remain ever in tension, with one side of the dichotomy ascending as necessary to resolve the question at hand. Both argue that common American principles upheld by masses of African Americans are the crucial links to African Americans' cultural and political progress. Thurman and Nugent's perspectives on Black art are so closely aligned, perhaps even symbiotic, that we may easily understand how they both claimed ownership of their analyses, unable to tell where they diverged intellectually. Both novels corroborate each other and lay equal claim to a history over which students of the Harlem Renaissance have argued. Read in tandem, they confirm the younger New Negroes' struggles with their artistic identities, struggles the authors shared.

CHAPTER FIVE

Editorial Collaboration and Creative Conflict in *Outline for the Study of the Poetry of American Negroes*

Shawn Anthony Christian

James Weldon Johnson and Sterling A. Brown's *Outline for the Study of the Poetry of American Negroes* (1931) is a compelling instance of New Negro or Harlem Renaissance editorial work. As a fifty-two-page "reader" for students and teachers, Johnson and his publisher, Harcourt, Brace, and Company, envisioned *Outline* as a companion text and study guide for his landmark *Book of American Negro Poetry* (1922). *Outline* not only emerged as Johnson and Brown collaborated on a revised edition of *Book* and as Johnson crafted the introduction to Brown's indelible first volume of poetry, *Southern Road* (1932), but the reader also followed the poet-editors' public debate about the value of dialect for African American literature. From Paul Laurence Dunbar's and Charles Chesnutt's late nineteenth-century popularity, to Johnson's and Brown's subsequent efforts to move African American folk speech from caricature and stereotype to authentic voicing and artistry, questions about the viability of dialect informed efforts at imagining and imaging the "New Negro" throughout the period. In terms of literature, the debates that ensued functioned between those, like Johnson, who felt the singular drive to versify Black speech restrained African Americans' poetic abilities and those, like Brown, who saw the use of dialect or the vernacular in poetry as essential in demonstrating the artistry of African American folk life.

109

110   SHAWN ANTHONY CHRISTIAN

In this context, it makes sense that Brown qualifies his interest in dialect as unsurprising in a letter to Johnson where he agrees to compile and edit *Outline*: "I am, as you probably would realize, interested in your distinction between traditional and authentic dialect," he writes. "I am very much interested in that problem."[1] In the preface to the first edition of *Book of American Negro Poetry*, Johnson is explicit about the problems of dialect. For him, dialect is limiting as a poetic form, bears the influence of slavery, and, ultimately, constrains the realization of the modern artistic expression that he feels African Americans need. Despite Johnson's critiques of misrepresentations of Black folk speech and advocacy for, even encouragement of, artistic autonomy and experimentation among African American artists in general and poets in particular, Brown reads Johnson's disavowal as premature and argues that dialect, instead, is an understudied and thereby easily misrepresented, cultural resource. In his 1930 *Opportunity* magazine feature, "Our Literary Audience," Brown pens a pointed rejoinder to Johnson's assertions in *Book* and reasons that the rendering of authentic dialect is a real measure of artistry and a signal element in realizing an African American literature. Though Johnson consolidates his initial perspectives on dialect in the revised edition of *Book*, Brown's sense about the value of studying dialect predominates in *Outline for the Study of the Poetry of American Negroes*. As I illustrate in what follows, their early 1930s letters to one another and the content of *Outline* reveal how Brown produces a study guide that deploys Johnson's structural aims, but also, diverging from Johnson, explicitly positions readers to explore dialect as imperative in African American poetry.

Intertextual Collaboration

By 1930, Johnson was an established educator, musician, lawyer, writer, and civil rights leader. In the years after the first edition of *Book*, Johnson developed editorial acumen and garnered respect as a literary historian and critic. Through anthologies such as *Book of American Negro Poetry*, *The Book of American Negro Spirituals* (1925), and *The Second Book of American Negro Spirituals* (1926), Johnson cultivates an ethos based on what he views as his experience "with the deepest revelation of the Negro's soul."[2] It shaped his choices of poetry and spirituals that he collected across

EDITORIAL COLLABORATION AND CREATIVE CONFLICT 111

these early volumes as well as his understanding of the need to contextualize them. In the preface to the first edition of *Book*, for example, Johnson not only details his sense that "[t]he public, generally speaking, does not know that there are American Negro poets," but he also situates poetry and African Americans' other arts, such as the cakewalk and ragtime, as "distinctive American products."[3]

The first edition of the *Book of American Negro Poetry* offers much to inform American readers, Black and white, and to respond to their then-increasing but complex interest in African American life and culture. Johnson's stated motivation for compiling the volume capitalizes as much on the limited knowledge that he describes as it does the interest that Harcourt, Brace, and Company engage and seek further to cultivate. In a 1922 "Dear Friend" promotional letter to the National Association for the Advancement of Colored People (NAACP) membership, for example, Harcourt notes *Book*'s potential appeal to anyone "interested in the artistic achievements of the Negro."[4] Even more, it echoes Johnson's arguments about the palpable and dual, racial audiences consuming African American literature yet also placing demands on it. After a reference to *Book*'s preface and Johnson's centering of African American arts within it as "recognized the world over as American products," the letter contends: "No white person can read this essay and fail to feel increased respect for the Negro. Every colored person who reads it will experience a new pride in his race and a new hope for the future."[5] In addition to his poetry, Johnson's success and subsequent influence as a critic stem from his ability to consistently name and write creatively and critically about these nuances of America's reading public.

Sterling A. Brown understands this dynamic as well. His poetry, criticism, and editorial work often explore and mirror African American experience in its racialized and racist contexts. The "dissenting voice" that Brown deploys in reading "popular representations of African Americans" often conveys his understanding of and serves as a response to white readers and writers.[6] "Though interested in all readers, whatever their background," as Robert O'Meally argues, "Brown most urgently desired the creation of a community of *black* readers who received from literature images expressing the meanings of their lives, and strategies for coping with them."[7] For example, Brown argues for the integrity of

112   SHAWN ANTHONY CHRISTIAN

his work in this regard when he addresses Johnson's early draft of the introduction to *Southern Road*. Brown finds the introduction appealing but voices concern that some readers might be led to view "folk ballads" as the primary source for his poetry instead of "folk experience," as the earlier draft appears to suggest.[8] For Brown, it is critical that readers know that, "for my raw material, I have dug down into the deep mine of Negro folk experience." As he emphasizes, "That is my unfailing source."[9] These commitments punctuate the criticism and editorial work that he produces in the years after the publication of *Southern Road* and that coincide with his long tenure at Howard University, especially his column in *Opportunity* magazine, literary histories *The Negro in American Fiction* and *Negro Poetry and Drama*, both published in 1937, and one of the most important compilations in African American literary history, *The Negro Caravan* (1941).[10]

Published within months of one another in 1931, the intentional dialogue that operates between *Outline* and Johnson's preface to the revised edition of *Book* functions as an early register of what George Bornstein describes as the "social component in textual construction and transmission."[11] Indeed, Johnson and Brown's concurrent work comprise linked but contrasting organizing principles born out of a shared appreciation for African American folk culture, mentorship and mutual support. Just a few months prior to the publication of *Southern Road*, for example, Johnson encourages Brown and writes that, "I would not have written an introduction at all, for that matter, had I not felt that they [Brown's poems] would stand."[12] He concludes his letter: "I hope that the book is going to make a ten strike. Certainly you ought to know anything I can do to help along I shall."[13] These representative lines from a 1932 letter capture some of the ways that Johnson mentors Brown as an aspiring poet. They also underscore Johnson's confidence in Brown's poetry or what Johnson describes in the introduction to *Southern Road* as "original and authentic poetry."[14] With its proximity to the other texts that reflect Johnson and Brown's editorial collaboration in the early 1930s, a version of what Noelle Morrissette describes as the "referentiality between [his] works," Johnson's introduction reads similarly to the preface and the biographical note for Brown in the revised edition to *Book of American Negro Poetry*.[15] Johnson situates Brown in the introduction to *Southern Road* as important among

EDITORIAL COLLABORATION AND CREATIVE CONFLICT 113

the "Younger Group" of (male) African American writers that he identifies across these texts and then celebrates Brown as an embodiment of contemporaneous African American artistry and, in effect, the future of African American dialect poetry.[16] As he argues, "Mr. Brown's work is not only fine, it is also unique. He began writing just after the Negro poets had generally discarded conventionalized dialect."[17] Even more, as Johnson concludes, "it is in his poems whose sources are the folk life that he makes, beyond question, a distinctive contribution to American Poetry."[18] If Johnson's introduction to *Southern Road* (and willingness to write it) document his "reluctant" admission of error regarding his claims about African American dialect poetry as Joanne Gabbin argues, then Johnson and Brown's tandem work likely contributes to Johnson's reconsideration.[19]

As their correspondence documents, Johnson enlists Brown to edit *Outline* and proofread copy for the revised edition of *Book*; Brown does this work while having, as he notes, "a heavy load of teaching this quarter (having an evening class as well) and plays to coach."[20] This means that at the time that he compiles *Outline* Brown reads Johnson's "draft of the second preface" and knows its aims.[21] Similarly, Johnson reads drafts of *Outline* as they develop and later its publication proofs. Page edits to the revised edition comprise parts of several of Johnson's and Brown's letters to one another and their publisher, Harcourt, Brace, and Company. It is not clear, however, whether Brown comments on Johnson's striking claims in the preface to the second edition of *Book*. As well, though Brown seeks and likely receives Johnson's feedback on *Outline* as he drafts it, their correspondence does not indicate that Johnson has many general or specific edits. As a result, I read Johnson's direction to Brown that *Outline* "will carry your name" as his respect for Brown's perspectives and support for the younger poet's developing career.[22] Johnson clearly provides guidance on—or his preferences for—the structure of *Outline*. As a result, Brown displays deference but exercises autonomy in crafting its substance and nuance.

As just one of Johnson and Brown's three, concurrent collaborations, *Outline* illustrates well what Ben Glaser describes as the New Negro Renaissance's "inter-textual underpinnings."[23] Additionally, it reflects the professional and personal relationships that often turn on the sometimes less visible, editorial expertise and tasks that several writers engage in as

114   SHAWN ANTHONY CHRISTIAN

they forge the period's literature into a tradition. Langston Hughes and Zora Neale Hurston's *Mule Bone* (1930) is an instructive complement to Johnson and Brown's work. With *Mule Bone*, Hughes and Hurston thought working together would allow them to formally merge their individual but related views on the artistry of African American folk speech and employ it to develop an African American theater tradition. In a 1931 letter to Hughes, Hurston writes pointedly that, "You say over the phone 'my version of the play.' Are not both copies my version? I don't think you can point out any situations or dialogue that are yours. You made some suggestions, but they are not incorporated into the play."[24] Hughes and Hurston's correspondence and notes across drafts of *Mule Bone* and related texts document how authorship, loyalty, and personality lead to an intractable dispute, their infamous "falling out," over the play. Hughes and Hurston's exchanges also point to the nature of their editorial work or their compelling, "manner of revising or transforming the oral tradition" as a means of affirming the operations of African American dialect, especially spoken in the South.[25] Such creative conflicts offer insights into the complexities of the period, specifically, as Lawrence Hogue notes, "the various literary and ideological forces that actually cause certain Afro-American texts to be published, promoted, and certified and others to be subordinated and/or excluded."[26] Given its context and content, I read *Outline for the Study of the Poetry of American Negroes* as the result of the creative conflict over dialect that shapes the period's literature, in this case poetry.

(Re)Framing the Anthology of African American Poetry

James Weldon Johnson's assertions about dialect in the first and revised editions of *Book of American Negro Poetry* underscore his aims to have poets and reading audiences cultivate interests beyond dialect. As he writes in the preface to the revised edition of *Book*, "The statement made in the original preface regarding the limitations of Negro dialect as a poetic medium has, it may be said, come to be regarded as more or less canonical."[27] He adds, "It is as sound today as when it was written ten years ago; and its implications are more apparent. It calls for no modifications, but it can well be amplified here. The passing of traditional dialect

EDITORIAL COLLABORATION AND CREATIVE CONFLICT   115

as a medium for Negro poets is complete."[28] Even with his later distinction between dialect of the "comic minstrel tradition or of the sentimental plantation tradition" and "the common, racy, living, authentic speech of the Negro in certain phases of real life," Johnson's claims of finality here illustrate well the potential permanence of his words or what Brent Hayes Edwards compellingly argues about an anthology's "power," which "is concentrated in its discursive frame—in its preface, introduction, or opening statement."[29]

Due in part to its preface, the success of the first edition of *Book of American Negro Poetry* adds even more authority to Johnson's claims about dialect, which he extends into the revised edition. Though *Outline for the Study of the Poetry of American Negroes* omits a preface, the sets of questions that open the study guide refer specifically to Johnson's prefaces for both editions of *Book*. This structure mirrors what Johnson notes to Brown in suggesting an outline for the study guide. Despite his claim that Brown "know[s] much more about a piece of work of this kind than I do," Johnson suggests content for the study guide and identifies four elements to feature with emphasis.[30] Johnson notes his preference that the guide, "embrace a study of the Preface" to both the original and revised editions of *Book*. As well, he writes, "there should, of course, be suggestions for supplementary reading from the works of the poets in the book."[31]

Brown's questions substantively prompt the "embrace" that Johnson advocates but also advances consideration of dialect as central to a reader's study. Through twenty-eight questions addressing elements of both prefaces, Brown compels reflection in seven of them on dialect generally and Johnson's assertions in particular. For example, the twentieth question about the preface to the first edition directs readers to "Summarize the author's opinions on dialect. Study these carefully, as they will be referred to frequently in considering Dunbar and his imitators in dialect verse."[32] Brown does not simply sustain consideration of Johnson's assertions about dialect through such questions. He also urges a greater degree of attention when he asks readers of *Outline* to, "study these carefully" and, later, to "analyze carefully."[33]

Perhaps less necessary because African American poetry had achieved a greater degree of visibility by the 1930s, rather than contribute to the creation of an infrastructure for it, *Outline* served to deepen

116   SHAWN ANTHONY CHRISTIAN

understanding of and appreciation for the diversity in African American poetic practices. Even though efforts to make African American literature viable as a school subject for American youth, and African Americans in particular, pre-dated *Outline*, presenting and organizing a study guide as a complement to an anthology of African American poetry or literature more generally was still a developing practice. Both poet-editors see value in, "prepar[ing] a handbook that [would] make the study of Negro poetry interesting for pupils."[34] Brown goes further and pointedly asks Johnson, "can't I make it a thing to serve both teachers and students? That would guarantee a wider use."[35] Since it follows his own approach, Johnson agrees with this rationale. Through his query, Brown echoes Johnson's earlier efforts to keep copies of the first edition of *Book* in the hands of African American teachers and students. In a July 1922 letter, Johnson notes to Harcourt, Brace, and Company that "some arrangement might be made for the selling of these books there. There will be perhaps three or four hundred teachers in attendance at the convention" for the National Association of Teachers in Colored Schools.[36] Given the success of the first edition of *Book*, *Outline* was poised to be a timely and useful addition to this effort and buttress marketing for and eventual sales of the second edition of Johnson's volume. Writing on behalf of the firm, James Reid conveys these ideas to Johnson when he notes that, "It will be necessary for you to get your suggestions to [Brown] at once, since we are rushing the pamphlet through the press."[37] Further evidence of *Outline's* viability as a reader for teachers and students comes from Brown in an early acknowledgement to Johnson that he also uses the first edition of *Book* in his own teaching at Howard University.[38]

As companion to a poetry anthology, *Outline for the Study of the Poetry of American Negroes* differs from the larger expanse of material that related textbooks cover, specifically Myron T. Pritchard and Mary White Ovington's *The Upward Path: A Reader for Colored Children* (1920) and Otelia Cromwell, Lorenzo Dow Turner, and Eva Beatrice Dykes's *Readings from Negro Authors* (1931).[39] *Outline* offers a series of questions to answer in studying Johnson's prefaces to the 1922 and 1931 editions of *Book*; contextual notes and bibliographies for "spirituals" and other folk cultural forms such as work songs; a study outline for selected poets and some of their poems that Johnson includes in the revised edition to *Book*;

EDITORIAL COLLABORATION AND CREATIVE CONFLICT 117

and, three appendices—a "glossary of poetic terms," a review of the "main tendencies in American poetry," and a list of "selected poems of Negro life by white authors."[40] In contrast, as multi-genre texts, *Upward* and *Readings* feature poetry, interspersed in the former and as the lead genre in the latter, but neither is solely devoted to it. Of the two textbooks, only *Readings* explicitly aims to guide readers in a study of African American poetry and its development; it specifically showcases twenty-five different poets and offers thirteen pages of notes, questions, and assignments in its "Suggestions for Study."[41]

Perhaps because Harcourt, Brace, and Company also published *Readings* in 1931, dialect was not among the thematic groupings organizing *Readings'* guided study of poetry. Though Dunbar's poetry, for example, appears in the textbook, *Readings'* editors direct readers instead to consider how "nature," "childhood and youth," "love," "the poet," "problems of life," and "lengthening shadows" inspire his selections.[42] Following Johnson's selection of poets and poems in the revised edition of *Book*, *Outline* advances its own version of *Readings'* notion that, "To form an estimate of a group of poets, one should have a basis of studying the entire group in its relation to one another as well as a basis of studying the entire group in its relation to other groups."[43] In *Outline*, this approach facilitates a reader's movement from one poem in a poet's corpus to another and recurs with each poet. For example, in the prompt for McKay's "The Tired Worker," Brown writes:

> a. Connect this poem with incidents in the poet's biography. b. Compare with other sonnets to sleep; e.g. Sidney's and Samuel Daniel's. c. Compare with McKay's other poems of protest. d. Is this poem racial or universal?[44]

In ways similar to the editors of *Readings from Negro Authors*, Brown guides readers of *Outline* to consider African American poetry through frequent review of a poet's biography, and comparatively, in relation to her own work and that of other poets, Black and white. Whereas race is an element in how Cromwell, Turner, and Dykes frame study prompts, Brown privileges it. Far from suggesting that it is the only organizing principle for his and Johnson's study guide, Brown, nevertheless, positions

118   SHAWN ANTHONY CHRISTIAN

race as salient. His question to readers about the racialness or universality of McKay's "The Tired Worker" is an extension of "the racing that must occur in the context of an anthology of 'Negro' poetry."[45] Brown's and Johnson's references to Elizabeth Lay Green's earlier *The Negro in Contemporary American Literature: An Outline for Individual and Group Study* (1928) in their correspondence are germane in this regard.

Early in their planning, Johnson suggests to Brown that Green's handbook has some adaptable features that he might consider for *Outline*.[46] It is not clear from their correspondence what Johnson has in mind specifically, and Brown does not indicate to what degree he models Green, if at all. Notwithstanding, when juxtaposed, one reads a similar use of brief, declarative sentences as prompts for study in *Negro in Contemporary American Literature* and *Outline*. As pre-texts for *Readings* but echoes of the first edition of *Book of American Negro Poetry*, Green's study guide and *Outline* compel their readers to review a poet's biography and comparatively read across a selection of his works. Green's treatment of Paul Laurence Dunbar, for example, provides useful illustration. Across four sections on poetry, some fourteen pages, Green features Dunbar as the exemplar of "Early Contributions of the Negro."[47] Noting the first edition of *Book* among the references for this section, Green is clearly aware of the volume and even echoes Johnson in establishing context for Dunbar's status in the section's headnote. Her contention that Dunbar's "use of dialect verse is his distinctive contribution, but his poems in the conventional manner must not be overlooked" reads similarly to Johnson's earlier assertion that "Dunbar's fame rests chiefly on his poems in Negro dialect. ... And, yet, dialect poetry does not constitute the whole or even the bulk of Dunbar's work."[48] As well, Green directs readers to Dunbar's biography (e.g., "Success of his readings from his own work. His personality.") and then to explore his dialect poems further. She writes: "The dialect poems, their phrasing, interpretation of the Negro. Is the author influenced by the white man's conception of the humor and pathos of the black? Read 'When Malindy Sings,' 'When de Co'n Pone's Hot.'"[49] *Outline* replicates but expands Green's focus on Dunbar.

Again, reflecting the structure of the revised edition of *Book*, *Outline* features Dunbar prominently as first among African American poets. Its section note amplifies the nearly two pages of biography that precede

Editorial Collaboration and Creative Conflict   119

Dunbar's poems in the revised edition of *Book* (not to mention Johnson's assessments of him in the preface to the first edition, which Johnson also includes in this edition). In another echo of the revised edition of *Book* but an element that contrasts *Outline* from Green's study guide, Brown opens the section on Dunbar with a lengthy quote from "The Negro in American Literature," William Stanley Braithwaite's contribution to *The New Negro* (1925). As is practice in treatments of Dunbar after his death in 1906, especially among other African American poets, Braithwaite's reflection venerates Dunbar for making "a people articulate in verse," but also situates the unrealized potential of his talent. For Braithwaite (and several others), Dunbar "expressed a temperament but not a race soul."[50]

Brown's decision to open with Braithwaite, an influential poet, critic, and editor himself, projects another sympathetic but critical voice to frame a reader's extended exploration of Dunbar's poetry beyond his own and Johnson's. Even more, Brown draws on the ideas that Braithwaite articulates to underscore the questions that Brown poses about individual poems. The prompts aim to return a reader to the balance of representative poems from Dunbar's corpus that the revised edition of *Book* achieves through nine selections, including "A Negro Love Poem," "Ere Sleep Comes Down," and "When De Co'n Pone's Hot." The prompts also compel consideration of Dunbar's own insights about dialect poetry— "For Dunbar's attitude to his dialect verse read 'The Poet,' *Life and Works of Paul Laurence Dunbar*"—as well as the complexity that Brown appears to read in Dunbar's life and work.[51] In this regard, Brown first asks a reader to "notice fidelity of dialect" when reading "A Negro Love Song."[52] He also stresses Dunbar's versatility when, aiming to guide further study about "The Haunted Oak," he compels, "Notice that when Dunbar deals with the tragic aspect of life in the South he does not use dialect. Have you any theory to explain this?"[53] The three-page section on Dunbar reflects Johnson and Brown's shared understanding of Dunbar's importance and the constraints to the fuller expression of his artistry. Through its reframing of dialect across the nine prompts, the feature on Dunbar also recasts his status as a pioneering African American poet whose influence stems as much from his popularity with white readers as it does his pioneering artistry as a dialect poet. In this regard, text placement and the structure of *Outline*'s components help make the case. Correspondingly,

120   SHAWN ANTHONY CHRISTIAN

Brown closes the section on Dunbar with the final poem selection in the revised edition of *Book*, "A Death Song," and writes, "It is one of the best known of Dunbar's dialect poems and deservedly so. c. Read aloud."[54]

Dialect as Tradition

In both editions of the *Book of American Negro Poetry*, Johnson includes selections of poems from three early but lesser-known poets—James Edwin Campbell, James David Corrothers, and Daniel Webster Davis— to contextualize the practice of dialect poetry among African American writers and to demonstrate that though extraordinary Dunbar is not singular. As a result, *Outline*'s extended treatment of dialect as central to Dunbar's legacy is not solely Brown's intervention. Biographical notes for these poets in the revised edition of *Book* describe Campbell, for example, as preceding Dunbar "as a writer of Negro dialect poetry" and contend that Corrothers's "dialect poetry is modeled closely after Dunbar's."[55] In these and other ways, both editions of *Book of American Negro Poetry* argue Dunbar's centrality and significance to African American dialect poetry. *Outline* extends this framing and nuances it further in grouping additional poets featured in but interspersed throughout *Book* as "Other Dialect Poets."[56]

In this subsection, too, Brown notes the complexity of African American dialect poetry and guides readers to consider it. With Ray Garfield Dandridge's "Sprin' Fevah" for example, Brown instructs: "Study the dialect for any inaccuracies."[57] Additionally, though the prompt for Charles Bertram Johnson's "A Little Cabin" only compels observation of "frequent references," its direction about Bertram Johnson's use of "traditional dialect poetry" to name and describe "angels, Heaven, Eden and biblical stories" invites, among myriad interpretations, the possible reading of the dialect here as an ironic, even critical, depiction of religion.[58] Just as with the section of prompts on Dunbar and related poets, "Other Dialect Poets" and the recommendations that follow it in "General Topics for Reports" reflect Johnson's distinction between "Negro dialect as a poetic medium" and "traditional dialect," which he notes stems from the "comic minstrel tradition" and "sentimental plantation tradition."[59] With the "General Topics for Reports," Brown offers eight prompts that further

EDITORIAL COLLABORATION AND CREATIVE CONFLICT   121

consideration of this distinction but also affirms "Negro dialect poetry," through repeated use of the phrase in this section, as a viable subject for study. In comparison with the revised edition *of Book of American Negro Poetry* then, *Outline* resituates Dunbar as central to African American poetry because of the complexities of his poetic practices, especially his dialect poems, and then frames such complexity as a signal character- istic of African American dialect poetry. *Outline*'s alignment of Dunbar, *et al.* as forging a sub-category, even sub-genre, of African American poetry reads against the almost simultaneous, postmortem prefacing that Johnson does in the revised edition of *Book*. *Outline*'s framing of Dunbar and related placement of probing study prompts are not the only ways that this companion volume casts as premature Johnson's assertion that the "Aframerican poet" does not consider African American dialect poetry "worth the effort."[60] An element of this measured perspective, which extends *Outline*'s contention about the worthiness of African American dialect poetry, is how Brown juxtaposes "folk idiom" and "dialect poetry."

A subtle instance of Brown's contentions about African American dialect poetry in *Outline,* the first, concurrent use of these phrases in the volume occurs in the "Questions Based Upon the Preface to the Revised Edition."[61] Here, Brown opens with a question about Johnson's distinction about dialect and then quotes from Johnson's consideration of "folk stuff."[62] In doing so, Brown repeats Johnson's emphasis of the folk as possessing "musical folk speech," in the first edition of *Book*, and as "creators" who generate "genuine folk stuff" in the revised edition.[63] The repetition of folk as an explanatory category in both editions of *Book* and in *Outline* reflects, as Mark Sanders argues, African American writers' efforts to deploy folk culture as a means of "reconstructing a cultural past that would help lay claim to full citizenship."[64] Whether displayed in his poetry such as the volume *God's Trombones* or his anthologizing of spirituals, Johnson under- stands the expressive power and artistic potential of these sources; for example, the preface to the first edition of *Book* considers these sources in the context of what Johnson argues is African American arts' "transfusive quality."[65] As I discuss above, Brown views African American folk experi- ence and the culture and cultural forms that result from it as worth *his* efforts as a poet, critic, and editor. Again, Brown stresses this to Johnson in their correspondence regarding Johnson's introduction to *Southern Road*.

122   SHAWN ANTHONY CHRISTIAN

As Brown writes to Johnson, he also wants to be known as a poet who "attempted to deal with it [folk experience] in a manner congruous to the productions of the Negro folk."[66]

Inasmuch as Johnson's uses of "folk" in the preface to the second edition of *Book* further his efforts to distinguish "traditional dialect" from folk speech and, more specifically, the sources of African American dialect poetry, then Brown's complementary uses of "folk" in *Outline* are compellingly in the service of the latter. Likely because Johnson names Brown specifically as a poet who has "dug his raw material from the great mine of Negro folk poetry" in the biographical note that precedes Brown's poems in the revised edition of *Book*, which Johnson echoes in the preface, Brown offers prompts about his own work that identify such material for readers.[67] The majority of *Outline*'s eight prompts name a source of folk experience or culture and then direct a reader to explore further or to consider the source(s) in reading or re-reading a given poem. For example, the first prompt for Brown's "Odyssey of Big Boy" reads, "Casey Jones, Stagolee, Jazzbo Brown, and John Henry are Negro folk heroes. Find out what you can about them."[68] Subsequently and relatedly, for Brown's eponymous "Southern Road" the prompt reads, "In this poem an attempt is made to catch the rhythm of a convict singing as he hammers. Read it aloud with this in mind. Retell the story."[69] For "Long Gone," Brown also notes, "There is a folk ballad on a fugitive from justice called 'Long Gone Lost Johnson,' which deals in humorous fashion with a Negro version of the seven-league-boots legend."[70] In each of these representative prompts, Brown offers brief notes that aim to guide readers to specific cultural contexts and texts. As they often are across Brown's poetry, the folk here are laborers making art through how they live and the conditions they navigate. In these ways, Brown nuances his deployment of "folk" and "folk culture" more than what Johnson conveys through his less precise and more general use of "folk stuff."

Brown's poetry and criticism frequently display folk culture as "material objects, cultural practices and linguistic idioms and forms created by poor and working-class African Americans in both rural and urban settings throughout the eighteenth, nineteenth, and twentieth centuries."[71] Even at this early point in his career, Brown's understanding of the artistry of African American folk culture, especially dialect poetry, compels him

EDITORIAL COLLABORATION AND CREATIVE CONFLICT   123

to treat it as viable for study. In addition to *Outline*'s framing of Dunbar and his poetry as well as Brown's own poetry through this perspective, the volume importantly advances Brown's assertions about the continued viability of folk culture as a source for African American poetry through the prompts it offers for James Weldon Johnson's poetry. Paired with the nine poems from Johnson that the revised edition features, the section "Study of J. W. Johnson's Poems" similarly interchanges "folk idiom" and "dialect poetry" and often names the sources for both in Johnson's poems.[72] Whether in directing readers to "Notice that the poem ['The Creation'] is not in dialect," and then asking, "Does this lessen the folk quality of the poem?" or in directing readers to "Notice how for this poem ['Listen, Lord'] too the poet has gone back to the folk for his material. Comment upon the convincingness of the folk idiom," *Outline* positions Johnson as central to the development of African American dialect poetry and a student of the folk culture that enables it.

In language similar to what Johnson employs in the biographical notice that accompanies Brown's poems in the revised edition of *Book*, Brown introduces or reaffirms for readers Johnson's ability to engage African American folk culture and fashion "something of lasting beauty" through it.[73] Since Brown is the only other biographical notice author in the revised edition of *Book* (Johnson's notice carries Brown's byline), his entry likely develops through drafts that he shares with Johnson. Brown welcomes the opportunity to write Johnson's biographical notice. He revises it significantly, however, to reflect how, in his estimation, Johnson's "life has been of such great variety and significance."[74] Their correspondence does not indicate whether Johnson comments on Brown's characterization of Johnson's contribution to African American dialect poetry. Johnson likely reads it as appropriate, however, especially as he prompts such characterization through his reflections in the preface to the revised edition. Johnson writes that the "blues," "work songs," "folk epics and ballads" are "unfailing sources of material for authentic poetry."[75] Offering a point that Brown echoes in the biographical notice that he pens for Johnson and, as I argue, refigures in *Outline*, Johnson adds, "I myself did a similar thing in writing *God's Trombones*. I went back to the genuine folk stuff that clings around the old-time Negro preacher, material which had many times been worked into something both artificial and false."[76]

124   SHAWN ANTHONY CHRISTIAN

An important detail in the context of his declarative framing of African American dialect poetry in the preface to the revised edition of *Book*, Johnson's statement here provides readers a window into his creative process and articulates the value he earlier views in "genuine folk stuff." In *Outline*, Brown recasts this idea in the study prompts related to Johnson's poems in *Book* and the "General Topic for Reports" that follow. Of the eleven suggested topics, more than half of them compel consideration of Johnson and folk culture or dialect poetry; "Compare James Weldon Johnson and Dunbar" and "Folk religion in *Green Pastures* and *God's Trombones*" are two examples.[77] Again, though phrased succinctly, when read together these topics project the recurring focus of African American dialect poetry that cohere *Outline*. One of the most pointed ways that Brown centers Johnson's poetry in underscoring the value of African American dialect poetry is through the prompt he offers for "Sence You Went Away." Brown writes:

> a. This is perhaps the best-known dialect poem of James Weldon Johnson. It has been set to music by his brother. A record of it sung by John McCormack has been issued by the Victor Company. b. Read other dialect poems in *Fifty Years and Other Poems*, in the section entitled "Jingles and Croons." c. Sum up again Mr. Johnson's attitude toward dialect poetry.[78]

Again, syntax and text placement convey much here. First, Brown opens the prompt by signaling the popularity of Johnson's dialect poetry and, compellingly, illustrating the "transfusive quality" that Johnson ascribes to African American creative practices in the preface to the revised edition.[79] That "Sence You Went Away" is set to music reinforces Johnson's own assertions about the interchangeability of African American musical and poetic forms, in this case dialect poetry. Brown then follows with a direction to read Johnson's dialect corpus comparatively with the caveat to revisit Johnson's "attitude toward dialect poetry." In this focused and dense prompt, Brown, again, argues his case about the viability of African American dialect poetry but does so through study of its, then, most skeptical practitioner and critic—Johnson himself. In doing so, Brown strategically employs *Outline* to counter Johnson's corresponding "death"

EDITORIAL COLLABORATION AND CREATIVE CONFLICT   125

call in the preface to the revised edition by positioning Johnson as chief among African American poets who employ the "cultural forms around them to reshape the past and the present" to envision "a future of greater possibility."[80]

Conclusion

Years after their collaboration on *Outline for the Study of the Poetry of American Negroes*, Brown reflects on Johnson's introduction to *Southern Road*, especially Johnson's reading of the sources for Brown's poems. As Brown relates to interviewer Charles Rowell,

> I wouldn't have phrased it in that way, but I'm glad he said I did that. I certainly believe a poet should do that. I didn't want to give any raw material. I wanted to use it. Take a poem like "Southern Road." I'm using the chain gang swing of the hammer, but I tell a story in there that no chain gang song tells.[81]

Compellingly, in *The Negro Caravan*, the 1941 anthology that he co-edits with Arthur P. Davis and Ulysses Lee, Brown commits to permanence this idea about his own contributions to African American dialect poetry while positioning Dunbar and Johnson, much as he does in *Outline*, as forebears. *Negro Caravan* notes that Dunbar "has long been the best-known American Negro poet. His best dialect poetry has kept a charming freshness over the years; his picture of rural Negro life, though it may seem idyllic, is peopled with likable human beings, not with clowns."[82] The editors also note that, "As a critic he [Johnson] was congenial to efforts at recording true folk speech. His own poetry is transitional: from rhetorical race defense, romantic lyricism, and conventional dialect it has gone to the dramatic portraiture of *God's Trombones*, in the idiom of the people."[83]

James Weldon Johnson made an earlier determination that the African American poet:

> needs a form that is freer and larger than dialect, but which will still hold the racial flavor; a form expressing the imagery, the idioms, the peculiar turns of thought and the distinctive humor

126   SHAWN ANTHONY CHRISTIAN

and pathos, too, of the Negro, but which will also be capable of voicing the deepest and highest emotions and aspirations, and allow [for] the widest range of subjects and the widest scope of treatment.[84]

This presents a challenge for Sterling A. Brown and other poets like him. It is a challenge that Brown meets through explicitly valuing African American dialect in his criticism, poetry, and anthologizing. Through how he edits and structures *Outline for the Study of the Poetry of American Negroes* in particular, Brown demonstrates that the use of dialect is not only essential in African American poetic traditions. He also argues and presents dialect poetry as a tradition on its own and worthy of study. In doing so, Brown re-presents Johnson as a complex but pioneering dialect poet across *Outline*'s pages and, ultimately, claims a different permanence for dialect as an essential resource for expressing modern Black subjectivity and artistry.

CHAPTER SIX

Jessie Fauset and Her Readership
The Social Role of *The Brownies' Book*

Jayne E. Marek

Flexible and responsive, magazines help enunciate and establish their cultural milieus. African American periodicals of the Harlem Renaissance reflected the era's exceptional artistic potential as well as its massive social unrest. Black editors had to gauge how to guide their readers, without overwhelming them, through the competing narratives of the times. As an editor, Jessie Redmon Fauset decisively influenced public discourse through *The Brownies' Book* (1920–21), a youth-oriented publication of the NAACP, and the NAACP's *The Crisis* (1910–   ), notably when she served as literary editor from 1919 to 1926. Under Fauset's hand, *The Brownies' Book* fostered education and modeled the value of critical thinking. Even in its short run, *The Brownies' Book* sampled the era's complicated forces; it frankly acknowledged racism, classism, and misogyny, but it also presented options for reaching one's personal potential, promoted a love of reading, honored children's points of view, affirmed Black identity, and offered hope for a better future. As such, *The Brownies' Book* showcased Fauset's positive vision for African Americans during a tumultuous period of American history.[1]

The Brownies' Book came to life in a context of changes that forced Americans to assess who they were and what they wanted the nation to be. Social and economic effects of the ongoing Great Migration radically altered the composition of communities nationwide, with many

128   JAYNE E. MAREK

Southerners moving to northern urban areas.[2] As demographic changes brought in fresh voters, consumers, and taxpayers, some of whom were unfamiliar with the parameters of urban living, Black civic leaders recognized the need for an informed electorate. As Katherine Capshaw Smith notes, education was "spotlighted ... as a chief factor in racial progress" and pursued through "industrial and technical" training, "liberal arts" studies, and other iterations across multiple levels of schooling.[3] This push for broad-based learning helped communities engage with disparate points of view. Libraries provided many valuable services to their public, offering reading materials and spaces for book groups, salons, and lecture series; churches and schools also housed such groups; and informal neighborhood gatherings and "street corner debates" addressed additional ideas.[4] Yet the public's ability to thoughtfully assess information was a moving target, especially for persons without much formal education. "Given the social and legal obstacles and racial violence prohibiting opportunities to read for nearly three centuries," Shawn Anthony Christian observes, "to produce a (more) literate African America in the early years of the twentieth century was a tremendous feat."[5]

Learning was already being promoted in *The Crisis*, which ran an "Education Number" every July and a "Children's Number" every October, although these issues were not necessarily aimed toward children. While the Children's Numbers helped introduce young people to topics of concern to adults, *The Crisis* was not always appropriate reading for youngsters—its analyses of topics such as lynching and rioting were explicit and sometimes included pictures.[6] *The Crisis*'s cultivated writing style also presented hurdles for less skilled readers. As a more accessible option, *The Brownies' Book* was meant to replace the annual Children's Number with a monthly magazine.[7]

At that time, there were few models of journals framed for youngsters, let alone Black youth, so *The Brownies' Book* had to create its own approach.[8] Fauset, herself a teacher, drew on types of materials that would entice children to learn and dream, and she mixed in practical information about social studies, sports, home economics, and professions. *The Brownies' Book* also meant to appeal to adults—parents, teachers, librarians, and those who were still developing skills in cultural literacy. Since many neighborhood adults joined library groups or otherwise got together with peers to discuss books and current events, information in *The Brownies' Book* could be expected to disseminate throughout a community. Word of mouth would have an additional advantage: inexperienced readers who were likely to find it difficult to parse *The Crisis*'s dense political and social analyses might turn to *The Brownies' Book* as easier to navigate. Fauset's editorial choices demonstrated that she intended *The Brownies' Book* to meet all such readers with respect.

When it appeared in January 1920, *The Brownies' Book* resembled *The Crisis* in format, but the periodical coding in *The Brownies' Book* signaled that its primary motivation was to reach its audience through enjoyment and education, as distinct from *The Crisis*'s consistently political ethos.[9] By its own account, *The Brownies' Book* reached out to "children of the sun."[10] It included tales, songs, dances, games, short plays, poems, articles, photographs, letters, and illustrations for "Kiddies from Six to Sixteen."[11] Such an age range for the stated target audience was not unusual. Many schools combined all students into one classroom, so instructional materials that could address all levels would have been familiar to many students and, presumably, parents who observed their children's work. *Brownies' Book* materials exemplify "cross writing," an approach by which literature for youth also addresses grownups while elevating the child's implied stature, through use of writings prepared for "a complicated and multiply determined audience," according to Smith.[12] This magazine repeatedly signaled that it welcomed parents reading aloud to children, adults deciding to subscribe for their homes or institutions, and persons who wanted to develop their skills in reading and critical thinking but might feel left behind by *The Crisis*'s erudition.

The Brownies' Book itself was not lightweight. The magazine addressed current events, Black history and biographies, ethics, and personal relationships. Regular offerings included Fauset writing as "The Judge," a column of news snippets titled "As the Crow Flies," and correspondence from the audience in "The Jury" and "The Grown-Ups' Corner." Fiction in *The Brownies' Book* tended toward adaptations from other languages, stories about daily life, fairy tales, or dialect stories. While the orthography of dialect renderings might have been challenging for some readers, idiomatic speech could make stories more appealing. Printing stories in dialect signaled that *The Brownies' Book*—published in New York—was

130   JAYNE E. MAREK

open to representations of regional speech and, by extension, of nonurban communities. Along with its strongly internationalist bent—there were stories and information about Spain, Mexico, China, Cuba, Scandinavia, and African nations—*The Brownies' Book* often printed items depicting children of various skin tones conversing and playing amicably.

Fauset's editorial choices were significant, especially in 1920–21, while fallout from postwar civic unrest continued across the globe. As a model for learning, *The Brownies' Book* provided good-natured and eclectic materials that encouraged its readership to test their ideas. As both an adjunct and a corrective to *The Crisis*, *The Brownies' Book* brought intellectual seriousness and encouraged imagination in previously underserved audiences—children, their elders, mentors, and readers seeking personal enrichment. Unfortunately, *The Brownies' Book* was expensive to produce. *The Crisis*, itself subject to financial straits, could not pay for *The Brownies' Book* indefinitely. Despite consistent appeals, *The Brownies' Book* did not bring in enough income to continue after two years. Yet it has earned historical prominence as the organ of a new "[B]lack children's literature" that gained nationwide readership. The journal actively solicited correspondence and creative pieces written by readers and provided "an early venue" for "major literary voices" of the Harlem Renaissance.[13] The era's movements to link African American communities, to attain educational and professional progress, and especially to create positive, powerful self-awareness for Black readers all found a platform in *The Brownies' Book*.

Reaching Readers

Fauset maintained positive emotional inflections in the journal, in part by treating her readership as willing participants in mutual progress. This approach echoed the uplift ideology that energized African American community organizations since the late nineteenth century.[14] Fauset believed in the power of curiosity and imagination. Creating the right mix in the journal required thoughtful selection of materials. Too great an emphasis on didacticism or on elementary-level contents would lose the more mature readers (children and adults alike) whom Fauset wished to invite. Too-high expectations of readers would leave behind the young whom Fauset wished to encourage. A magazine offering solid, deeply textured writing for children—especially Black children—was a new venture; bridging wide disparities in readers' abilities was also an innovation. Fauset struck a balance by presenting an eclectic roster of contributions in a substantial format of thirty-plus pages per month. Issues were eagerly anticipated by subscribers, and each issue took time to consume. Correspondence from readers indicated that entire families would take turns perusing, then discussing, the journal's contents. The arrival of *The Brownies' Book* epitomized shared learning.

The cover of Issue 1 in January 1920 presents a figure of literal "uplift": a young ballerina in a white fairy costume, on her toes, stretching her arms overhead with fingers at an angle as if ready to grasp the future— or the viewer. This image was surely intended to be positive, but it is not uncomplicated, for it hints at ambiguities likely to circumscribe the lives of *Brownies' Book* readers. On one hand, the young woman's posture and half-smile convey a sense of pleasure in strength. These qualities echo a primary motivation of *The Brownies' Book* as a vehicle for Black youths' self-confidence. Yet a closer look at the dancer's face reveals strain at holding the posture *en pointe* for the duration while being photographed. Her sustained pose suggests the effort required for personal improvement, the inherent pain of reaching for something past her grasp. As a thumbnail representing African American life in 1920, this image's contradictory, compelling qualities signal the world that enveloped *The Brownies' Book*.

The magazine combined seriousness with a sense of humor about the foibles of human nature. While tolerant amusement may be expected in a publication for children, it was also useful to put grownups at ease. Persistent undercurrents indicated the journal's appeal to mature readers. This journal, it was clear, would not be a smaller version of *The Crisis*, relentlessly calling for reform of injustices; *The Brownies' Book* proffered a kindly tone by relying on the instructional potential of storytelling as well as on factual information and direct address.[15]

For instance, one narrative in the first issue, "Over the Ocean Wave," portrays children asking their Uncle Jim questions as a result of seeing a newsreel segment about young Filipino women attending the University of Chicago.[16] This detail prompts discussion about geography and other people of color, leading the group to look up items in an atlas (curiosity is a perpetual motivation for characters depicted in *The Brownies' Book*). In this piece, the adult Uncle Jim is not simply a purveyor of instruction; the point of view indicates that Uncle Jim does not know as much as he wants to, so he avoids answering some questions and joins in as the children share information they find. Like youngsters, this grownup wants education. He knows some things, although not everything, and is willing to learn, prompted by an understandable desire not to embarrass himself. Readers of this story can enjoy it for several reasons. Youngsters see adults using hedging tactics just as children might; the story's characters all learn more about geography; and the lesson about ongoing self-education benefits from a dose of humorous surprise. Adults find Jim a sympathetic figure who models how to deal with mild discomfiture about a temporary dearth of knowledge by taking steps to learn more. Jim also demonstrates patience when responding to the children's repeated questions. Persons who might be practicing their reading skills using *The Brownies' Book* can be reassured of the value of persistence, while teachers' and tutors' efforts are implicitly reinforced. Finally, this sample from the journal sets a friendly yet directive tone that remains consistent throughout the run of *The Brownies' Book*.

The figure of Uncle Jim reappears in the March 1920 issue, confidently discussing geography with the children and thereby modeling increased comfort with his own abilities. Such cross writing offers practical information and aspirational coaching. Similar effects occur when articles explain balanced meals for children (which could be useful for adults who might not have known much about nutrition if they had experienced privation) or demonstrate word choices that create positive reinforcement instead of blame (a good skill to have at all ages).

"The Grown-Ups' Corner" represented adult views directly. From the beginning, the column notes that *The Brownies' Book* is for children, but parents are the ones who best grasp children's needs, therefore the magazine invites constant communication from parents. Both adults and children responded positively to the journal's approach. In April 1920, a librarian states she is glad to subscribe to *The Brownies' Book* because it is hard to find good stories for children's hour at her library, and an instructor from the Tuskegee Institute notes that he "read [the first issue] with much pleasure, from cover to cover."[17]

JESSIE FAUSET AND HER READERSHIP   133

In "As the Crow Flies," squibs about postwar conditions, economics, politics, business developments, labor, education, women's suffrage, deaths of notable people, and similar topics were distilled into plain language. This news digest prompted broad cultural literacy, sampling the multitudinous currents sweeping across the world, introducing concepts and vocabulary that would allow someone to recognize a word or name later and perhaps pursue more understanding of its significance. "As the Crow Flies" probably would not hold the attention of *The Brownies' Book*'s youngest readers, but Fauset believed that even grade-schoolers could usefully be informed about such matters. Having a column such as "As the Crow Flies"—likely from the pen of W.E.B. Du Bois—probably seemed essential to Fauset, who compiled a similarly wide-ranging assembly of newsy segments titled "The Looking Glass" for *The Crisis*.[18] Most of the magazine's contents represented Fauset's choices; Dianne Johnson-Feelings notes that Fauset wrote "many signed and unsigned essays, poems, stories, and biographies" for *The Brownies' Book* and monitored unsolicited submissions, selecting "the ones that would appear in each issue."[19]

"The Judge" was Fauset's most consistent means to communicate the virtues of self-improvement and self-control through the pleasant device of anecdotes. In April 1920, during a discussion of what the children think of as "fun," the Judge responds with a whole paragraph on the importance—and challenge—of reading:

> so few people learn how to read; they skim and skip and half understand and don't use the dictionary; and then, worse than that, still fewer people know *what* to read. It is fine to have a friend, and yet you would not make friends with a burglar or a scamp—that is, not usually. It is fine to read, but there are some things not worth reading, and there are other things more than worth.[20]

Naturally, the Judge's young interlocutors inquire about what they should read. The Judge indicates he will say more about the topic later, thereby creating a bit of a cliffhanger for *Brownies' Book* readers, who might follow up among themselves by debating possible recommendations. It is a brilliant rhetorical tactic to stimulate interest in books and make readers

134   JAYNE E. MAREK

anticipate the next journal issue. For Fauset as the Judge, the epistemic question of what to read encoded issues of personal effort as well as cultural value. She urged individuals to thoughtfully take control of their personal literacy.

May 1920's column for "The Judge" defers the discussion of books in favor of another literacy skill—writing. The concept of "fun" reappears, as the Judge and his young audience discuss the enjoyment of "making things." The Judge notes that, while the girl Wilhelmina might like to be a great singer right away, or while the boy William might prefer that things be "ready-made," there is value in personal effort—"the big task always ahead and always growing bigger," leading to the "fierce, sweet, tired, biting joy" of achievement.[21] Fauset's language makes clear that such beneficial efforts include critical thinking:

> The world is full of things to be touched. It's fuller of things seen— it's fullest of things thought. The Thought World is without end in space or time. And we grasp it by writing. It's hard to write well— that is, clearly,—because Thoughts are always big, shadowy, dim things. But try getting hold of them and reducing them to words. Oh, but it's glorious. Did you ever keep a diary? Or write poems? Or stories? My! but what you've missed in Fun![22]

Attaching "fun" to writing may well have derived from Fauset's experience as a teacher who had to overcome student reluctance; it also directly ties into *The Brownies' Book*'s repeated exhortation that readers send in their creative efforts.

Although easier than writing, reading also requires a particular type of adherence. The Judge stood ready to show the way. After a two-month wait, *Brownies' Book* patrons discover some of the Judge's suggestions in June 1920. First come ground rules for practicing reading: "1. Don't skip; 2. Read straight through; 3. Finish ... in reading, as in other things, when you start a job finish it—get the habit."[23] One of the children asks what to do if he does not understand a piece, and the Judge responds, "Stick to it." The column then offers specific recommendations for progressive levels of reading, starting in youth. The Bible, Aesop's *Fables*, Mother Goose, and fairy tales made up the initial set. For slightly more experienced

JESSIE FAUSET AND HER READERSHIP   135

readers, the Judge names *Gulliver's Travels*, Kipling's stories, Stevenson's verses, *Robinson Crusoe*, and the like, making sure to add "above all dear old 'Uncle Remus' … although to really enjoy 'Uncle Remus' you ought to have a grown-up tell it to you in dialect." For the older children, who are developing individual tastes, the Judge mentions *Morte d'Arthur, Alice in Wonderland, Huckleberry Finn*, and tomes of natural history. At this point, the Judge pauses to state:

> when it comes to half-growns and grown-ups, picking out books is like picking out lives. There's not only a world full but all the mighty worlds that have gone have left us their books and we can range amid endless beauty and wonder and knowledge as far as we will. Only most people don't.[24]

This particular column holds up reading culture as it has come down through canonical traditions—although Uncle Remus is an extension of that canon—and emphasizes the value of training oneself to make choices based on the development of ever more skillful comprehension as well as on personal interests.

The next month, in July 1920, *The Brownies' Book* prints a letter from one youth about his own choices, which include books by Paul Laurence Dunbar, Booth Tarkington, Robert Louis Stevenson, Rudyard Kipling, Mark Twain, and journals such as *The Crisis, The Etude, Literary Digest*, and *Competitor*.[25] When in the summer of 1921 "The Judge" repeatedly returns to the question of serious readings, the column reveals that Africa is the Judge's favorite subject. Over the course of three months, Fauset's series sketched the continent's ancient civilization, technology, and folklore, dropping hints also about its hardships. That the Judge prefers to learn about Africa above all would come as no surprise to *The Brownies' Book*'s regular readers, since Fauset included many African stories, adaptations, and photos representing various regions of that continent. Still, despite the Judge's penchant for "serious" African-oriented materials, Africa appears as a vague symbolic presence, at least for the Judge's young interlocutors.

> "[O]ne is able to get nowadays a pretty definite array of facts concerning that wonderful and mysterious land [*sic*]. Some of it

136   JAYNE E. MAREK

is rather sad reading, but all of it is interesting, and I'm not sure but that even the sadness has its good points, because it may cause some gifted young men of this generation to turn their thoughts toward remedying the causes of that sadness."

"And gifted young women too," Wilhelmina puts in jealously.

"By all means, the young women; we can't do anything without them."[26]

Adding a deft reminder of women's essential roles in society, Fauset signals that "The Judge," like her journal's more sophisticated followers, grasps the several implications of such "sadness."[27] Racism and oppression were problems that her readers had to navigate regularly, but, even if the problems were presented simply, Africa required attention and thought from Harlem Renaissance readers. Along with the history of the slave trade, colonial exploitation, and intertribal conflicts, about which *The Crisis* had printed many pieces, in the early 1920s there was a contemporary argument about what Africa meant for the Black diaspora. Marcus Garvey had built up his United Negro Improvement Association (UNIA) in part by encouraging Black Americans to move to Africa; Garvey was raising money for his Black Star Line of ships for that purpose. Du Bois thought of Garvey as a charlatan, as readers of *The Crisis* knew from his repeated editorials. Fauset, well aware of the issues, chose to treat African materials like any other pieces for *The Brownies' Book*. While there were some dissonances in depictions of African clothing, customs, lifestyles, and values, the overall treatment was inquisitive and multifaceted. Africa, which could not be ignored, was at least introduced to younger readers and treated as an emblem for those more knowledgeable.

Reading was the predominant aspect of the personal growth and self-discipline at the core of the Judge's ideology. As the Judge, Fauset repeatedly pointed her audiences toward the qualities nourished by books (for *The Crisis*, she prepared the "What to Read" column and put together recommended book lists). Abby Arthur Johnson writes that Fauset "could appreciate the changes and new expressions" of modern Black Americans and "tried, while on the staff of *Crisis*, to encourage diversified interests and to attract large numbers of readers."[28] Fauset's linguistic sophistication helped her filter and arrange materials for *The Brownies' Book* as well. Much of what the journal printed involved multipage stories, relatively large vocabulary, occasional nonstandard orthography, contradictory ideas, and suspense. *The Brownies' Book* modeled the appeal of being comfortable with this level of literacy.

For several decades leading up to the Harlem Renaissance era, according to Elizabeth McHenry, the increasingly popular women's clubs and societies had encouraged reading but expressed uncertainty about what to read, since the canon of so-called "good" literature did not include African American authors. In the late nineteenth century, "[w]arnings about the dangers of 'bad books' and, more to the point, about the imperative of choosing wisely lay at the base of public statements about reading."[29] Such sentiments echoed the idea of "lifting as we climb," the "uplift" ideology that informed the leadership style of women's clubs, which Fauset emulated in her editorial choices. Fauset, however, rejected the insecurity of nineteenth-century "racial projections that designated black women [or men] incapable of the sophisticated thought required for serious intellectual inquiry."[30] Fauset published many pieces by Black authors in *The Brownies' Book* and, as The Judge, made sure to recommend additional readings, both canonical and extracanonical.

The Brownies' Book printed much work by Black contributors and showcased children's and youths' initiative, using excerpts from letters and printing creative pieces by youngsters. More than one story in *The Brownies' Book* portrayed a young person, and sometimes an adult, who wanted to attend school but had to overcome obstacles, or exercise considerable patience, to do so. Yet formal education, while valuable, appeared as just one way to improve intellectually. Fauset cleverly invites her readers to embrace discovery beyond the classroom. In the magazine's first issue, her poem "After School" depicts two children who resist studying what the teacher dictates but are enthusiastic about doing "sums," finding countries on a globe, or drawing maps by themselves.[31] Other parts of *The Brownies' Book* discussed aspects of natural history—for instance, animals and birds, or details of farming, gardening, or household chemistry. For readers intrigued by the idea of flight, in November 1921, "The Judge" experientially described flying in an airplane—something most *Brownies' Book* readers had probably not experienced. At times, too, young readers

138   JAYNE E. MAREK

were encouraged to question, inform, or instruct adults—a classic outcome in families where children received schooling while parents had little education.[32]

While enthusiasm for learning pervaded *The Brownies' Book*, the curious young characters in "The Judge" or in the fiction sometimes appeared lazy or recalcitrant—that is, they reflected familiar aspects of human nature. Therefore, it is no surprise to find selections that were didactic as well as informative, most notably through her persona as "The Judge." Nor was all the learning positive in nature; negative or equivocal content appeared on occasion. For instance, white activist Lillie Buffum Chace Wyman's extended family chronicles in *The Brownies' Book* sometimes depicted failures as her ancestors and other historical figures attempted to correct injustices. One segment depicts an escaped slave who makes friends with white sailors in a free state but cannot be saved from recapture; the story focuses on his white friends' angry response without detailing the slave's return to the South (and his likely punishment).[33] More commonly, "As the Crow Flies" conveyed unhappiness about world problems through its brief updates on international and domestic matters. Its dry tone tamped down its didacticism, although a sample from 1921 demonstrates how the column framed its data for effect. One entry notes the gathering of the Second Pan-African Congress in Europe, stating: "Representatives from groups of colored peoples all over the world will be present to discuss their problems."[34] The Crow's voice interjects, "No matter how sweet the sunshine or how gay the waters, storms will come. What of it? I fly through them blithely and seek the sun again." The next news entry reads, "In race rioting in the Negro section at Tulsa, Oklahoma, thirty persons were killed and 300 wounded; the property loss is $1,500,000. The cause of the riot was the successful effort of the colored folk to prevent a lynching." As with the African references, the full implications of these data can be grasped by mature readers, whereas children are being alerted to topics of significance that they can ask their elders about. At the least, youngsters would notice and learn when such topics arose amid adult conversations. This sort of cross writing provided additional emotional texture to *The Brownies' Book*.

Like the prose and poetry selections, illustrations in *The Brownies' Book* reflected an inclusive, inquisitive editorial aesthetic. Fauset often printed artwork by women, children, and foreign artists and photographers. Drawings could be realistic or fanciful, some draping across an entire page or filling up the margins. Images of clothes, farms, homes, and social gatherings conveyed the textures of life across the world. The photography repeatedly celebrated Black figures—in formal poses, in school pictures, in various homes, at parades. Some of the photographed figures were opulently dressed—as in pictures of princesses and other international leaders—while others were clad simply, implying that the subjects were of modest economic stature. The range in such images indicated pleasure in the beauties of art and a general determination to educate readers about contemporary global life. Prompted by these illustrations, even less-skilled readers, or illiterate observers, could gain enjoyment and develop their willingness to learn more.

Yet, as with written materials, the images in the aggregate conveyed psychological density. For example, in July 1921, Fauset inserts a full-page photo of a young, Black boy, dressed in fancy cowboy garb, pointing a pistol toward an adult white man, dressed like a "tenderfoot" in a suit and hat, holding up his hands. The child depicted is "Sunshine Sammy," an actor whose real name was Ernest Morrison, a successful Hollywood figure who later became the basis for the "Our Gang" series.[35] The caption under the photo reads, "'Sunshine Sammy' would never do this in real life, but it's all right in the movies."[36]

Fauset surely calculated the implications of this photo, which—despite the caption's disclaimer—contains several problematic subtexts. To begin with, the disastrous race riots of 1919 were barely two years past, and one might find it ill-advised to show a Black person holding a firearm on a white person (or vice versa). The figure of the boy "playing" mutes but does not obviate the implications of ethnic violence, especially since racist whites blamed African American communities for the rioting. For many readers, the photo could trigger a real sense of anxiety. The caption straddles the picture's text and subtext by, on one hand, refuting the image of potential violence yet, on the other hand, expressing a dangerous fantasy world in which such a pose is "all right." The phrase "in the movies" also suggests how childhood play reflects ideologies of popular culture. Cinematic characters at the time were often clichéd figures presented in racist and classist ways. Children pretending to be cowboys might indulge in

140   JAYNE E. MAREK

play with toy guns, perhaps to "fight Indians," which replicates a dynamic of imperialist genocide. Even though the caption softens the photo's meanings by acknowledging that Sunshine Sammy would not threaten someone "in real life," this qualification points out the illusions in Hollywood imagery even though it nominally reinforces proper conduct. The cross writing in *The Brownies' Book* in this problematic picture expresses conflicting messages of dominance, control, and powerlessness.

Fauset nevertheless chose to include this photo in *The Brownies' Book* as a way to draw attention to the achievements of African Americans, particularly children. The picture appears to be a promotional still for the silent feature *Whirl o' the West*, which was released in January 1921 and starred popular comedian "Snub" Pollard and Morrison. An article printed in February 1921 discusses Ernie Morrison's success as "Sammy."[37] By featuring "Sammy," whom her audience might well have seen in films, Fauset reminds her readers that many people nurture daydreams of great success—and in this case, she offers a role model who, ostensibly, knows better than to provoke harm even as he has achieved fame and fortune. A short surviving digitized clip does not contain the scene in the photo, but it develops the story in ways that support the likelihood that Fauset sees Sammy as a positive figure.[38] Supposedly set "out West," the story depicts a visiting "dude" (Pollard) whom Sammy befriends. He teaches Pollard to box and, later, fires a pistol to sever a rope when a gang tries to hang Pollard for flirting with a young woman. As Pollard and the woman rush onto a coach to drive out of town, Sammy is seen hopping into the back, presumably to avoid the antagonists and stay with his new friend. Sammy's brave acts save the day for the bumbling Pollard.

Reference to a popular Hollywood figure echoes *The Brownies' Book*'s inclusion of regional and folk materials. Fauset drew on humor and familiar aspects of human nature repeatedly when reaching out to readers. For instance, several stories printed in *The Brownies' Book* involve characters—both children and grownups—who believe in superstitions. Often, the characters eventually see the error of their ways, but some do not. The superstitious characters in *Brownies' Book* tales were not necessarily tied to rural settings and might not use local idioms, so the journal avoided some of the hazards of stereotyping. However, literary use of dialect was a vexed topic in uplift ideology and among writers.[39] Fauset's choice in this regard came down in favor of entertainment that would engage readers. Stories about superstitions, like fairy tales and formulaic stories involving Br'er Rabbit, Br'er Fox, and other animals, surely delighted certain segments of *Brownies' Book* consumers. In each case, there was didactic purpose in using magic, luck, traditional beliefs, and other folkloric elements to convey the stories' main points.

By presenting dialect writings, *The Brownies' Book* appealed to audiences who would recognize and enjoy the regional evocations; regionalisms would likely have called to mind the extremely popular poetry of Paul Laurence Dunbar and, by extension, would show respect for such linguistic traditions. Yet Fauset also provided correctives. In a story of September 1921, Fauset included a tale in which dialect usage led to a traumatic misunderstanding, when a girl who didn't understand an older woman's pronunciation mistakenly killed a chick.[40] In October 1921, the Judge expounded on the importance of knowing and using proper English.[41] By printing dialect works as well as providing guidance about various registers of language usage, Fauset allowed her readership to enjoy and learn about linguistic and cultural variations.

Clearly, Fauset wished for all readers of *The Brownies' Book* to appreciate the joy and usefulness of learning. Enthusiasm for *The Brownies' Book* demonstrated the journal's value for readers at all ages, as letters to the editor verified. The variety of materials in the magazine not only fed the audience's curiosity but provided multiple ways to think about the contending forces of Black identity and modern history. Considering the magazine's value for youngsters, its "intricacy, multiplicity, and ambiguity reveal [publisher] Du Bois's and [editor] Fauset's faith not only in the capacity of [B]lack children to handle various articulations of cultural ideologies but also in children's literature's capacity to serve as a viable stage for theoretical debate."[42] From adult readers' points of view, *The Brownies' Book* offered a digest of entertainments and news items, enunciated an array of opinions, gave families and schools reading materials to share and promoted global awareness. This last quality was especially important. From our twenty-first-century outlook, we may not realize to what extent information gathering was much slower and more uneven a century ago. Many African American library collections were in early stages, and Black-run newspapers (a main source of information) were

142   JAYNE E. MAREK

subject to limitations in distribution, even proscription (the *Chicago Defender*, for example, was prohibited in many sectors of the South).

Conclusions

Although *The Brownies' Book* had acquired over 3,500 subscribers and was widely known through repeated mentions in *The Crisis*, which had an exceptional circulation of roughly 100,000 at the time,[43] subscriptions never reached the hoped-for levels, and the December 1921 issue was the last. "The Judge" in December 1921 takes a metatextual tack, as the fictional children bemoan the demise of *The Brownies' Book* while the Judge responds that "it's life" and that progress requires "all of us together" to make things happen—and it's "never too late" to try to enact change.[44] In "The Jury" that month, with a final encouraging flourish, Fauset printed a reader's poem, a letter from young person stating that she wished to be a writer, and a short piece submitted by yet another child. Fauset then appended her own note, "Goodbye dear Brownies! How I shall miss your letters!" and signed it.[45]

Jessie Fauset's years as an editor helped shape public discourse about African American lives in ways that reached far beyond her success as a novelist. As editor, the ways she wrote about and framed issues of race, class, and gender signal her sense of the "multiple, contradictory, and competing truths about [B]lack people's lives."[46] Behind the conventions that often directed Fauset's point of view, one detects her "more challenging concerns," Wall notes, although Fauset could be "reactionary" as well as forward-thinking.[47] Some aspects of *The Brownies' Book* did not fully transcend the limitations of its era. While some materials questioned traditional gender roles, there was no obvious interrogation of sexual identity or disabilities, and some of the stories' standards of "beauty" seem regressive now. Even so, Fauset repeatedly championed women's autonomy by printing stories about self-assured female characters, indicating the potential of women's suffrage and of the era's "New Woman."

Appealing to a broad range of readers—children and adults—was key to the relevance of *The Brownies' Book*. Fauset's editorial choices fostered submissions that enacted a psychological complexity that connected with readers of various ages. While *The Brownies' Book* shielded its younger

JESSIE FAUSET AND HER READERSHIP   143

readers from the harshest truths in life, as children's literature may be expected to do, the magazine also offered modulated, multifaceted political awareness that provided a steadying influence for youth and adults alike. Most importantly, it affirmed its readers' desire to hope and achieve despite life in a world of struggle.

Fauset's editorial achievements in *The Brownies' Book* proved fundamental to the Harlem Renaissance. No single assessment can fully plumb the journal's riches. Future scholars might return to *The Brownies' Book* to consider, for example, how this magazine's composition influenced literary monuments such as *The Messenger, Opportunity, Fire!!, Harlem,* and *Survey Graphic/The New Negro.* Some researchers might wish to trace the songs, musical scores, and dance descriptions that appeared; others might consider the breadth and variety of the international stories and games. Cultural historians might assess *The Brownies' Book*'s series of articles about the Girl Reserves, an organization formed to correct the gender and racial segregation of Boy Scouts and Girl Scouts at the time, or the data in articles about child-welfare initiatives. Other scholars might be curious about how Pauline Hopkins's work at *Colored American Magazine* and *New Era* might have influenced the biographical articles that graced many pages in *The Brownies' Book.* As more archives come to light or are digitized for scholars' use, we can anticipate further discoveries about this manifestation of the Harlem Renaissance and its long-term influence. Fauset reached out to a public negotiating the complexities of African American identities in a social environment of vigorous change. By doing so, she honored Black youth, community, the power of literacy, and critical thinking—then, as now, keys to a future that offers America hope.

CHAPTER SEVEN

Pure Essence without Pulp
Editing the Life of Langston Hughes

Joshua M. Murray

In an April 1956 letter to his close friend and fellow Harlem Renaissance contributor Arna Bontemps, Langston Hughes describes the process of editing *I Wonder as I Wander*, his second autobiography, as "[t]he kind of intense condensation that, of course, keeps an autobiography from being entirely true, in that nobody's life is pure essence without pulp, waste matter, and rind—which art, of course, throws in the trash can."[1] In this letter, Hughes pinpoints the anxiety and pressure of his experience with autobiography—a genre that purports to be unabridged fact yet in practice must collapse years and decades into a compelling and easily consumable volume. A methodology of "intense condensation" and editorial creativity appears clearly within Hughes's autobiographical texts, as they emphasize international travel and a diversity of experiences, while downplaying an expected emphasis of his literary career and eliminating many of the more controversial elements of his life. Indeed, his extant compositional notes, draft documents, letters, and promotional materials indicate the editorial construction of his life writings was thoughtful and calculated.

Hughes's process for creating his autobiographies therefore serves as a compelling illustration of the editorial nature of life writing, and an in-depth study of the autobiographical products, as well as Hughes's epitextual materials, demonstrates the innate disconnect between the lived

145

146 Joshua M. Murray

life and the written life. At various points in the available documents, we witness Hughes wrestling with the confines of the genre that forces him to edit and recontextualize his life experiences. While his poetry and other writings certainly stem from personal life experiences, his autobiographical materials are arguably the *most* personal of his works, destabilizing the notion of a single, objective self and establishing the acts of memory recollection and self-writing as innately creative and editorial. By studying Hughes's specific case of autobiography creation, my study sheds light on the tenuousness of autobiography and the editorial nature of rewriting oneself for public consumption.

Autobiography

Sidonie Smith and Julia Watson, scholars who have dedicated decades to theorizing the production and reading of autobiography, explicate the innate multiplicity an autobiographer experiences during the composition process and within the finished product. As we willingly distance ourselves from false assumptions of autobiography—namely, that of autobiography as simple, objective fact—we can begin to understand it as an act of authorial self-editing and textual memory manipulation. In parsing out the various roles of the autobiographer, considering the layers formed by way of a person consciously composing a narrative about himself or herself, Smith and Watson delineate four distinct roles, which they identify as unique antecedents for the autobiographical "I": the "real" or historical "I," the narrating "I," the narrated "I," and the ideological "I."[2] In application, the textual artifact itself transtemporally combines the moment of writing with the written product, establishing the real/historical Hughes as the person sitting at the typewriter composing the draft, "whose life is far more diverse and dispersed than the story that is being told";[3] the narrating Hughes is the omniscient, omnipresent "voice" of the text; the narrated Hughes is the protagonist of each scene throughout the text; and the ideological Hughes is "at once everywhere and nowhere," behind the scenes supplying the "potentially conflictual" assumptions about "identities marked through embodiment and through culture; gender, ethnicity, generation, family, sexuality, religion, among others."[4] Crucially, we must remain consciously aware that "the ideological 'I' is only apparently stable and the possibilities for tension, adjustment, refixing, and unfixing are ever present."[5] Cognizance of these layered personae reveals the complexity of autobiography and its artificiality by way of being a created product more so than an organic outgrowth. This concept is further complicated by highlighting the subjectivity and interrelatedness of the various personae as the autobiographer, in this case Hughes, whether consciously or unconsciously, attempts to direct public response and interpretation of the narrative.

In the case of Hughes's autobiographical materials, the need to edit his life and package it as a marketable narrative leads Hughes to settle upon the primary identity as a cosmopolitan world traveler instead of his fame as a literary figure. Most obviously, Hughes titles his two autobiographical volumes *The Big Sea* and *I Wonder as I Wander*, evoking images of sailors, explorers, adventurers, and global trekkers. While he explores his growth as a poet in his autobiographical writings, this storyline takes a thematic backseat to his travels. Unsurprisingly, then, Hughes refers to *The Big Sea* as an "autobiographical travelogue"[6] in a letter to Arthur Spingarn dated January 20, 1940—seven months prior to the publication of his first autobiography.[7] To understand Hughes's writings as travelogue or travel narrative therefore alters our interpretation of his editorial acts and the subsequent layered personae he creates. Smith and Watson emphasize the broadness of travel narratives—a term that can encompass "travelogue, travel journal, (pseudo)ethnography, adventure narrative, quest, letter home, [and] narrative of exotic escape"—and the specific ways the genre molds the subject's life:

> Subordinating other aspects of the writer's life, [travel narratives] typically chronicle or reconstruct the narrator's experience of displacement, encounter, and travail and his or her observations of the unknown, the foreign, the uncanny. In this way they become occasions for both the reimagining and the misrecognizing of identity ... and for resituating the mobile subject in relation to home and its ideological norms.[8]

Reading Hughes's autobiographies through this lens informs our interpretation as both readers and critics. If he views his autobiographies as

148   Joshua M. Murray

a chance to convey himself candidly to the reading public—whether he actually accomplishes this or not[9]—then his emphasis on travel points to what he deems central to his identity.

Two additional necessary considerations are Hughes's use of emplacement and emplotment, autobiographical concepts that enable the discerning reader to examine the editorial decisions the autobiographer makes in funneling a dynamic, subjective, and unconstrained experience into a linear, finite form. Similar to the ideological self outlined above, autobiographical authors unavoidably carry all components of their multifaceted identities into their creations. Emplacement, then, is "the juncture from which self-articulation issues, foreground[ing] the notions of location and subject position, both concepts that are inescapably spatial."[10] The travel narrative genre clearly lends itself generously to this consideration, as Hughes places his spatial positioning and repositioning as the key determiner of his self-definition. However, while this "concept of location emphasizes geographical situatedness ... it is not just geographical site. It includes the national, ethnic, racial, gendered, sexual, social, and life-cycle coordinates in which narrators are embedded by virtue of their experiential histories and from which they speak."[11] The related theory of emplotment consequently directs our view of the narrative structuring of autobiographical plot. While a strictly chronological approach might seem obvious and assumed, autobiographers (Hughes included) frequently eschew a linear timeline in favor of more creative patterns that spotlight central moments of experience.[12] Sans an achronological structure, the disparity between the narrator and the narrated subject consistently reiterates the artificial nature of autobiography in general. Practically, emplacement and emplotment provide us with significant tools in the study of life writing, as they uncover the processes by which autobiographers place themselves within a setting, in three distinct modes: first, physically, through retroactive storytelling; second, temporally, through that same act of recalling a previous experience; and third, authorially, through the conscious or unconscious emphases, details, and omissions that provide the reasoning behind the recollection in the first place. Awareness of these devices encourages reader scrutiny and brings questions of authorial intention into a genre traditionally devoid of such critique.

With this in mind, I examine Hughes's editorial process for his two published autobiographies as well as his plans for a third autobiography that never materialized. By unpacking Hughes's life writings from the perspective of literary construction and self-representation, in conjunction with key theories of autobiographical studies, we can extend editorial theory to incorporate the autobiographical process, taking into account Hughes's multifaceted identity and thereby formulating a thorough explication of the self-editing of his protagonist-persona and the self-fashioning of his marketed persona. Additionally, other letters and archival materials demonstrate Hughes's keen awareness of autobiographical editing, as he planned his life story deliberately and edited the texts meticulously with an eye to the finished products and their eventual public reception. Such an approach sheds light on the editorial nature of autobiography, while also granting an unusually candid glimpse behind the curtain at Hughes's understanding of the tension at play when self-identity, literary art, and public marketability intersect.

The Big Sea (1940)

Though he had been encouraged to write an autobiography as early as 1925, Hughes finally began crafting his first life narrative in 1939.[13] Even in the initial draft, he seemingly viewed his life in terms of the places he had traveled more so than the writings he had published or the people he knew. By all accounts, the structure of his drafts and finished books places location as the primary component. In a 1939 letter to Noël Sullivan, Hughes references his progress on *The Big Sea* by stating he is "not yet quite up to that first trip to California and the departure for Russia," which would ultimately be cut from the book and reserved for the later *I Wonder as I Wander*.[14] The research notes and early drafts repeatedly indicate this emphasis on travel, including a series of pages showing the itemized trips and total mileage calculations (53,799 miles) for the period of 1931–33 covered in *I Wonder as I Wander*.[15] This fascination leads Joseph McLaren to posit that "Hughes's internationalism, his global vision, underlies his creative articulations in the two autobiographies."[16] It should therefore also influence our understanding of Hughes's authorial self-creation.

150   Joshua M. Murray

The better known of Hughes's two published autobiographies, perhaps because of its scope encompassing his adolescence and the Harlem Renaissance, *The Big Sea* as a literary text enacts key first steps to establish his identity as a global citizen. The three chapter groupings provide us with key details on the first three decades of his life, granting insight into his personal and literary development while constantly underscoring their transitory elements. Arnold Rampersad aptly describes the book and Hughes's writing style as "a study in formal sleight of hand, in which deeper meaning is deliberately concealed within a seemingly disingenuous, apparently transparent or even shallow narrative."[17] Brian Loftus also recognizes the creative compositional choices, claiming that "Hughes uses irony, omission, and distortion to reconstruct his subjects. Ironically, omissions function to produce meaning rather than to repress it."[18] The first obvious distortion appears at the opening of the book, when Hughes begins *in medias res* with a scene of his twenty-one-year-old self's departure aboard a freighter. Significantly in the first chapter, Hughes details his departure from New York aboard the S.S. *Malone*[19] and acts upon the desire to throw all of his books into the rushing waters.[20] Hughes evinces the impetus for this dramatic act multiple times, explaining that "books had been happening to me" and "books began to happen to me" throughout his adolescence.[21] In a 1951 correspondence to Ing Zdenko Alexy, the translator of the Slovak edition of *The Big Sea*, Hughes provides further clarification on the repeated phrase's implication, writing, "My life had been largely influenced by books up to that time—I had read a great deal rather than lived. Vicarious experiences in books. So I threw the books away preparing to live through actual experiences."[22] An anticipated experience that likely encouraged the offloading of his books was the ultimate destination of the freighter on which Hughes voyaged: Africa.

The first chapter then climactically concludes with Hughes's arrival in Africa where the locals call his presupposed identity into question by "not believ[ing he] was a Negro."[23] This shocking moment opens the door for Hughes to continue down the path of an achronological autobiography by detouring back in time to a brief genealogy of his recent ancestors, followed by a review of the significant moments in his adolescence, all leading back up to his African voyage. This dramatic and creative introductory section causes *The Big Sea* to appear more like a novel than a memoir, yet it serves the purpose of attracting the reader while also emphasizing the import of this "big sea" in Hughes's personal identity construction, a move that edges the text more toward the genre of *Bildungsroman*, wherein Hughes details his "journey from boyhood to manhood."[24]

The central and most vital grouping of chapters is simply titled "Big Sea." Here, perhaps more significantly than any other part of his autobiographies, the recursive act of emplacement through the process of life writing foregrounds our understanding of Hughes and his many personae. Scrimgeour recognizes this layering, describing Hughes as

> at once the individual, unembittered autobiographer white reviewers desire and the sterling leader of his race that black reviewers expect. Such a self-creation is fraught with dangers and elisions—Hughes, for example, must keep his ambiguous sexuality a secret, since neither audience would have been receptive to it—yet it demonstrates an impressive, necessary, and striking creativity in response to the expectations of African-American autobiographers.[25]

Ultimately, the tensions of genre and audience influence Hughes's creation of self within his life writing. The resultant site lies somewhere between fiction and nonfiction, as Hughes attempts to insert himself into the narrative, but the created character lacks the dimension and depth of the reference model. Nevertheless, the most prominent and memorable scenes, by design, are Hughes's trips to Africa and through Europe, including his extended stay in Paris. Hughes's work as a poet and literary figure remains conspicuously absent through the majority of the narrative and appears only tangentially at times until the final third.

The last chapter grouping of *The Big Sea*, titled "Black Renaissance," begins to address Hughes's literary experiences and artistic circles. Understandably, this section likely houses the content that fans of Hughes anticipated. Though brief and only a fraction of the completed work, the back third of the volume grants important firsthand insight into the Harlem Renaissance. Hughes fought to keep these chapters in the published book, arguing that the "material was important historically

152   Joshua M. Murray

and had not been written before," and "it was the background against which I moved and developed as a writer, and from which much of the material of my stories and poems came."[26] To this day, *The Big Sea* remains significant as a historical account of the period, "never [to] be surpassed as an original source of insight and information on the age."[27] Still, the majority of *The Big Sea*'s final section employs an episodic rather than a comprehensive approach to Hughes's involvement in the Harlem Renaissance. The first several chapters of "Black Renaissance" establish the milieu of 1920s Harlem, as Hughes details his literary connections and the prominence of rent parties and speakeasies during a time "when the Negro was in vogue."[28] Though more cursory than his treatment of Paris, the details of his tour around the United States finally provide information about his popularity as a poet and his interactions with other key figures of the Harlem Renaissance. Regardless, when taken as a whole, Hughes prioritizes his travels and the portions of his life that do not relate to the Harlem Renaissance.

Despite his apparent confidence in establishing the traveler persona of his protagonistic, narrated self, Hughes remained uncomfortable with the genre's presentation of memory as objective fact. His caution and tentativeness may not overtly appear throughout the text of his autobiographies, but his reticence to divulge certain intimate details or to offer emotional signposts in various scenes underscores his tendency to withhold a more subjective narration. In a folder titled "Research materials and notes/1926–40," a small slip of paper written in the third person addresses *The Big Sea*. Though the scrap has a long red line struck diagonally through the center of the paragraph with what appears to be "no" or "not" written in the middle of the line, the text sheds light on Hughes's hesitancy and self-consciousness in placing himself at the center of a narrative:

> If somebody else were writing this book about Langston besides Langston they would perhaps say other things about him that he [unintelligible] can not say, or does not know ^how^ to say, or is ashamed to say. ~~There are people who know other things.~~ Maybe some of the people he writes about in this book would not write about themselves as he writes about them. Maybe what he writes about them is not as true as what they would write about

EDITING THE LIFE OF LANGSTON HUGHES   153

themselves, but it is true to him. And Langston thinks now that a book cannot ever be true to anybody except to the one who writes it. And sometimes even then[.][29]

The torn sheet concludes mid-sentence, but the incomplete paragraph sheds light on Hughes's concern with appearing overly subjective or less-than-factual. The anxious and apologetic tone attempts to assuage any potential conflict before the public (or those named within the narrative) can inspect the manuscript in the first place.

Perhaps stemming from this same anxiety, when Alfred A. Knopf published *The Big Sea* in 1940, Rampersad notes, Hughes "seized every opportunity that came his way to promote" it.[30] Despite these efforts, *The Big Sea* was a commercial failure in Hughes's eyes, not obtaining the success of Richard Wright's contemporaneous *Native Son*, as Hughes had hoped.[31] The reviews themselves were varied, often split along racial lines, with many of the people and writers Hughes admired lamenting its shallow discussion of social issues and its conspicuous omission of his radical views and publications of the time.[32] The book would go on to receive various language translations throughout the 1940s, and "[e]veryone, it seemed, wanted to read the story of his life"; still, *The Big Sea* was not profitable, and Hughes "lived close to poverty."[33] This letdown would have been particularly painful for Hughes, especially considering his confession at the end of *The Big Sea*: "I'd finally and definitely made up my mind to continue being a writer—and to become a professional writer, making my living from writing. So far that had not happened."[34] The disappointment of his autobiography's reception served as an awakening, reinforcing his desire to present his autobiographical self attractively to the reading public. William Charvat, the pioneering scholar who introduced economic considerations of the influence money and "awareness of audience" had on a writer's literary output,[35] delineates how the profession of writing sways the act of creation itself: "The problem of the professional writer is not identical with that of the literary artist; but when a literary artist is also a professional writer, he cannot solve the problems of the one function without reference to the other."[36] During the long gestation period for his second autobiography, then, Hughes certainly desired to avoid a similar letdown with the publication of *I Wonder as I Wander*. His

154   Joshua M. Murray

reinvigorated involvement in the promotion and marketing of the book, as evidenced through his letters and other archival materials, demonstrates the ways his quest to succeed as a professional writer impacts a deliberate construction of his character-identity, both in the text and in its publicity.

I Wonder as I Wander (1956)

Soon after the publication of *The Big Sea*, Hughes knew he would write another autobiography and began the planning process almost immediately, despite several false starts and an ultimate delay in completion. Over the course of sixteen years, he kept the second volume in mind even when he needed to prioritize other projects. The final necessary push for Hughes was the $2,500 he received from Rinehart to publish the autobiography, "by far his largest advance ever."[37] For Hughes's second autobiographical effort, Carl Van Vechten suggested that he attempt to include more information specifically addressing race relations in America; in a 1941 letter, Hughes responds, "I agree with you about the second part of The Big Sea. Only I don't want it to get so weighty that it weighs me down, too."[38] At play within the construction of *I Wonder as I Wander*, then, is the tension between Hughes's personal experiences and more general commentary regarding the racist laws and societies of his travels. Hughes conveys the challenge of this balancing act in the 1956 letter to Arna Bontemps, in which he explains:

> My No. 2 LIFE is going to be good. ... I've now cut out all the impersonal stuff, down to a running narrative with me in the middle on every page, extraneous background and statistics and stories not my own gone by the board. The kind of intense condensation that, of course, keeps an autobiography from being entirely true, in that nobody's life is pure essence without pulp, waste matter, and rind—which art, of course, throws in the trash can. No wonder folks read such books and say, "How intensely you've lived!" (The three hundred duller months have just been thrown away, that's all, in this case; as in THE BIG SEA, too. And nobody will know I ever lived through them. They'll think I galloped around the world at <top> speed.)[39]

As autobiographer, he discovers the falsity of the text that mounts with each cut and consolidation. With this in mind, Rampersad considers the effect Hughes's edits have on the finished book, proposing that

> *I Wonder as I Wander* raises questions about the tension between truth and design—about the relationship between the facts of Hughes's life and the art of autobiography, which inevitably involves selection, suppression, and more than a little invention, as the writer seeks both to make his or her story vivid and to present a self-portrait that is compelling and also credible.[40]

With an eye to Hughes's editorial work as professional writer aware of audience expectations and the business of marketing, we can gain insight into his creative process from the published text and even more so from the ancillary epitexts.

In terms of chronology, the 1956 published version of *I Wonder as I Wander* follows a more traditional path than *The Big Sea*, opting to pick up almost exactly where the first book left off with his decision to become a professional writer. Instead of opening with another attention-grabbing scene of a definitive moment in Hughes's life, then, the initial chapter serves as a quick refresher of Hughes's life in 1929 and 1930, before settling into a slower rhythm to recollect his Caribbean voyages to Haiti and Cuba. Despite a more straightforward start, Hughes ultimately follows a similar overall structural pattern to his first volume, organizing the eight chapter groupings around his mostly transnational travels. Though covering a much shorter period of time than *The Big Sea*, his denser second autobiography encompasses a truly global narrative, following Hughes through the Caribbean, to Russia and Uzbekistan, to Japan and China, to California by way of Hawaii, to Mexico, and finally to Spain, with briefer, inconsequential stops along the way. His self-editing still paints him as the consummate wanderer, with his literary endeavors appearing as more of a side project. By his own admission, Hughes considers his life writings to be autobiographical travelogues; by definition, then, their emphasis on Hughes's transnational exploits makes them a success. Nonetheless, the tension between unabridged, historical, lived experience and a consciously edited narrative intended for a

156   Joshua M. Murray

public audience conspicuously underlies the autobiography's creation. The diversity of locales enables Hughes to address a wider range of topics and experiences than he had previously, yet many of his more radical beliefs and writings again appear watered down or altogether deleted. Indeed, Hughes dedicates roughly two-fifths of the book to the retelling of his time in Soviet Asia, yet his own Communist leanings are nowhere to be found. Juan J. Rodriguez Barrera illuminates Hughes's retroactive self-editing as an autobiographer–narrator in the McCarthy-era 1950s who attempts to smooth over and mute "his radical consciousness by omitting or altering a number of experiences and observations" he had in the 1930s.[41] Though more willing to give Hughes the benefit of the doubt by claiming he does at least "expose himself partly" in his two autobiographies, R. Baxter Miller recognizes that "though we catch rare glimpses of Hughes the man, this narrator does withdraw often into obscurity and silence, leaving the reader to make his or her own sense of social or historical disorder."[42]

Interestingly, despite the actual content of the published volume in 1956, Hughes chose to double down on his self-promotion efforts by relying upon various sensationalized elements in an attempt to gain a broader readership; in the available materials, he takes advantage of the compelling momentum afforded his autobiographies via the omission of the "duller months." In contrast to the supposed complaint in his letter to Bontemps, this practice purposefully avoids a holistic consideration of the book. At this moment, Hughes appeals to the business of literature. Whereas we might consider Hughes's self-articulation of his autobiographical persona complete at the moment of publication, we can alternatively see how Hughes attempts to continue his self-fashioning by maintaining authorial control even after its publication. Likely as a result of his experience with the reception of *The Big Sea*, then, Hughes inserts himself into the publicity and promotion of *I Wonder as I Wander* on a much larger scale, moving away from the self-editing of a protagonist-persona within an autobiographical text into the self-fashioning necessary for marketing and sensationalizing that text for public consumption. For this reason, I focus less on another close reading of *I Wonder as I Wander* and instead formulate a critical engagement with Hughes's attempt to mold audience interest and reception.

This attempt directly relates to Hughes's continual crafting of his identity through his life writings. For instance, a synopsis included in his archival materials—appearing to have been written by Hughes himself, based on the handwritten edits accompanying the draft—embraces sensational marketing tools to emphasize, and even misrepresent at times, various elements of the book:

> I WONDER AS I WANDER is a personal narrative of travel and adventure in the world of both poetry and politics from the America of the depression period to Russia of the famine years, from Harlem around the world to Samarkand and back via the Golden Gate, from Topeka to Tashkent. It is the simple yet dramatic chronicle of a Negro writer's wanderings from the Caribbean to Soviet Asia, China and Japan, with poetry as a passport and the written word as a ticket into the cities and homes and hearts of people around the world. ... This book contrasts, too, the handling of the color line in such varied places as Haiti and Uzbekistan, the United States and the USSR, but always in terms of people not problems, of incidents not social theory. ... [T]his is a book about the men and women and children and dogs around the world whom the author, regardless of class, color, or politics, liked or disliked in his years of wandering. It is a warm and intimate and almost continuously amusing book revealing the personality of an American writer in his journeying around and about this warm and human and exciting ~~world~~ ^earth^ he loves.[43]

As a theme in Hughes's *I Wonder as I Wander* promotional materials, international travel appeals to the audience's sense of adventure while mentions of race and politics seek to engage readers on a deeper level. Hughes purposefully calls upon the controversial political milieu of Asia to entice potential readers, yet Hughes neglects to reveal many details regarding his leftist tendencies and ties to the Communist party during the 1930s. Though the scenes mentioned in the synopsis technically exist in the book, it verges on false advertisement if the readers come to expect lurid details from within the Soviet Union. With the Second Red Scare

158   JOSHUA M. MURRAY

fresh in the minds of contemporary Americans, this fact surely raised some interest in prospective readers.

Continuing this mode of inquiry, Hughes's archives include an undated list of blurbs and a list of publicity ideas, the latter of which Hughes sent to Theodore "Ted" Amussen, his editor at Rinehart, two months before the autobiography's publication.[44] These promotional materials demonstrate his desire to gain a broad audience while foregrounding certain themes in *I Wonder as I Wander*. In each of these cases, the advertisements emphasize a variety of elements from his second autobiography, often amplifying minor scenes or details as a way of creating a diverse series of statements. In his list of blurbs, for instance, Hughes primarily employs general and ambiguous statements that offer little insight into the book itself, as can be seen in six examples: "the story of a story teller whose stories are not stories but <u>real</u> stories"; "the saga of a soul carrying a body about the globe cue-balled by its times—and eight-balled now and then"; "the narrative of a journey around the world from capitalism to communism and back"; "the canvas of finding the same blue sky and the same stars everywhere"; "a simple history of our complex times"; and "the beginning and the end of a book, with something, between the first word and the last word, called LIFE."[45] The list sent to Amussen follows a different format by offering reasons the book might interest potential readers. The quick snippets continue to prioritize transnationalism and sensationalism, though the first does reference Hughes's literary pedigree. Subtitled with the parenthetical suggestion "Possibly for an Ad or a Mailing," the list includes, among others: "If you want to know how to become a <u>PROFESSIONAL WRITER</u> read I WONDER AS I WANDER"; "If you want to know how they make <u>LOVE IN UZBEKISTAN</u> read I WONDER AS I WANDER"; "If you want to know how <u>LIFE IN THE SOVIET UNION</u> impressed a Negro writer read I WONDER AS I WANDER"; "If you want to know about <u>COLOR LINES AROUND THE WORLD</u> read I WONDER AS I WANDER"; "If you want to know about the <u>HORRORS OF SHANGHAI</u> read I WONDER AS I WANDER"; "If you want to travel around the whole wide world, <u>TOPEKA TO TASHKENT, HARLEM TO HELSINKI, SAMARKAND TO SPAIN, ^MEXICO TO MADRID,^</u> read I WONDER AS I WANDER."[46] In each case, regardless of his apparent motive for universality or controversy, these introductions to the book

EDITING THE LIFE OF LANGSTON HUGHES   159

remain consistent with the autobiographical self he began fashioning in *The Big Sea*.

Hughes's archival materials include other examples of his desire for input and control over the publicity of his autobiography, including a *Chicago Defender* advertisement proposing the book as "<u>AN IDEAL CHRISTMAS GIFT</u>"[47] and an invitation to an "<u>AUTOGRAPHING PARTY</u>" in honor of the newly released autobiographies by Hughes, Eartha Kitt, Pauli Murray, and Henry Armstrong.[48] Ultimately, the bulk of these marketing materials serve two functions. First, each time Hughes summarizes or presents the contents of his autobiography, he does so in terms of a global, transnational identity. He highlights the travel aspects explicitly, while downplaying his controversial views of the period. These materials, therefore, contain multiple syntactical constructions of transition. In fact, these locations and the act of travel appear more prominently than Hughes's name or his status as a literary figure. Even the blurbs that discuss the book in the most generic of terms offer an image of a book worthy of consumption by anyone capable of reading, regardless of race, nationality, or gender. These concepts lead organically into the second function of these pieces. Not only do these glimpses of the book continue the self-construction Hughes begins in his first autobiography, but they do so alongside the idea that the consumers could be first-time readers of Hughes. In this way, the brief synopses of the life of Hughes are more accessible than either of his published autobiographies. For some readers, the first idea they consider regarding Hughes could be the fact that he traveled globally, spending a good deal of time in Soviet Russia. Yet, while *The Big Sea* begins Hughes's work of self-editing and self-creation, the external publicity materials begin to play a similar role in establishing his identity for a potential audience. As a result, we can see that Hughes clearly views his globetrotting identity as important and compelling for telling his life story.

Despite his attempts to create a bestseller, however, his second autobiography followed in the footsteps of his first by failing to live up to his expectations. In a review of *I Wonder as I Wander*, dated December 23, 1956, J. Saunders Redding provides a mixed critique, arguing that the book "is frank and charming, though neither events nor people are seen in depth. Mr. Hughes, it seems, did more wandering than wondering."[49]

160   Joshua M. Murray

In a 1943 letter to Bontemps, thirteen years prior to the publication of the second autobiography, Hughes appears to admit the same thing: "'I Wonder As I Wander' might even now be published, if I did not wander even more than I wonder."[50] For other critics, "[t]he two main points of critical disagreement were the quality of genial detachment that was central to the narrative and ... his treatment of radicalism."[51] Here, as in *The Big Sea*, Hughes's propensity for withholding certain intimate details widens the chasm between Hughes and his constructed self.

Potential Energy

Though the available secondary criticism of Hughes's life writing is limited to *The Big Sea* and *I Wonder as I Wander*, in consideration of Hughes's autobiographical corpus, it is worth noting that he originally planned to continue his autobiography past the two volumes. Hughes mentions a third autobiography in passing several times, such as in letters to Maxim Lieber in 1956,[52] to Roy Blackburn in 1956,[53] and to Bontemps in 1954[54] and 1962.[55] Not to limit himself to only three volumes, Hughes writes to Bontemps in 1963, "I myself plan to do perhaps a third autobiographical volume in due time; maybe even a fourth."[56] Despite archival materials and letters referencing Hughes's intention for a third autobiography, this fact and its related information remain conspicuously absent, even in Rampersad's exhaustive two-volume biography and Miller's useful consideration of Hughes's autobiographies.[57] The recently published *Selected Letters*, edited by Rampersad and David Roessel, contains no editorial footnote or explanation when Hughes mentions a third volume explicitly. James A. Emanuel, in his biography *Langston Hughes* (1967), written with Hughes's consent before his death, makes one of the few external references to an additional autobiography when he claims that "the sequel that he hopes to record should rival" his first two autobiographies.[58] In a copy of a letter addressed simply to "L.G.,"[59] Hughes discusses his personal understanding of his autobiographies, as well as his thoughts for a potential third: "My first autobiography, THE BIG SEA, was about trying to become a writer, my 2nd, I WONDER is about being a writer, and my third will ~~be about~~ concern trying to remain a writer."[60] Interestingly, Hughes frames his autobiographical journey in terms of his identity as a writer, despite the fact that any discussion of literary endeavors comprises the minority of his writing, taking a backseat to his journeys of the 1920s and 1930s. Based on the available materials indicating his plans for continued work on his autobiography, however, Hughes maintained a fascination with his global travels, and he tied this interest to his self-edited identity. While a third autobiography never moved past the idea stage, the information we have contributes to the complexities of Hughes's autobiographical life and writings.

Fortunately, Hughes found the archiving of his letters and other writings to be important, leading him to donate the majority of the available archival materials himself.[61] These vast stores of letters and research notes enable us to understand his thought process in the preparation of his works. Even prior to the publication of *I Wonder as I Wander*, Hughes had the idea for a third volume in mind. For instance, on a list of possible titles for his second autobiography, "3rd Volume" appears at the bottom of the page next to the titles "TOMORROW'S NOT TODAY" and "COME TRAVEL WITH ME."[62] Perhaps the greatest information along these lines comes from several folders in Hughes's archives containing research and preparation materials for a proposed third autobiography. The materials include a chronology of Hughes's travels during the 1930s and 1940s, indicating that Hughes planned for a third autobiography while he was still preparing *I Wonder as I Wander*. Containing a red pencil line dividing a page of events from 1935 to 1942, the page shows the words "2nd 'Big Sea'" written above the line and "3rd 'Big Sea'" below.[63] While most references simply address the volume as "3rd Big Sea," the materials also demonstrate that Hughes considered other possible titles such as "50 Years a Negro"[64] and "DON'T WORRY ABOUT THE SUNSET GUN," a reference to Dorothy Parker's 1928 volume of poetry, *Sunset Gun*.[65]

At one point, then, Hughes apparently planned for his third volume to continue the story where his second left off. More than a chronological endeavor, however, the folder indicates a reevaluation of his entire life. No official draft or outline for a third volume exists, but the materials in this archive include more than direct references to the possibility of an autobiography. If categorized, the notes and excerpts housed in this collection could perhaps more accurately be considered a scrapbook. The largest folder contains a diverse assortment of writings and clippings, including Archibald Rutledge sonnets, a map of Paris, childhood drawings, and career test score sheets, in addition to numerous handwritten notes. Taken as a whole, no coherent narrative or chronology presents itself. This collection of information offers no skeleton of a third volume; if anything, the folder presents a palimpsest in which the disparate articles emphasize the diversity of Hughes's interests and lived experiences. Most importantly here, as with his two published autobiographies, Hughes yet again finds himself confronted with the question of how to recreate himself through the autobiographical act. While many of the artifacts appear to be sentimental ephemera, their inspiration holds the potential energy of recollection and rewriting.

The discussion here only scrapes the surface of the various notes and materials in the Langston Hughes Papers, many of which appear not to have an obvious purpose for inclusion in the archives. Yet, in seeking the author's own sense of selfhood and identity, there is no better place to look. Miller contends, "It would be an oversimplification" to believe "that Hughes wrote two autobiographies without revealing himself."[66] In a way, this is true. However, the concern resulting from an examination of Hughes's life writings is not that he refused to reveal himself, but that he revealed multiple selves while remaining at arm's length. Nonetheless, Hughes the autobiographer undertook an extremely personal endeavor. His techniques (and choices) suggest that we must reevaluate our tendency to use autobiographical texts as reliable, historical documents, when in fact they are as created as any poem, story, or play. Yet, as a result of what is edited out, we gain a new appreciation for the genre that still points back to the author, a man who understood his role in the business of literature and the business of being a Black writer in America. As we scrutinize the words on the page, we can ultimately seek—and often find—a more insightful glimpse into the author's mind, self-estimation, and creative process.

III Editorial Frameworks

CHAPTER EIGHT

Desegregating the Digital Turn in American Literary History

Korey Garibaldi

Like many of his early twentieth-century peers of color, Arturo Schomburg was captivated by powerful narratives of Black life published across the Atlantic World. Schomburg catalogued related texts obsessively, which often refused racial, ethnic, and literary categories. Nor did he limit his book collecting to "Black" literature published in English. In 2000, James Briggs Murray, the Founding Curator of the Schomburg Center's Moving Image and Recorded Sound Division (New York Public Library), published "Democratizing Education at the Schomburg: Catalog Development and the Internet." In this essay, Murray took pains to describe the early years of the Schomburg Center's "digital turn" as guided by its namesake's open-minded, painstaking approach to recovering the past:

> There were no online catalogs for him to peruse—indeed he could find no manual catalog through which he could readily search Africana. Eventually, therefore, he traveled the globe in search of documentation of Africa and its peoples, gathering all that he could find that was either by or about the global Black experience. He dreamed of disseminating that documentation to anyone and everyone thirsting for knowledge of the glory of Africa's past, as well as the accomplishments of her descendants

in the African Diaspora, dispersed throughout the globe largely via the business of enslavement.[1]

Schomburg's broad interpretation of Afro-diasporic literary culture was informed, in part, by his own story. Schomburg's heritage was Afro-Latinx and German, and he did not immigrate to Brooklyn from Puerto Rico until the relatively mature age of seventeen in 1891.

From a quantitative and historical perspective, Schomburg would have cherished how accessible texts with Black cultural themes, and Black writing, have become after close to four decades of digital humanities (DH) scholarship. Humanities computing in the form of database construction in this amorphous literary genre was initiated by the Project on the History of Black Writing (HBW) in the early 1980s; in the twenty-first century, early, ongoing, and related initiatives are complemented by a host of digital technologies enabling the recovery and analysis of more digitized texts than ever before.[2] And yet there is a lot more cynicism in the DH field than these achievements might otherwise suggest. This includes frequent—highly publicized and highly politicized—infighting within the unwieldy, faction-ridden sphere of digital literary research. Inequitable allocations of institutional support and resources are at the center of most of these tensions. At the same time, some of these problems in the digital field surely bear some relation to much earlier separatist tendencies both in and outside of the American academy. But even some of the most astute commentaries on the "digital divide" have not perceived either race or gender as factors that may be exacerbating unequal access to DH resources.[3]

A cohort of leading scholars in traditional literary studies have been unequivocal in calling for "desegregation" in their areas of specialization.[4] Moreover, similar critiques are by no means entirely absent from recent critical assessments of socio-cultural challenges in the digital field. In 2020, Howard Rambsy II argued that in addition to a general marginalization of Black scholars in the DH, there is "also the matter of segregation—or persistent exclusion from projects and opportunities that are ostensibly open to all but invariably involve primarily white scholars."[5] Despite how important observations like these are, it remains uncommon to attribute difficulties and fractures in the DH to segregation.

One consequence of this paradigm is that any potential "desegregation" of the digital field remains woefully undertheorized.[6] More problematic still, many authoritative and influential digital humanists—including some underrepresented minorities, and a growing number of women— still equivocate on sympathizing with critiques of racial (and other forms of) homogeneity in the field. Cynics might argue that the current list of problems and challenges is so depressingly long that imagining an inclusive digital future is pointless. But building equitable partnerships in the DH is by no means a lost cause, and it would be a mistake for scholars and other practitioners to treat it as such.

The primary aim of this chapter is to consider how racial segregation in twentieth-century American society and print culture has informed and undermined numerous achievements made possible by the digital turn in the humanities. As just one valuable yet under-examined historical example, literary interracialism in the early twentieth century could offer DH practitioners countless generative cases studies for considering when and where racial lines and related categories blur in the digitized past.[7] Despite numerous problems and setbacks, there were countless experiments with literary pluralism in the forms of writing and working across racial divides in the first three decades of the twentieth century. Investigating the roots, dismantling, and re-emergence of segregation in literary culture—as well as shifts in how persons of Black African descent were racialized—offers a valuable case study for contextualizing the need for inclusive DH designs and professional collaborations.

Somewhat ironically, computational studies supported by "big data," which often fails to register blurred racial lines in the literary record, may be the best resource for building on Schomburg's capacious methodologies.[8] While Schomburg made it his life's work to collect "all that he could find that was either by or about the global Black experience," an array of boundaries has inhibited similar orientations in DH research in the field of literary history. To be sure, DH work on African American literary history is one of the most racially inclusive sectors in the broader digital field. Still, it bears keeping in mind that at least some of its antiracist, well-meaning practitioners characterize their African American DH work (at least rhetorically) as unequivocally "Black."[9] In other DH sectors, which are typically far less diverse than the Black DH, claims that this work is

168   KOREY GARIBALDI

both collaborative and firmly committed to increasing "access" have been regarded with suspicion by marginalized groups. Indeed, neither claim has stopped numerous critics from questioning why institutional funding, support and other resources are disproportionately granted to white men in computational literary studies.

The following sections of this chapter imagine what the future of DH research might look like if scholars were more diligent in marking race, segregation, and interracialism in the literary past.[10] A written exchange between the "dean" of the Harlem Renaissance, Alain Locke, and Claude McKay, who rebuffed racial labels for his writing, illuminates how complex this professional dynamic once was by the second half of the 1920s. Locke wrote McKay in April 1927, "The movement suffers—but that is your prerogative. I hope you will find the abstract universal [i.e., non-racial-ized] recognition you desire. My opinion is that your previous work and acceptance of racial representativeness and spokesmanship will follow you through life and posterity."[11] The "movement" in question is what had become commonly known by the late 1920s as the "Negro Renaissance." Like Jean Toomer, Jessie Fauset, Isaac Fisher, Nella Larsen, W.S. Braith-waite, and several other critically acclaimed Black writers, McKay wasn't abandoning his racial identity by rejecting Locke's marketing and inter-pretation of Black authorship. Sharing much in common with Toomer in particular, McKay was simply refusing a racialized classification that limited his work to one side of the color line. Rather than building on the racial barriers Black writers broke in the 1910s and 1920s, gener-ally speaking, the DH have over-determined "Black" and "white" racial categories for authors of color like McKay and Schomburg. But markedly dissimilar from our own social, professional, and academic standards in the twenty-first century, the majority of intellectual "gate keepers" working in the ivory tower prior to the 1930s were unquestionably racist, sexist, and hostile to cultural interracialism. Moreover, scholarly inatten-tion and disagreements over Jim Crow in the literary field during the early twentieth century arguably still haunt the present, but are rarely, if ever, interpreted as such.

Segregated Origins of a Divided Literary Field

A broad, progressive definition of "interracial" literary culture stands in sharp contrast to the segregationist tendencies in the publishing world after the turn of the twentieth century. After the 1970s, this term dropped from common use, as readers, teachers, and critics affirmed logics whereby "African American" and "American" lives, literature, and culture were frequently separate, segregated, or distinct. Today, common use of the term generally describes either sex or romance across racial lines. Before the 1960s, authors and literary professionals used the term to describe a much broader range of cultural ephemera, including: writing and narratives that crossed racial lines which did not affirm racial hierarchies; cross-racial contact that was not characterized (exclusively or primarily) by animus, abuse, or violence; cross-racial collaborations on book projects; friendships between authors and literary professionals of different backgrounds; productive cross-racial dialogues; and organizations and governance that was not racially homogeneous or exclusive. Black authorship and productions that were critically and commercially successful with readers and audiences across the color line were also perceived as interracial and credited for promoting cross-racial thinking and habits. In twentieth-century literary studies, interracial print culture and networks are associated with the 1920s "Harlem Renaissance" far more than any other decade or time period.[12]

On the eve of the "Black Power" era, undercounting interracial literary culture in the United States became standard practice on both sides of the color line. White writers who echoed related claims affirmed common assumptions that Black authorship was unquestionably narrow and irregular during the first half of the twentieth century. In a 1966 essay on Jewish American authors, literary critic Alfred Kazin claimed in *Commentary* magazine that "A Historian of the Negro novel in this country says that most Negroes who have published one book have never published another." Kazin also noted, "and one might well wonder what, until the sudden fame of James Baldwin, would have induced any Negro writer in this country to keep at it except the necessity of telling his own story."[13] Kazin's conspicuously limited awareness of a powerful African American literary tradition belie at least two key elements of this genre. There were,

170 KOREY GARIBALDI

in fact, numerous Black writers prior to the 1960s who published multiple books. Braithwaite, Toomer, Larsen, McKay, Fauset, and many, many others published more than one book. Not only did they do so as individuals, rather than as simply "Negro" authors, they were also by no means committed to telling their "own story" in these published texts. Adding to countless other distortions of both early and mid-twentieth-century literary history, misrepresentative assessments like Kazin's implied that white authors did not figure into the genre of African American literature at all. But Schomburg was far from alone before the late 1950s in recognizing how important white authors were in penning both fictional and nonfictional narratives of Black life in book form. Kazin's essay, "The Jew as American Writer," simply ignored Gertrude Stein's early contributions to twentieth-century Black literary culture with "Melanctha," the novella-length love story of two bi-racial African Americans at the center of her first book, *Three Lives* (1909).

Overall, Kazin's unwitting biases made plain in his attempts to comprehend American writers, by imposing racial and ethnic categories on their published work, were much less prejudiced than some of the most prominent criticism published decades earlier. After the turn of the century, it was far from uncommon for racist white intellectuals to argue that the United States and Europe's most esteemed writers of African descent were poor, or inaccurate, representatives of Black people, as a race. A typical white supremacist critique published in 1908 by Southern planter and politician Alfred Holt Stone warned that writers like Alexander Pushkin and Alexandre Dumas, and other "so-called [mixed-race] Negroes of distinction," were "not real Negroes at all." Stone, alarmed that whites might misinterpret the novels of Dumas as "a demonstration of Negro capacity," cautioned: "thousands read his books or listen to his spoken words, or engage him in social intercourse."[14] The popularity of canonical Black authors, Stone insisted, threatened white allegiances to Jim Crow and recognitions of racial hierarchies. From a quantitative perspective, it remains difficult to estimate how frequently white commentators attacked "so-called" Black authors "of distinction" like Pushkin and Dumas. Nevertheless, it is clear that Stone perceived value in obscuring and minimizing the importance of their "Negro" heritage. Of course, the DH could be an invaluable resource for ascertaining how common this was. New computational technologies can easily map book distribution and determine word frequencies for globally recognized novelists like Dumas. But, in reality, Stone's criticisms—and fears of—influential Black authorship are little more than a poignant reminder of the methodological challenges complicating the creation of massive data sets that are able to do this work. Put differently, big data DH projects on Dumas, Frank Yerby, Malcolm Gladwell, and other phenomenally successful Black authors would surely benefit from experts who were trained in using race and racialization as categories of analysis. But according to two leading DH scholars, such interconnections are still too rare. Richard Jean So and Edwin Roland observed in 2020 that "distant reading and the critique of race" are both methods "of cultural-literary analysis that have yet to be fully integrated" with one another.[15]

Scholars advocating for a fuller digital recovery of Black writers and narratives published in the early twentieth century should take these gaps and imbalances in expertise on race and literary studies seriously. Back in the 1920s, young, canonical African American authors frequently discussed blurring racial lines as a means of messing with, and evading the expectations of, authoritative elders on both sides of the color line. In 1929, Langston Hughes jokingly cautioned in a letter to Wallace Thurman, the author of *The Blacker the Berry* ... (1929), that not even his dear friend would be able to decode his cross-racial literary experiments and influences. "I took up Gertrude Stein and now I'm changing style altogether and you need not expect to understand my next book unless you too have lost your mind and are no longer [physically] sick but mad." Hughes frequently referenced his appreciation for Stein's capacious, ill-defined, and impenetrable writing at the end of the twenties. In the same letter, Hughes explained that he was planning a review of Thurman's latest book manuscript "in the style of Stein so that the colored papers will find it too erudite for their attention." Such exchanges were common among formidable Black writers when they discussed their incredible range of literary inspirations with one another.[16] But we can safely assume that Alfred Kazin would have never imagined a dialogue like this between two African American intellectuals before the sixties.

Hughes had nothing but praise for Wallace's writing on the eve of the Depression. But both men and many of their generational peers were far

172 KOREY GARIBALDI

more ambivalent about how their literary achievements were racialized, on both sides of the color line. Hughes thus joked in a summary of Thurman's exceptional potential after reading an unidentified manuscript:

> It's a gorgeous book that nobody but a brand new nigger would dare write and I am sure it will complicate things immeasurably for all the associations, leagues, and federations ... And what with two more plays and another novel, you yourself are a great and noble example to the Negro race, going in boldly for a literary career and not deigning to hit a tap of any other kind of work. ... And you are only 21 or is it 23 and Youth and Blackness ought to make you the marvel of the age. ... and you still have fifty years yet in which to be a young and new Negro.[17]

Somewhat eerily, Hughes also predicted that literary historians far into the future would follow his contemporaries in essentializing the connections and influences he shared with Thurman and other young Black authors. "[I]n 2650 when we're the prey of research experts from the antique department of Tuskegee his heirs will receive a tremendous sum [of money] for the lot [of the magazine, *Fire!!*], all first and last editions of original copies containing source material on the whole Negro renaissance."[18] It is Hughes's references to "the whole" Harlem Renaissance that seemingly poke fun at what literary historians in the twenty-seventh century would miss. For the rest of his life, and despite his deep admiration for Black culture, Hughes remained skeptical of conventional preoccupations with race and racial categories—including oversimplified conceptions of Black renaissancism—that became so dominant by the late 1920s.

Such fetishes had indeed transformed Harlem in this era, and many of those changes were not welcomed by Black contemporaries. In another letter to Thurman offering a brief summary of related developments, Hughes noted on the eve of the thirties, "as for Harlem, alas, all the cabarets have gone white and the Sugar Cane is closed and everybody I know is either in Paris or Hollywood or sick. And Bruce [Nugent] wears English suits!"[19] Hughes's report also suggested that some recent developments were making his peers reject what being a preeminent "Negro" author based in the United States entailed. "Nella Larsen is right for more and more we are passing and now even you [Thurman] say that you won't live in Harlem upon your return. That's right, desert the race that made you what you are today."[20] Hughes wasn't chiding Thurman. He was simply lamenting that burgeoning white interest in what might best be described as "authentic Negro culture" was pushing skeptical Black writers away from a neighborhood that was curiously beholden to white supremacist norms. A letter of recommendation Sinclair Lewis wrote on behalf of Claude McKay to the latter's white benefactor a few years earlier indicates that astute white interlocutors were aware of these frustrations.

> About his [McKay] coming home [to the United States]. It seems to me that that is something he must decide. ... As he is a negro, he has here [in Paris] an ease, a chance to forget social problems and consider the vast material he has already accumulated, which he would never have in America.[21]

American "social problems" (e.g., racism and segregation), Lewis's reflections suggest, followed Black writers and intellectuals anywhere they lived, worked, or traveled in the United States. Perhaps this white author's capacity to speak candidly about the specter of Jim Crow might serve as an early model for DH practitioners willing to assess—and counter—twenty-first-century manifestations of related tendencies in their own field.

Toward Multiracial Narratives of the Digital Turn

To be clear, it would be a mistake to simply conflate or misconstrue current barriers in the DH with racial prejudice, sexism, or other forms of discrimination. On the other hand, neither should scholars ignore that lamentations of "segregation"—e.g., critiques of professional teams in the digital field that are either racially homogeneous, and/or male-dominated—have certainly haunted the academic DH for years. The title of literary scholar Moya Bailey's 2011 essay, "All the Digital Humanists Are White, All the Nerds are Men, But Some of Us Are Brave," offers a clear sense of how exclusionary tendencies have been characterized by one of the DH field's leading Black practitioners. It is also noteworthy that scholars from a wide range of backgrounds have echoed Bailey's framing.

This includes Tara McPherson's "Why are the Digital Humanities So White? or Thinking the Histories of Race and Computation," a widely discussed essay published the year after Bailey raised similar questions. At the beginning of the early 2010s, these two scholars were veritable trailblazers in shedding new light on how "deeply siloed" race, gender, and computational studies still were in the early twenty-first century.[22]

More recently, criticisms directly related to these assessments have prompted some of the most heated DH debates in recent memory. Nan Z. Da's interrogation of a refereed sample of dubious questions and findings, that were nevertheless enabled by the relatively cloistered big data sector, was summarized in an essay titled "The Computational Case against Computational Literary Studies" (2019): "Misclassifications become objects of interest, imprecisions become theory, outliers turn into aesthetic and philosophical explorations, and all merit more funding and more publications."[23] The prominence of Da's findings inspired a vociferous backlash. Methodological differences aside, Da's skepticism of structures in the academy affirming computation shares much in common with Bailey's and McPherson's concerns a decade ago.[24] But the fact that few of the leading commentators who have denounced Da's thesis have publicly acknowledged how race and gender figured into their unusually acrimonious responses is a timely reminder of how limited socio-cultural reforms have been over the past decade.

Swift (and arguably disproportionate) attacks on this woman of color—primarily, though not exclusively, by white men who specialize in quantitative literary research—suggests how relevant earlier criticisms remain.[25] Offering a sense of how unpopular questioning these structures are in some DH circles, a female scholar responding to Da's essays asks: "Why is literary studies so hung up on (whether in favor of, or opposed to) this individualistic, masculinist mode of statistical criticism?"[26] Digital humanist Daniel Shore's "The Form of Black Lives Matter" (2020) has productively connected Da's recent DH work to scholarly investigations of racial injustice. But most of Da's prominent detractors have either ignored or overlooked both race and gender in their engagements with her provocations.[27] Two years earlier, Elizabeth Losh and Jacqueline Wernimont argued that the DH needs more "forms of intellectual engagement that confront structural misogyny and racism." Women and minorities, these scholars contend, continue to be "relegated to the status of fringe concerns" in the field.[28] Not only is this statement an apt summation of this academic sector, the scholarly DH needs many more intersectional observations and calls to stand in solidarity like these. Nevertheless, it also bears remembering that recent furor stemming from Da's willingness to question the power dynamics underpinning current inequities demonstrates that underrepresented scholars can indeed become central actors in the digital field—as targets of scrutiny.

One of the defining characteristics of contemporary DH is that there is little consensus among practitioners about how privilege functions, who has it, and how to "disrupt" dominant power structures.[29] In 2015, Armand Marie Leroi published an op-ed in the *New York Times* cheering how the DH had elevated "humanities scholars," a group often perceived as "second-class citizens" in the academy. Leroi then hailed: "a new breed of scholar able to both investigate Cicero's use of the word 'lascivium'" while "cod[ing] in Python." Whether or not this statement can be characterized as "masculinist" is debatable. But the racial connotations of celebrating "a new breed" of academics who could investigate Ancient Roman thought while juggling computation are arguably clearer. Recognizing his own privilege, Leroi boasted that the "digital humanities have captured the imaginations of funders and university administrators."[30] Not surprisingly, many Black scholars have found themselves shortchanged by the new genetic mix Leroi outlined and celebrated. Three years earlier, in 2012, Mark Anthony Neal lamented, "[w]hen all these deans and provosts are looking around for the folks who are going to do cutting edge work [in the digital humanities], the last folks they think about are black folks." As Kim Gallon explains, "Neal's comments touch on the unspoken assumption that African Americans are technophobes, even in the midst of the information age."[31] Gallon's analysis of Neal's comments arguably help clarify why Black scholars were virtually absent from the cohort of scholars that was so concerted and insistent on rejecting Nan Z. Da's "case" against computational literary studies in 2019.

Debates aside, few would disagree that computation has become the most prominent subfield in the digital humanities. Its experts promise— and not infrequently, deliver—tools enabling the digital interpretation of thousands of texts at one time. Computer programs generating quantitative

176   KOREY GARIBALDI

data and findings on this scale do indeed hold enormous potential. And yet it would be remiss to heap praise on this sector without acknowledging the incessant infighting inhibiting inclusive progress in this sector. When critics have pointed out shortcomings and imbalances stemming from competition over resources, unsympathetic practitioners have responded that commentators can't, or shouldn't even attempt to, compare sectors of the "digital humanities."[32] As just one example of this paradox, one recent essay, Michael Piotrowski's "Ain't No Way Around It: Why We Need to Be Clear About What We Mean by 'Digital Humanities,'" unambiguously embraces the use of Black vernacular English, while completely sidestepping any discussion of race whatsoever.[33] The disjuncture between recent commentaries and scholarship suggests an urgent need for new narratives and histories of the digital turn indicating more awareness of a capacious, pluralist DH.[34] In terms of the latter characteristic, researching and writing about early achievements in Black literary DH would introduce both new and seasoned practitioners to a variety of digital humanism that dates back to the early 1980s. Not least important in this respect is an ongoing need to challenge perceptions in and outside of the academy that Black intellectuals and professionals are "technophobic."

Todd Presner's frequently cited 2010 essay, "Digital Humanities 2.0: A Report on Knowledge," is emblematic of how the genealogical roots of the digital humanities are usually described in the computation sector. "Digital Humanities 2.0 introduces an entirely new discipline, featuring convergent fields, hybrid methodologies, and even new publication models that are not often derived from, or limited to, print culture." Foregrounding recent technological advancements, Presner also claims that "the first wave of Digital Humanities scholarship in the late 1990s and the early 2000s tended to focus on large-scale digitization projects and the establishment of technological infrastructure."[35] One need not deny the utility of these genealogies and achievements to seriously interrogate what milestones in the DH are missing. Indeed, it is particularly telling how conspicuously absent pioneering DH work in Black literary studies and related African American fields were from similar reports prior to the late 2010s. Arguably the most influential resource that essays following Presner's lead rebuffed accounting for was the "Computer Assisted Analysis of Black Literature" (CAABL) founded back in 1983. After two

DESEGREGATING THE DIGITAL TURN 177

name changes, this collective is now a research unit in the Department of English at the University of Kansas that is currently known as the "Project on the History of Black Writing" (HBW). One of this group's most important interventions in digitization technologies in this early era of scholarly computing was its development of a "digital database" of Black writing. From its initial base at the University of Mississippi in 1983 under the direction of literary scholar Maryemma Graham, with support from the Cooperative Research Network in Black Studies, the group achieved, among other things, an electronic database of over 1,000 "verified" Black novels. This adjective is used advisedly. Here it is important to remember that Black authorship is not always clearly marked by race. The anxiety of white supremacists like Alfred Holt Stone prompted by writers like Alexander Pushkin and Alexandre Dumas offers a particularly apt example of why recovering "verified" Black texts in the 1980s was important.

Digital humanists and students can and should learn much more about how Black scholars (and any scholar who has specialized in Black DH work for that matter) have built on these gains since the early 1980s. On the eve of the twenty-first century, the development of new software by practitioners, in conjunction with new technologies and equipment, was crucial in supporting exponential growth in public access to Black history and literature. Between the mid- to late 1990s, the ascent of CD-ROM-based sources was instrumental for the growing number of scholars and digital humanists who contributed to this work. Among many other noteworthy outcomes in this era was HBW's CD-ROM prototype, "Neither Bond Nor Free: An Anthology of Rare African-American Texts," which the group describes in its self-published history (online) as a "completely digitized anthology."[36] HBW's short narrative of this epoch also characterizes the group's activities in these years as "expanding digital access" via its production and worldwide distribution of "Neither Bond Nor Free." In 1999, the collective supported these efforts by joining Henry Louis Gates, Jr.'s *Encarta Africana: Library of Black America*, which enabled seventy-five novels from HBW's digitized collection to be included on the mass-produced *Encarta Africana* CD-ROM. James Briggs Murray's "Democratizing Education at the Schomburg" sheds light on how similarly expansive digitization projects were implemented at the Schomburg Center in this period.

178   Korey Garibaldi

Murray observes that G.K. Hall's CD-ROM publication of the Schomburg's existing holdings in 1995 increased the public's awareness of its collection and did so in a way that was much more coherent than its computer-generated catalogs dating from the early 1970s. In our own time, investigating and attempting to narrate the early history of digitization in Black literary studies is by no means cutting edge scholarly work. Even so, there are still remarkably few common considerations clarifying how these interrelated histories intersect with newer narratives—e.g., Todd Presner's—of how the broader field of computational literary studies has developed since the turn of the twenty-first century.

Recovering Pluralist Worlds

More so than is generally recognized, recent scholarly debates in the DH, however groundbreaking and important, parallel older patterns that have kept innovations in the digital humanities separated. In 2012, Tara McPherson observed, "the difficulties we encounter in knitting together our discussions of race (or other modes of difference) with our technological productions within the digital humanities (or in our studies of code) are actually an *effect* of the very designs of technological systems." McPherson attributes the "partitions" of "considerations of race" in the DH to "computational culture" in the United States that emerged after the Second World War. Yet, over a century before the most recent digital turn, most white Anglophone literary experts certainly "cordon[ed] off race" and "contain[ed]" it, as McPherson has observed in relation to the "very structures of digital computation."[37] Moreover, given how impermanent these designs are, DH scholars and practitioners are particularly well-positioned to help research, recover, digitize, analyze, and publicize countless more texts published by forebears with similar progressive commitments. And these new challenges to the color line in the digital era will inevitably enrich DH technologies, methodologies, and professional practices. One of the only factors that remains uncertain is the rate at which these contributions will occur. This will necessarily require honest assessments of barriers to initiating this work, and thus encourage specialists like Armand Marie Leroi to move beyond exclusionary, celebratory accounts of nascent DH technologies.

Here too, there are progressive forebears that DH scholars can and should become familiar with as they consider implementing desegregationist frameworks. A year after Arturo Schomburg's *Bibliographical Checklist of American Negro Poetry* (1916) appeared as the second volume in white publisher Charles Heartman's *Bibliographica Americana* book series, a white doctoral student, Newman White, reviewed it for the *South Atlantic Quarterly*. Newman titled his impressive and comprehensive eighteen-page essay: "American Negro Poetry." Giving a sense of how diverse the poetic works Schomburg catalogued were, White estimated, "Omitting the considerable number of volumes published in French and Spanish, there are 173 titles in English." Even after scaling down Schomburg's list, and excluding the "numerous books published since 1916," White noted, "the total volume is rather surprising to the average [white] person who has taken it for granted that the negro is not interested in poetry." Not least important among those factors inhibiting a broader awareness of creative Black authors was the fact that "about a fourth of [Schomburg's cited texts] can not be located in the combined collection of the three largest libraries in America."[38] Surely enthusiastic and provocative primary sources like these would be useful for more digital humanists to gain at least some familiarity with.

The recovery of literary artefacts like White's with various tools made possible by technological advancements in the DH will eventually make it impossible to ignore the interracial character of both the "American" and "African American" canons—even for those who will prefer to. Digital recoveries and analyses of texts from the 1910s in particular—a decade which is fully accessible based on the temporal parameters of American copyright restrictions—is especially valuable for considering when and where racialized canons confound classifications as such. Beyond specialists in African American literary studies, most scholars and commentators are unaware of the sheer number of Black-authored narratives, and texts with Black themes, produced before the classical 1920s periodization of the Harlem Renaissance. Indeed, a range of distinctive books and print commodities were published in the years leading up to the First World War that were intentionally designed to challenge Jim Crow and other forms of racial subordination both in and beyond the United States.

Editor Dusé Mohamed Ali's first issue of the *African Times and Orient Review* was initially printed in July 1912. The front page of this periodical featured classical type and a white angel sitting on a globe, joining hands with two imperial subjects that were clearly distinct from one another. The first cover of this internationally distributed publication also advertised its "principal contents," including writing that ranged from "Charles Rosher on 'Morocco'"; "The Negro Conference at Tuskegee"; and "Articles on 'The Hawaii Islands,' etc., etc., etc." Editorial gestures that were this global, cosmopolitan, and interracial in character anticipates several of DH scholar Alan Liu's recent recommendations for diversifying the digital field:

> A specific research direction for DH related to diversity might be to train machine learning on image collections representing different nations, cultures, and epochs. This would allow for comparatist data analysis of depicted objects (e.g. What objects are in pictures? How many of each are there?), formal structures, color patterns, perspective systems, and material media. The goal would be to seek unexpected relations among images not accommodated as 'movements' or 'styles' in standard cultural histories segregated by Western, Eastern, African, indigenous, and other [categories of] art.[39]

What best characterized Black and interracial texts from the teens exemplifying commensurate, non-segregated, transnational perspectives was their frequent appearance as high-quality periodicals or bound books. Progressive critics and everyday observers alike perceived these innovations as virtually unprecedented. Regardless of what precursors there were to new, sophisticated, and engaging anti-racist texts, at the time, the growing number of print titles in this unwieldy genre represented a radical transformation of contemporary standards. Back in the first decade of the twentieth century, Black access to printing technologies—and financial resources—to produce comparable works had been much more limited. As Black and interracial literary culture expanded during the 1910s, these texts were much less ephemeral than pamphlets.

Although W.E.B. Du Bois's *Crisis* (est. 1910), the *Pullman Porters' Review* (est. 1913), W.S. Braithwaite's short-lived *Poetry Journal* (December 1912–July 1913), and the London-based *African Times and Orient Review* (1912–20) were early outliers, the landscape of periodicals directed by people of color in and well beyond Harlem thickened rapidly by the mid-1910s. As another early example, prize-winning essayist Isaac Fisher's *Negro Farmer* (1914) was also thoroughly forward-looking, despite the agricultural connection its title signals. Toward the end of its first year in print, the *Negro Farmer* was described by the *American Missionary* as "bid[ding] fair to become one of the most [influential] journals in the life of the race."[40] Plans for several Black magazines were announced in this era. One announcement of Nashville's *New Negro Magazine* in February 1915 described the concept for this periodical as a monthly that "will be devoted to literature, art, science, music, agriculture, and sport."[41] The following year, the men and women responsible for editing a woefully understudied, popular, Chicago-based Black magazine, *The Champion* (1916–17), refused to limit their contributions and coverage to the reigning elite—or, in their case, "the talented tenth." The periodical's editor, Black poet Fenton Johnson, and his staff thus insisted in *The Champion*'s first issue, published in September 1916, that: "We realize that it is not possible to bring about a literary Renaissance by holding ourselves aloof from those aspiring, nor can we gain results by publishing [material] which does not measure up to [this] standard." Its editors thus encouraged readers to "send us your manuscripts, your drawings and your photographs; we have plenty of time to devote to the discovery of new talent."[42] Despite how important records like these are, even specialists in African American literary studies don't have regular or reliable access to these materials in digitized form. Curiously, given how many of these short-lived texts are preserved in physical archives, *The Crisis* is the only African American journal represented by "The Modernist Journals Project" sponsored by Brown University and The University of Tulsa. Du Bois would have welcomed the project's tagline, "modernism began in the magazines." But this praise wouldn't have stopped him from protesting how limited the project's digitized materials are for journals sponsored and produced by communities of color throughout the Anglophone world.

In addition to heightened theoretical scrutiny for the growing number of scholars interested in building and applying DH tools, addressing racial imbalances like these deserves far more attention. Overall, teachers and scholars need many more digital platforms to connect books, periodicals, newspapers, and other forms of printed matter that are too often either arbitrarily segregated by race or missing altogether. I gained access to most of the works cited or mentioned above by searching digitized databases. After realizing how limited scholarship on Black and interracial literary texts published in the 1910s remains, I have directed my own research and recovery efforts to scouring public domain resources. Although many searches end in frustrating circles, it is not uncommon to find newly digitized texts on Google Books, Hathi Trust (www.hathitrust.org), and the Internet Archive (https://archive.org) that are available for both viewing and downloading. Scholarly digital humanities projects such as the Black Press Research Collective, the Black Book Interactive Project (originating from the HBW), the Harlem Shadows Project, the older Charles Chesnutt Archive, the Colored Convention Project, and the Mapping the Stacks archival project founded by literary historian Jacqueline Goldsby have complemented my reliance on much-larger corporate and institutional digital resources. It would be difficult to overestimate how generative better coordination between these resources would be. Often in the case of Black and interracial texts published before the 1920s, the only alternatives to digitized records are physical first editions that are regularly sold by rare booksellers for hundreds—if not thousands—of dollars. Langston Hughes would not be surprised by this latter development.

It is heartening that a growing number of scholars are calling for more room for Black authors, texts, and practitioners to contribute to new and existing computational research. Be that as it may, leaders in the digital field have been much slower in either admitting or assessing how biases in the DH have perpetuated contemporary inequities. Renewed commitments to desegregating literary studies, histories of the academic DH, and professional collaborations holds the potential to revolutionize access to racially and gender-inclusive American culture. DH scholarship and projects operating in this spirit would be an honor to writers like Arturo Schomburg, Gertrude Stein, and Claude McKay, who regularly challenged how literate Americans perceived and accessed Black life, culture, and accomplishments. Moreover, Hughes and Wallace Thurman's correspondence from the late 1920s offers an important reminder of why scholars need to stay vigilant in how they mark and interpret racial distinctions between American and African American literature. Stubborn inattention to where these two genres overlap in the digital humanities have made it much too common for well-meaning colleagues to reify, rather than counter, invisible prejudices and professional hierarchies.

CHAPTER NINE

(Re-)Framing Black Women's Liberation in the Classroom

Nella Larsen, Zora Neale Hurston, and Twenty-First-Century Editorial Frameworks

Emanuela Kucik

Today, Nella Larsen and Zora Neale Hurston are among the most famous African American and American authors. However, their journeys to reaching canonical status were tumultuous. In "Nella Larsen's Erotics of Race" (2007), Carla Kaplan writes that, although Larsen's two novels, *Quicksand* (1928) and *Passing* (1929), "were favorably received" when they were published, the texts "certainly never generated the celebrity now accorded Larsen as one of the central figures of the African-American, modernist and feminist literary canons." Kaplan adds that "Larsen's [current] status among early twentieth-century black women writers is rivaled only by Zora Neale Hurston's."[1] Today, Larsen's *Passing* and Hurston's *Their Eyes Were Watching God* (1937) are firmly established within the canons of African American, American, and other literatures. Students in colleges and universities across the United States are regularly transported into the world Larsen created around Clare Kendry and Irene Redfield and the one Hurston drew around Janie Crawford. In guiding students into those worlds, professors around the country often assign twenty-first-century editions of *Passing* and *Their Eyes*. While such a detail might sound insignificant, it is crucial for gaining

185

a fuller understanding of the legacies of these novels and their authors, as twenty-first-century editions of both texts often include introductory and concluding frameworks providing context about the Harlem Renaissance, the authors, and relevant scholarship, all of which influence how students encounter and interpret the stories in their hands. This chapter elucidates how including the aforementioned additional material is akin to an act of editing; although the novels' original contents are not altered, these frameworks dramatically shape readers' interpretations of the books in ways that mirror the shifts and changes produced by editing. While the impact of Conclusions and Notes that follow the texts are important, I focus on Introduction and Forewords in copies of *Passing* and *Their Eyes*, as these introductory materials precede the novels and form the first encounters that readers have with the books.

In this chapter, I use *Passing* and *Their Eyes* as case studies for illuminating the editorial significance of the twenty-first-century frameworks that accompany recent printings of Harlem Renaissance literature and the transformative capabilities of analyzing said literature within the context of those frameworks. While the novels work well as the aforementioned case studies, this chapter also highlights how these texts are important in deeply specific ways. The chapter argues that today's students are performing expansive, emancipatory readings of these novels, as they enter these classic texts *after* reading introductions that urge them to think about the novels' protagonists and authors within the context of Black women's liberation. These introductions guide students to think about how Clare, Irene, and Janie challenge the categorizations and limitations society tries to impose upon them, and this guiding produces a practice of reading in which students approach the novels focused on the emancipatory capabilities embedded within their pages. Additionally, these guided readings provide students with an amplified understanding of the ways that Larsen and Hurston pushed for robust, flexible, and liberated imaginings of Black womanhood.

Before diving into analyzing the introductory frameworks, it is important to note the importance of studying these texts and authors in conversation with each other. While Larsen is often at the center of conversations around mixed-race identity and wealthy, cosmopolitan Black life, and Hurston typically anchors discussions around Southern Black

American life and dialect, both women subverted the Harlem Renaissance's showcasing of wealthy, educated, heteronormative Black families in Northern cities. Larsen imbued *Passing* with undercurrents of a sexual and romantic attraction between her protagonists and criticisms of Harlem's Black "elite," and Hurston embraced Southern Black communities and refuted respectability politics and the criticisms of multiple Black male authors in *Their Eyes*. Considered together, the novels showcase a push for capacious understandings of Black womanhood that upend conventional binaries, such as Southern and Northern, rural and cosmopolitan, formally and not-formally educated, and others. Considered independently, each text showcases the need for a broader understanding of Black womanhood within its particular niche; however, taken in conjunction with one another, the novels call for an even wider emancipatory expansion regarding how we view Black women, their lives, and their interiority. That said, it is not only the content of the authors' novels that provides a meaningful lens of analysis for understanding the importance of their work and the significance of how introductions address that work—their biographies also present crucial information for understanding how the introductions to their novels function.

Larsen and Hurston were both born in 1891, and accounting for the details of both women's lives has proven difficult for those who have attempted the feat.[2] Two of Larsen's main biographers, Thadious M. Davis and George Hutchinson, have laid out some of the basic facts of her life. Larsen was born in Chicago, Illinois, to a Black West Indian father and a white Danish mother. Larsen's father died when she was two years old, and her mother re-married a white man. Larsen reportedly felt as though she existed on the perimeter of her own family, and that sense of singularity courses through both of her novels. When Larsen's mother and stepfather had a child, her peripheral existence within her family structure was seemingly solidified, as she was the only Black person among them. Larsen studied at Fisk University for one year and, later, completed training to be a nurse and a librarian through the Lincoln Hospital Training Program and the New York Public Library's librarian training program, respectively. She traveled to Denmark but did not find that she fit in particularly well there, either. In 1919, she married Elmer Imes, who was part of the "elite" of what is now widely known as the

188   EMANUELA KUCIK

Harlem Renaissance. After publishing *Passing* in 1929, Larsen became the first Black woman to receive a Guggenheim Fellowship. Unfortunately, after plagiarism accusations were leveled against her in 1930, Larsen ceased writing fiction, her books went out of print, and she lived the remainder of her life as a nurse in Brooklyn, New York. She died in 1964, and, approximately five years later, her books resurfaced in American publishing markets. In "The Many Lives of Nella Larsen" (2018), Lynn Domina writes: "During the Civil Rights Movement ... many African American texts were rediscovered and brought back into print. Three new editions of *Passing* appeared between 1969 and 1971. Literary critics approached Larsen's work with a new seriousness, publishing articles on both novels."[3] Larsen's grave was unmarked until 2006, when author Heidi Durrow marked it in the tradition of Alice Walker marking Zora Neale Hurston's previously unlabeled grave.[4]

Like Larsen, Hurston was born in 1891; however, while Larsen was a child of the Midwest, Hurston was born and raised in the South, and she spent much of her childhood in Eatonville, Florida.[5] The facts of her life are also often disputed, but her primary biographer, Robert Hemenway, has etched out its details for us. Hurston grew up in a mostly Black town—a town of which her father became the mayor. While her childhood seemed to be a joyous one, her mother died when she was thirteen years old. Years later, Hurston went on to attend Howard University and Barnard College, earning a B.A. in anthropology. While she was in New York, Hurston became part of the Harlem Renaissance crowd. True to her anthropological roots, she spent her life traveling to various Black communities and studying their culture. Like Larsen, she won a Guggenheim Fellowship—in fact, she won two. Her work interviewing the last known survivor of the transatlantic slave trade, Cudjoe Lewis, was published in 2018 under the title *Barracoon: The Story of the Last "Black Cargo."* Hurston published numerous works throughout her life, but she was paid less than she deserved, which led to her living in poverty. The publication and reception of Hurston's work was impacted by her decision to use Southern Black dialect in her writing. Some Black male writers— with Richard Wright leading the charge—thought the use of dialect would negatively impact white populations' perceptions of Black Americans. Hurston, however, believed that Southern Black communities who spoke in said dialect should be represented accurately and that their manner of speech was valid, beautiful, and worthy of honoring and celebrating. Like Larsen's novels before her, Hurston's work went out of print for decades and was brought back into public consciousness in the 1960s. In Hurston's case, interest in her work was revived after Alice Walker published "In Search of Zora Neale Hurston" in 1975. Two years before publishing the essay, Walker marked Hurston's grave with:

ZORA NEALE HURSTON
"A Genius of the South"
1901–1960
Novelist. Folklorist
Anthropologist

While this information about Larsen and Hurston provides only the barest of facts about their lives, deaths, and journeys to literary popularity today, these details and many more are typically present in the introductions of almost every twenty-first-century edition of their works. The sheer volume of versions of both *Passing* and *Their Eyes* makes it difficult to choose which editions to use here. Many late twentieth-century editions of both novels included new introductory and concluding material, and I could have oriented this study around the second half of the twentieth century. However, while many texts from that period included these additional frameworks, almost all twenty-first-century versions of the texts have them. As such, I have focused my study on the twenty-first century. In this chapter, I analyze Carla Kaplan's 2007 Norton Critical Edition of *Passing* and the HarperCollins 2004 eBook version of *Their Eyes*. Kaplan's Norton Edition of *Passing* is often assigned in college and graduate school classrooms because of the comprehensiveness with which it contextualizes the novel. The HarperCollins eBook of *Their Eyes* represents the rise in digital content that is currently available to students—and to which many of them are gravitating. Through in-depth analyses of both works, I consider how the ways in which college and graduate school students today are presented with these now-classic texts are drastically different than how students in earlier decades encountered the material. Moreover, I illustrate the

190 EMANUELA KUCIK

ways that this difference carries within it the potential for a liberatory re-imagining of the world that centers and celebrates Black womanhood in all of its expansiveness, complexity, and beauty.

Nella Larsen's *Passing*

Once understood solely—or at least primarily—as a novel about racial passing, Larsen's *Passing* is now largely seen as a story of racial, sexual, and class-based passing.[6] The sexual and romantic tension barely below the surface of Clare and Irene's relationship has been analyzed by many scholars, and it is now included in the introductory material to many versions of the text, including Kaplan's introduction to the 2007 Norton Critical Edition of the novel. Although the Norton presents a significant amount of new material that provides elaborate context for the novel, it is Kaplan's introduction that precedes the text of *Passing*. The first time that I studied Larsen's novel was in a doctoral course that assigned Kaplan's edited volume; the first assignment was to read Kaplan's introduction. Thus, Kaplan's essay was my initial formal encounter with Larsen's *Passing*, and it dramatically shaped my understanding(s) of and reaction to the text.

Kaplan's introduction is titled "Nella Larsen's Erotics of Race," which immediately presents a link between race and sexuality, indicating a connection in the two themes before one even opens the novel. As noted earlier, Kaplan starts her introduction by stating that Larsen's current status as a crucial part of multiple literary canons is "rivaled only by Zora Neale Hurston's." Kaplan also notes, however, that this is "in spite of Larsen's comparatively slim output and the fact that after 1930 she ceased to publish and dropped out of New York's literary circles altogether."[7] Kaplan then explains *Passing*'s significance:

> Larsen's writing, and *Passing* especially, is now hailed for helping create modernist psychological interiority, expanding our uses of irony, challenging marriage and middle-class domesticity, complexly interrogating gender, race, and sexual identity, and for redeploying traditional tropes—such as that of the tragic mulatta—with a contemporary and critical twist. Most importantly, Larsen's work is now prized for its portrayal of black,

female subjectivity and for its depiction of the social and psychological vertigo caused when identity categories break down.[8]

Due to this introduction preceding the novel in the Critical Edition, readers' first encounters with Larsen's text are shaped by all of the following: a description of Larsen's current status within numerous literary canons; a note about the obscurity her work once endured; and a summary of the themes of race, gender, sexuality, and class that reside at the heart of the novel. Kaplan zeroes in on the theme of race and argues that "*Passing* questions the very *idea* of race, exposing it as one of our most powerful—and dangerous—fictions."[9] This astute analysis is one of the most important to note in Kaplan's introduction, as it presents students with a popular theory about Larsen's intentions in relation to racial discourse before they have begun their journeys into the novel. While the words that comprise Larsen's text have not been altered by Kaplan's introduction, this introductory material provides a framework that is an act of editing, as it changes the way that readers enter the text. Reading *Passing* without an introduction such as Kaplan's means that the reader's first experience with the novel will be the text's first page. However, when Kaplan's introduction—or anyone's introduction—is added, and, often, assigned as mandatory reading for students *before* beginning the novel, it is the content of Kaplan's work that actually forms students' inaugural forays into the book. That is, before students read a page of the novel, they know that the story they are about to enter is one in which the idea of race is exposed as a "dangerous fiction," and it is this background that begins their experience with Larsen's famous novel.

While many contemporary students might already be aware of the racialized plot at the core of *Passing*, due to the novel's current popularity, there is still significance to readers being given such astute, incisive analyses of Larsen's work before they begin it, as the depth of those analyses allows readers to form a fuller understanding of all that Larsen was doing and all that her critique continues to do. The opportunity to engage with this fuller understanding prior to reading the novel is a gift that was not given to earlier readers. Kaplan notes that "the extent to which Larsen was criticizing prevailing racial assumptions, announcing an identification with Clare Kendry ... and attempting to

192   EMANUELA KUCIK

unsettle her readers, was rarely noted by early reviewers."[10] In direct contrast with these early reviewers, Kaplan clearly presents her argument for what Larsen is trying to say regarding race: "It is Irene's racial ideology, not Clare's, which is truly problematic. More than problematic, Irene—race woman, devotee of 'security,' fixity, and a world of black and white, right and wrong—proves deadly."[11] Kaplan continues and notes that "Larsen condemns Irene's racial ideology, in part, by having Irene's language mimic ... the discourse of some of the most notorious white racists of her day."[12] Considering the depth of Kaplan's analysis of how Larsen deploys race in the novel, even students who were aware of the novel's central conceit—a woman who is legally "Black" (Clare) lives her life "passing" as "White"—will most likely have their interpretation of the ways that race functions in the novel expanded and enhanced by Kaplan's introduction. Since Clare is often assumed to be the character who has made problematic life decisions based on race, many students would most likely be surprised by the theory that Irene is actually the one whom Larsen is casting as problematic.

In addition to her astute analyses regarding race in the novel, Kaplan's introduction also presents exploration of a second, intertwined theme that is of particular importance, as it was not part of the original conversations around the novel: sexuality. Kaplan notes the intersections of race and sexuality in *Passing*, stating:

> an erotics of race takes the place of the ethics of race that we find in most other passing stories. Irene's response to Clare's "appealing" and "seductive" "way," is, as Deborah McDowell has compellingly argued, an "onrush of affectionate feeling" for the "lovely," "beautiful," "incredibly beautiful," "tempting," "arresting," "languorous," "tortured loveliness" she believes she disapproves of. Irene's powerful erotic response to Clare allows also a positive response to unfixed, uncategorizable racial identity ... which Irene otherwise cannot, or will not, allow herself to approve. By the same token, Clare's "longing to be with you again, as I have never longed for anything before" (Larsen 7), allows Clare, who eschews all categories, received ideologies, and fixed identities, to embrace what she has repudiated and renounced.[13]

(Re-)Framing Black Women's Liberation   193

Students who read this introduction before they read the novel will now have a sense of the novel's engagement with the theme of sexuality, which they might not have had if they simply had jumped into the novel on their own. This is not to say that many students would not have picked up on the sexuality aspect without guidance, as countless students have done and will continue to do; rather, it is to say that students who read Kaplan's introduction prior to reading the novel have now explicitly been guided toward examining sexuality within the text, and they will dive into it with an expanded understanding of what constitutes the "passing" of the novel's title. Moreover, since it is quite difficult to secure a copy of *Passing* today that does not come with an introduction by an esteemed scholar in literary criticism who summarizes the novel's engagement with themes of race, sexuality, and class, it is likely that twenty-first-century students will be entering Larsen's classic text with a significantly broadened conception of the novel's themes than that which was possessed by readers from decades past whose copies of the novel did not include introductions such as Kaplan's.

While it might seem as though introductions that guide students toward particular readings are participating in a limiting practice that leads to less originality on the part of student thinking, that does not have to be the case. To the contrary, introductions such as Kaplan's provide students with expanded understandings of the novel—through that expansion, they produce an emancipatory reading that is in line with the liberatory aims of Larsen's work. *Passing* is about challenging social categorizations and their rigidity; it is a novel about crossing societally imposed boundaries, whether those are racial, sexual, or class-based in origin. Larsen's novel urges us to imagine a world in which we are not profoundly limited by unyielding categorizations that ultimately function on a fatal level—a reality that remains true in 2020. While laws dictating racial categorization are no longer in practice, their reverberations remain, as discourses of race are still dominated by rigid notions of inflexibility. Similarly, while discourses about the fluidity of sexual identity are more popular today, suicides of people who identify as part of the LGBTQIA+ community also abound, as abuse against those communities runs rampant. Additionally, murders of transgender women—particularly transgender Black women—continue at alarming rates. This violence maintains, at

194   EMANUELA KUCIK

its core, a belief in a lack of fluidity and flexibility; it promotes and (re)
produces a rigidity borne and reminiscent of that which Larsen so aptly
criticizes in *Passing*. Thus, it is important that today's students enter the
novel with an understanding of how strict categorizations along identity
lines resulted in the death of Clare and the psychological disintegration
of Irene. The knowledge students glean from introductory material about
the fatal enforcement of societal delineations can lead them to approach
the novel with an ingrained empathy that imagines a world that embraces
a capacious notion of Black womanhood—a world where Irene's mind
didn't have to disintegrate, and Clare didn't have to die. As such, introductions that guide students toward an understanding of this broadened,
empathetic reading before they encounter the text are performing acts of
crucial, emancipatory expansion.

Zora Neale Hurston's *Their Eyes Were Watching God*

As noted earlier, Kaplan's introduction to Larsen's *Passing* states that Lars-
en's current popularity is matched only by Hurston's. Although Hurston
produced a large body of work, she is most famous for her 1937 novel,
Their Eyes Were Watching God. While there are countless editions of the
text circulating today, I analyze the 2004 HarperCollins eBook. In my
courses, well over half of the students use digital copies of books, and I
anticipate that this percentage will continue to grow, as many publishing
houses have released eBook versions of texts that have been deemed "classics." In studying an eBook version of *Their Eyes*, I illustrate the ways that
these introductory frameworks are present in multiple formats; they do
not only accompany "fancier" editions of texts, such as Kaplan's Norton
volume. These introductions are omnipresent within the literary world.
The HarperCollins eBook provides a particularly rich ground for analysis
of prefatory material. Before presenting the text of Hurston's novel, this
edition includes an "eBook extra" reading group guide, which is comprised
of an introduction and discussion questions. The questions are then
followed by two forewords—one by Edwidge Danticat and one by Mary
Helen Washington. After the forewords, the novel begins. While many
reprintings of canonical texts include discussion questions, they typically
come after the source material. Concluding frameworks are important

(Re-)Framing Black Women's Liberation   195

to consider in these discussions as well, but, as I argue throughout this piece, introductory ones are the most significant, as they precede readers' encounters with the material and, therefore, shape and mold their readings in a way that follow-up material does not.

In the HarperCollins eBook of *Their Eyes*, the reading group guide begins with an introduction. The introduction, a concise two pages in length, opens with a brief summary of the controversy around Hurston's birthplace. In her autobiography, *Dust Tracks on a Road* (1942), Hurston writes that she was born in Eatonville, Florida in 1901; however, her biographers have claimed that "she was, in fact, born in Notasulga, Alabama, on January 7, 1891."[14] The introduction notes that "Hurston's ... political statements, relating to racial issues or addressing national politics, did not ingratiate her with her black male contemporaries. The end result was that *Their Eyes Were Watching God* went out of print not long after its first appearance and remained out of print for nearly thirty years."[15] Through this information, readers are now set up to understand that the book they are about to read was the site of controversy, though they do not yet have all of the details about those controversies (those will come in the forewords). The central contribution of the introduction comes next, through its presentation of the question that has surrounded Hurston's career for decades:

> Henry Louis Gates, Jr., has been one among many to ask: "How could the recipient of two Guggenheims and the author of four novels, a dozen short stories, two musicals, two books on black mythology, dozens of essays, and a prizewinning autobiography virtually 'disappear' from her readership for three full decades?"[16]

The introduction offers no answers—instead, it states that this question

> remains unanswered. The fact remains that every one of Hurston's books went quickly out of print; and it was only through the determined efforts, in the 1970s, of Alice Walker, Robert Hemenway (Hurston's biographer), Toni Cade Bambara, and other writers and scholars that all of her books are now back in print and that she has taken her rightful place in the pantheon of American authors.[17]

196   EMANUELA KUCIK

Through the discussion of this central question, readers are primed to approach the text with an eye toward producing their own answer to this question; what might *they* find in *Their Eyes* that could explain its disturbing disappearance—or, more accurately, removal—from the literary world for so long? Even if they find nothing, they will, most likely, read the novel looking for an answer (even if only subconsciously), due to the presentation of this question as a central aspect of understanding the legacy of Hurston and her most famous piece of writing. Thus, even without the more detailed information that will come in the forewords, students now know the broad strokes of some of the controversies of Hurston's life and work. Through this short introduction, students are guided toward a reading of the novel that is rooted in questioning why this classic work by a Black woman was rendered obsolete for decades.

This introduction is followed by a list of discussion questions. While the inclusion of discussion questions is a fairly common feature of twenty-first-century copies of books, their placement before both of the forewords and before the novel is striking. As a form, discussion questions often guide readers in their thinking; they can vary greatly in specificity and type, but, in one way or another, they typically lead readers in a direction (or away from a direction). As such, placing them at the end of a text allows readers to use the questions to help them synthesize their thoughts and meditate on elements of the material they might have missed—or to think differently about an idea they thought they had solidified. HarperCollins' prefacing of the text with the discussion questions presents readers with specific ideas *before* they encounter the material. Some of the questions are as follows:

> What is the importance of the concept of horizon? How do Janie and each of her men widen her horizons? What is the significance of the novel's final sentence in this regard?
>
> To what extent does Janie acquire her own voice and the ability to shape her own life? How are the two related? Does Janie's telling her story to Pheoby in flashback undermine her ability to tell her story directly in her own voice?
>
> What are the differences between the language of the men and that of Janie and the other women? How do the differences in

(Re-)Framing Black Women's Liberation   197

language reflect the two groups' approaches to life, power, relationships, and self-realization? How do the novel's first two paragraphs point to those differences?

How important is Hurston's use of vernacular dialect to our understanding of Janie and the other characters and their way of life? What do speech patterns reveal about the quality of these lives and the nature of these communities? In what ways are "their tongues cocked and loaded, the only real weapon" of these people?[18]

Each of these questions asserts an idea about the text and pulls readers in a certain direction in terms of analysis; thus, the questions function as another introduction of sorts. The questions indicate important themes and direct readers to particular readings, as each question embeds a theoretical idea within it. For instance, the last question I quote above does not simply present a query about vernacular dialect; inherent within the question are the claims about which it is asking. That is, by asking about the importance of Hurston's use of vernacular dialect and the significance of speech patterns in understanding the communities, the question is stating that Hurston's use of dialect is important and that it reveals something crucial about "the quality of these lives and the nature of these communities." The question allows for the level of importance of that dialect and the specific revelation of what, exactly, the dialect says, to be debated, but the notion that said speech patterns are important is implicit within the question.

While it might seem that questions such as these direct students so strongly in one direction or the other that they limit their ability to think for themselves, the opposite can also be true, and the questions can be read as a tool for providing an emancipatory reading of the novel. For instance, if we remain with the example of the question about dialect, we see that it can be used to ask students to enter the novel thinking about the power and possibility inherent within Southern Black dialect. Many students have told me that they struggle to understand some of the dialect in the novel—and, because of that, they skip over portions of it. Questions such as the one in this Reader's Guide implicitly implore students neither to skip nor to dismiss the dialect; in fact, the aforementioned question guides them toward viewing the dialect as a priceless asset to the people

198   EMANUELA KUCIK

who use it. This reading primes students to approach Janie's story from the perspective of an expanded understanding of Black womanhood that includes Black women in Southern towns who speak in Southern Black dialect—Black women who are often ignored and deemed less important than wealthier Black people living in cosmopolitan areas.

As the questions set up a particular type of reading, the forewords that follow them continue in that tradition. The first foreword, by Edwidge Danticat, presents a tribute to Hurston's novel, its characters, and Hurston herself. Danticat's opening brings the reader directly into a sense of communal space with Hurston and Janie: "Much like the porch sitters at the beginning of the book who are the first to see Janie arrive, Janie, Pheoby, and Zora Neale Hurston form their own storytelling chain, and it is through their linking of voices that we are taken on this intimate yet communal journey that is *Their Eyes Were Watching God*."[19] Danticat then expertly weaves in Hurston's biography in a way that does not focus primarily on the controversies surrounding her reading or her work, but that focuses on her extraordinary talent, her time in Haiti (Danticat's home country), and the story she created in less than two months:

> I have always been extremely proud to remind all who would listen that Zora Neale Hurston's masterpiece, *Their Eyes Were Watching God*, was written, by her own account, in seven weeks, in my homeland, Haiti ... Of course Hurston's own account of how long it took to compose the novel has been debated and contested. However, I am awed by her ability to have found the time during her anthropological travels and constant research in Haiti to produce a novel—at all. ... Many of my contemporaries, including myself, often complain—sometimes with book contracts in tow—about not having enough time, money, and space to write. Yet Zora battled to write and she did, knowing, as Janie Crawford must have also known, that "there is no agony like bearing an untold story inside you."[20]

Danticat's decision to gloss over the debates regarding how long it took Hurston to write the novel in favor of expounding upon the unprecedented talent and determination it required to produce the novel in any amount of time is a much more poignant decision than it might seem. By framing this introductory material through a tribute to Hurston's talent that does not omit the controversies surrounding her accounts of writing the novel, but, rather, briefly mentions them and then essentially states that those controversies don't matter, Danticat brings readers into Janie's world with admiration for Hurston at the forefront of their journey. She also quotes Alice Walker, who said, speaking of Hurston, "A People do not throw their geniuses away."[21] By meditating upon Hurston's immense skill and talent and identifying her as a genius, Danticat implicitly urges students not to dismiss the novel. Through this foreword, Danticat pulls students away from the dismissiveness and degradation that Hurston and her work faced and moves them toward an emancipatory reading of *Their Eyes* that names its author a Black woman genius—and, by association, asserts that its protagonist, who is also a Black woman, has a life story worth telling.

Danticat continues her tribute by showing that she is impressed not only that Hurston wrote *a* novel in such quick fashion, but that she wrote *this* novel. Danticat describes reading the book both in high school and in college and the discussions that surrounded those readings. She explains that, during her time at Barnard College, she and her classmates asked questions around Janie's significance:

> We brought up issues that concerned us as young feminists and womanists. Was Janie Crawford a good female role model or was she solely defined by the men in her life? Many of us argued that Janie did not have to be a role model at all. She simply had to be a fully realized and complex character, which she was.[22]

Here, Danticat eloquently summarizes the emancipatory reading that is at the core of this introductory material to *Their Eyes*. Danticat explains that Janie was not required to be a role model. The sentiment expressed here is that Janie is a full person, and she is a full person who became so on her own; she did not need respectability politics, men, a particular social class, or anything else to complete her. She makes mistakes, but those mistakes are borne of decisions that she makes based on what she feels is best for her at a particular moment. While those decisions do not necessarily bring

200 EMANUELA KUCIK

her the full range of love and joy that we desire for her, they are still active decisions. Thus, after reading this portion of Danticat's foreword, students are primed to examine all the ways that Janie is a full person, a reading practice that is inherently emancipatory because it releases Janie from the critics who said that the author who created her should have used different speech patterns or written about the North and its cities instead of the South and its charms.

Danticat's foreword frees Janie from the dismissiveness of those who were opposed to Janie's assertiveness and power—a power that flowed from Hurston, a Black woman, just as Clare's strength was infused by Larsen. Discussing Tea Cake's abuse of Janie, Danticat writes that

> in spite of Janie's choices concerning Tea Cake, or perhaps because of them, she experiences more freedom than most women (certainly most poor women) of her time. And as much as she loves Tea Cake, she ultimately chooses to live and not to die with him, and her final act is not to follow him to the grave, but to bury him and return alone to a community that will not embrace and welcome her without first being given an explanation as to where she has been and what she has been through.[23]

Danticat continues her analysis of the novel's significance, arguing that

> this is a novel with an overpowering sense of exigency and urgency in its layered plot, swift pace, intricate narration, and in the raw anguish evoked by the conflicting paths laid out for Janie Crawford as she attempts to survive her grandmother's restricted vision of a black woman's life and realize her own self-conceived liberation. Like all individual thinkers, Janie Crawford pays the price of exclusion for nonconformity, much like Hurston herself, who was accused of stereotyping the people she loved when she perhaps simply listened to them much more closely than others, and sought to reclaim and reclassify their voices.[24]

In these sections of her foreword, Danticat links Janie's story with Hurston's, and she asserts the strength and independence of both women.

Throughout the entirety of her foreword, Danticat meditates on the ways that Hurston wrote not only a strikingly complex novel, but a transformative one in which the hero is a Black woman whose heroism lies in her fullness, complexity, and determination to chart her own path in a world that has tried to predetermine her fate through patriarchal norms that she ultimately rejects. By arguing for Janie's importance as an independently thinking protagonist and then linking Janie to Hurston, Danticat effectively establishes the importance of Hurston's "nonconformity" as well, leading readers to embark upon Janie's journey with a concrete understanding of the inarguable significance of Janie's character and of the genius who created her.

This emancipatory reading centered around guiding readers toward an understanding of the novel that is rooted in claiming the genius of both Hurston and Janie is continued by Mary Helen Washington's foreword, which follows Danticat's in the eBook. Washington's foreword spends more time summarizing the main arguments around the novel, giving detail to the information hinted at in the introduction and Danticat's foreword:

> Black male critics were much harsher in their assessments of the novel. From the beginning of her career, Hurston was severely criticized for not writing fiction in the protest tradition. Sterling Brown said in 1936 of her earlier book *Mules and Men* that it was not bitter enough, that it did not depict the harsher side of black life in the South, that Hurston made black southern life appear easygoing and carefree. Alain Locke, dean of black scholars and critics during the Harlem Renaissance, wrote in his yearly review of the literature for *Opportunity* magazine that Hurston's *Their Eyes* was simply out of step with the more serious trends of the times. ... The most damaging critique of all came from the most well-known and influential black writer of the day, Richard Wright, [who] ... excoriated *Their Eyes* as a novel that did for literature what the minstrel shows did for theater, that is, make white folks laugh. ... By the end of the forties, a decade dominated by Wright and by the stormy fiction of social realism, the quieter voice of a woman searching for self-realization could not, or would not, be heard.[25]

202   EMANUELA KUCIK

Washington succinctly summarizes how multiple Black male authors tore Hurston's book apart because it wasn't the book *they* wanted. This information moves readers toward an empathetic reading of the novel before they have read one page of it. As a direct contrast to the derisive readings of Hurston's novel that Washington summarizes above, she follows said summary with an analysis that mirrors Danticat's in its exploration of Janie's significance to Black women across the country:

> What I loved immediately about this novel besides its high poetry and its female hero was its investment in black folk traditions. Here, finally, was a woman on a quest for her own identity and, unlike so many other questing figures in black literature, her journey would take her, not away from, but deeper and deeper into blackness, the descent into the Everglades with its rich black soil, wild cane, and communal life representing immersion into black traditions. But for most black women readers discovering *Their Eyes* for the first time, what was most compelling was the figure of Janie Crawford—powerful, articulate, self-reliant, and radically different from any woman character they had ever before encountered in literature.[26]

Here, Washington explicitly asserts that, to her, and to many Black women, Janie was a hero. In emphasizing Janie's "self-reliance," Washington's foreword reinforces Danticat's description of Janie's "self-conceived liberation." Taken together, these readings present the most powerful example of an emancipatory reading practice, as they directly assert that Janie's strength lies in large part in her "self-reliance" and that it is this self-determinacy that allows her to liberate herself.

Washington concludes her foreword by addressing Hurston's rocky road to the canon and emphasizing the significance of Janie's character to multitudes of Black women:

> Because *Their Eyes* has been in print continuously since 1978, it has become available each year to thousands of new readers. It is taught in colleges all over the country, and its availability and popularity have generated two decades of the highest level

of scholarship. But I want to remember the history that nurtured this text into rebirth, especially the collective spirit of the sixties and seventies that galvanized us into political action to retrieve the lost works of black women writers. ... Janie telling her story to ... Pheoby suggests to me all those women readers who discovered their own tale in Janie's story and passed it on from one to another; and certainly, as the novel represents a woman redefining and revising a male-dominated canon, these readers have, like Janie, made their voices heard in the world of letters, revising the canon while asserting their proper place in it.[27]

As I noted in my analysis of the frameworks around Larsen's novel, while neither Danticat's nor Washington's foreword—nor, for that matter, the discussion questions that precede both—edit the content of Hurston's novel, their comments provide a framework that functions as an editing device by shaping readers' interactions with the material *before* they come into contact with it. Danticat and Washington directly depict Hurston as a genius who refused to bow to the intersecting forms of oppression with which she was faced, and they paint Janie as a Black woman hero who, like the author who created her, makes her own rules. These forewords increase the probability that students will enter Hurston's famous novel looking for all of the ways that Janie carves her own path. They will, most likely, be rooting for Janie before they even open the book—and, in doing so, they will engage in an emancipatory reading that refuses to entertain the possibility that Janie (or Hurston) will be judged by patriarchal, racist, classist, or other problematic standards and that guides them toward focusing on Janie's independence, strength, and quest for freedom.

Conclusion

The Introduction and Forewords of Kaplan, Danticat, and Washington emphasize the ways that the women at the hearts of *Passing* and *Their Eyes* want to free themselves from rigid categorizations around race, gender, sexuality, and class; additionally, they seek freedom from the oppressive structures and limitations those categorizations produced. Clare and Janie actively fight for that freedom, while Irene can be read as someone who

204   EMANUELA KUCIK

is desperate to break free of social expectations but cannot quite bring herself to take action toward challenging the ideals Clare and Janie reject. Clare and Janie's subversions of societal expectations are not free of pain and sacrifice, however; Clare dies a horrifying death, and Janie suffers immensely throughout various points in her relationships and her life. All three of these Black women pay a price for engaging in any capacity with breaking society's rules and regulations regarding race, sex, and class. While we cannot travel into the worlds of Clare, Irene, and Janie (and all of the Black women they represent) to offer them something better than what they were given, we can guide students toward understandings of their lives that foreground the limitations placed upon them as Black women—and the ways that they pushed back. It is in this guiding that we find the emancipatory capabilities of reading introductions and forewords before entering Harlem Renaissance texts.

Through this prefatory material, students are gifted with the opportunity to approach these texts with knowledge of all that the authors had to overcome to write these stories and all that their protagonists faced in the worlds the authors created for them—worlds that reflected the realities of Black womanhood in the twentieth century. These introductions and forewords help students understand the restrictions placed upon Black women during the early twentieth century, and they urge them to think about the ways society continues to try and place Black women in boxes made of intersectionally oppressive preconceived notions and confining categorizations.

Moreover, these materials tell today's students that the work of Larsen, Hurston, and other Black women is responsible for much of the progress that *has* been made for Black women; in daring to challenge the status quo on paper, these authors challenged it in their everyday lives. Through their characters, they imagined a world in which Black womanhood was celebrated for its expansiveness, complexity, and nuance. These introductions and forewords allow students to enter the texts with that better world on their minds—one that is shaped by the inarguable genius and skill of Larsen and Hurston. *Passing* and *Their Eyes* make substantial progress in guiding us to that better place, and the introductory material to the twenty-first-century printings of the novels brings students directly into the fold of Larsen's and Hurston's project of creating a space in which a more liberated version of Black womanhood was able to move into existence. Ultimately, the prefatory material shows students not only the ways that both novels highlight how far we have come in building that space but also how far we have to go before we have created a world where Black women's stories are consistently deemed worthy of telling and their lives are indisputably deemed worthy of celebrating.

CHAPTER TEN

Editing Edward Christopher Williams

From "The Letters of Davy Carr" to *When Washington Was in Vogue*

Adam McKible

Walking into a bookstore often prompts joyful anticipation. Shelves and tables offer books on almost every conceivable topic and by authors from around the world. If you cannot find the book you came in to buy, you can ask a salesperson to order it for you. But I experienced only a modicum of joy when I visited my nearest megabookstore on the publication date of *When Washington Was in Vogue*, the novel by Edward Christopher Williams I had been working to get republished for nearly a decade. Instead, what I experienced was more akin to despair and a feeling of insignificance. Yes, when I finally did find a few copies of the novel tucked in alphabetically with the other W's, I was happy to see Williams's book finally on the shelves. But only the spines were on display—without a forward-facing front cover—and there were no copies of it on one of the several "New Hardback Fiction" tables. In that vast Brooklyn Barnes and Noble, the text I had worked on for so long was an almost entirely imperceptible drop in a gigantic sea of commodities, coffee, and printed matter. Over the next few days, I traveled to booksellers large and small across New York City to see how, and if, *When Washington Was in Vogue* was being sold. And, like many newly published authors, I checked the Amazon rankings obsessively. For a few blissful moments, the novel reached as

208   ADAM McKIBLE

high as #4,960. As I write this today, *When Washington Was in Vogue* is ranked at #1,026,365. A bestseller it never was.

Despite the relatively small public notice Williams's novel has attracted over the years since it was published by Amistad, an imprint of HarperCollins, I remain convinced of the novel's significance as a document of African American life in the 1920s. More than that, I consider *When Washington Was in Vogue* a rich text worthy of study and, best of all, it's a damned good read. But whatever the novel's reception was in the past and will be in the future, I am proud to have made it available, because *When Washington Was in Vogue* deserves a place in the classroom, in scholarship, and in various literary canons. For this essay, I would like to provide a historical account of the novel's journey from its initial publication in *The Messenger*, through its multiple layers of publication and publicity, and to the subsequent stewardship of the novel's reception and legacy. Innumerable decisions, and some significant compromises, were made along the way, and this volume offers an excellent opportunity to memorialize the entire process. I will also describe what transpired after the novel's publication, including media appearances and the novel's reception in and out of academia. As the recent publications of Zora Neale Hurston's *Barracoon: The Story of the Last "Black Cargo"* and Claude McKay's *Amiable with Big Teeth* and *Romance in Marseille* demonstrate, there are still gems to be found from the New Negro era; a narrative of my own experiences, I hope, might help future scholars and editors shepherd their own discovered treasures through the publishing process.

Some of what I write here repeats information included in my 2003 introduction to Williams's novel, but I also want to use this opportunity to address an important concern raised by David Chinitz in his 2006 *Modernism/modernity* review about the novel's lack of scholarly apparatus. *When Washington Was in Vogue* was initially packaged as a trade book aimed at the broadest possible audience; while both my introduction and Emily Bernard's "Commentary" provide readers with a good deal of literary and historical contextualization, the book does not include exhaustive explanatory scaffolding. Chinitz's critique of this absence is both accurate and fair:

My one complaint about this edition is that it makes so few concessions to the teachers and scholars who are bound to form a large part of the audience for any rediscovered Harlem Renaissance novel. From the design of its dust jacket and its repeated billing as "A Love Story" to the tenor of its introduction, the book is clearly being marketed to a general public. That in itself is not a problem. But if a reader happens to be unfamiliar with, for example, Tosti or Shand, or does not know the provenance of "Duna" or "the pitiful story of Dechelette and poor little Alice Doré," or has not read Dorland's *Age of Mental Virility* or Stribling's *Birthright*, the book provides no help at all. The assumption seems to be that readers would rather not know, if enlightenment requires the insertion of a footnote.[1]

Williams's epistolary novel is narrated by the erudite and worldly (but also emotionally obtuse) Captain Davy Carr, a widely traveled veteran of the Great War who has an extensive education and a deep love of the written word. Davy fills his letters to his friend Bob with literary allusions and historical minutiae, and many pages of *When Washington Was in Vogue* could invite multiple, deeply detailed notes. But because HarperCollins was trying to sell as many copies as possible, it did not want the book to appear too stuffy or abstruse. My editor never suggested the inclusion of detailed explanatory material, and I was frankly more interested in getting the novel into readers' hands as quickly as possible, not in producing a more time-consuming definitive edition. I wanted to publish a living thing, not a museum piece. Edward Christopher Williams wrote "The Letters of Davy Carr" for a general readership, and I believe *When Washington Was in Vogue* still deserves that broad audience today.

Michael Nowlin's observations about James Weldon Johnson's literary efforts are applicable here. Nowlin argues that the

> Harlem Renaissance is ... more accurately understood as a movement on behalf of a "normal" African American literature ... [a] ... regularly produced literature recognized as such by its

210 ADAM McKIBLE

aesthetic intent, its fictionality, its entertainment (and edification) value, its commercial viability, its potentially "universal" appeal.[2]

For Johnson (who was born just a few months after Williams, as it happens), a vibrant Black literary movement would achieve mass market appeal rather than cater to the more limited pool of coterie modernists in the 1920s who found value in exclusivity and avant-garde inscrutability. Even though Williams published his novel serially in a little magazine with a limited circulation, he clearly wanted to address a number of knotty issues in the language of popular fiction, and I did not want a critical apparatus to get in the way of either a pleasurable read or pleasing sales.

But I must also confess that I was moved by Chinitz's critique when it first appeared. I forwarded his review to the editorial team at HarperCollins and asked if it would be possible to follow the commercial release with the publication of an annotated edition. The response was quick and firm: as a trade house, HarperCollins would only be interested in producing academic editions for much more successful novels that had already achieved far greater sales, such as *Their Eyes Were Watching God*. And even with a perennial seller like Hurston's, HarperCollins is clearly not inclined toward providing a robust scholarly apparatus. The most recent paperback edition of *Their Eyes* provides a foreword by Edwidge Danticat, an afterword by Henry Louis Gates, Jr., and a reader's guide at the back of the book that includes brief essays by Valerie Boyd, but it contains no contextualizing or explanatory endnotes. Although this essay will not provide the missing material Chinitz calls for, it will, at least, fill in some of the gaps left empty by the original introduction.

Anonymity and Disappearance

Edward Christopher Williams was born to a mixed-race couple in Cleveland, Ohio, in 1871. An accomplished student and athlete, he graduated valedictorian from Western Reserve University in 1892, rapidly became head librarian at his alma mater, and studied librarianship in Albany, New York, thus becoming history's first professionally trained African American librarian. Williams left Cleveland in 1909 and settled in Washington, DC, where he was principal of the M Street School until 1916, when he began his career at Howard University. At Howard, he ultimately served as head librarian, and he also taught classes in library science and foreign languages and literature. Coming to DC when he did, Williams was well positioned to participate in the burgeoning New Negro era, and he became an active figure in the city's cultural life and literary scene. Three of his plays were performed at Howard, and he published an unknown number of short pieces in magazines. From January 1925 through June 1926, *The Messenger* ran "The Letters of Davy Carr: A True Story of Vanity Fair," which Williams published anonymously. *The Messenger* ceased publishing in 1928, Williams died in 1929, and "Davy Carr" remained almost entirely forgotten for nearly eighty years. As I will explain below, Williams's novel was retitled *When Washington Was in Vogue* when it was first published in codex form in 2003.

In addition to being a delightful, witty, and polished work of fiction, *When Washington Was in Vogue* merits serious critical and scholarly attention because of its unique position in African American literature and American literary history. First, while other books written by African Americans are at least partially set in the District—W.E.B. Du Bois's *The Quest for the Silver Fleece* (1911) and Jean Toomer's *Cane* (1923) being two prominent examples—*When Washington Was in Vogue* is perhaps the only novel-length text about Washington's Black middle class in the 1920s. No other novel of the period sheds so much light on that time and place. It is also most likely the first African American epistolary novel and the only novel of the Harlem Renaissance with an exclusively Black cast of characters, both major and minor. With its light-skinned protagonist, Davy Carr, who was born in the South and became a commissioned officer in France during the First World War, *When Washington Was in Vogue* also draws on historical events that contributed to the development of the Harlem Renaissance, including the Great Migration and African American military experience abroad. Because Davy can pass for white, the novel also explores the skin tone politics of the era, and through Davy's love interest, Caroline Rhodes, we encounter portrayals of jazz, youth culture, and the rise of the flapper. And, because the novel is set in 1922 and was originally published in 1925, it can serve as an almost perfect counterpoint to F. Scott Fitzgerald's *The Great Gatsby*. If my own experience is any guide, the two texts work very well together in the classroom; students cannot

212   ADAM McKIBLE

miss the similarities between Caroline and Daisy Buchanan as flappers, for example, and they are fascinated by how Williams and Fitzgerald both use first-person narrators to register their profoundly mixed feelings about modernity. *When Washington Was in Vogue*, in other words, is a rich and rewarding text, equally worthy of teaching, pleasure reading, and sustained scholarship. Certainly, this textual complexity could invite, as Chinitz suggests, an annotated edition, if there were indeed a public appetite for such scaffolding.

Despite its many merits, Williams's novel languished in obscurity for almost eighty years, and I have always suspected two accidents of history as the culprits for this obscurity. First, *The Messenger*, the small-circulation magazine that serialized the novel, underwent a radical transformation in the middle of publishing "The Letters of Davy Carr," and I suspect this diminished the novel's original audience considerably. In *The Big Sea*, Langston Hughes describes *The Messenger* as "a Negro magazine that had a curious career. It began by being very radical, racial, and socialistic, just after the war. ... Then it later became a kind of Negro society magazine and a plugger of Negro businesses, with photographs of prominent colored ladies and their nice homes in it."[3] In January 1925, when "The Letters of Davy Carr" began its run, the magazine was deep into this second phase. But, in July 1925, one of its two publishers, A. Philip Randolph, became involved in the Brotherhood of Sleeping Car Porters, and *The Messenger* entered its third and final stage, this time as a union organ. The look and feel of the magazine changed dramatically. Hughes thus characterizes the magazine's focus as "God knows what"[4] because it did not maintain a unified tone or appeal to a consistent audience during its eleven-year history. For most months of the novel's original serialization (during *The Messenger*'s close relationship to organized labor) "The Letters of Davy Carr" was an ill fit for a periodical that was no longer interested in the romantic lives of two middle-class characters with ample leisure time to read, attend parties, and choose between riding in a Mitchell touring car and a Packard limousine.[5] Indeed, the novel often seems like a well-heeled but unwanted bourgeois stepchild in the pages of the labor-oriented *Messenger*. The novel's incompatibility with the magazine's final political stance can be inferred by how the editors handled its conclusion. After running "The Letters of Davy Carr" continuously, issue after issue, for

EDITING EDWARD CHRISTOPHER WILLIAMS   213

a year and a half, *The Messenger* published the final installment without any fanfare whatsoever, and the editors seemed to have harbored so little regard for Williams's novel that they buried its final sentences in a tiny jump cut toward the back of the issue. In other words, there was probably only a handful of people in 1925 and 1926 who actually read "The Letters of Davy Carr" from first page to last. When *The Messenger* closed shop, the novel faded from memory and slipped into almost total obscurity.

The other primary reason for the novel's disappearance, I suspect, can be attributed to Williams's untimely death; he was only fifty-eight when he succumbed to a swift, unexpected illness. Because his novel is so polished, I find it easy to imagine that he might have enjoyed a longer and ultimately less anonymous literary career. Perhaps, like James Weldon Johnson, who did not claim authorship of his 1912 *The Autobiography of an Ex-Colored Man* until 1927, Williams would have written more fiction, and he might have republished a codex version of his novel with his name attached. This is mere speculation on my part, but I cannot help but wonder what would have happened if Williams had lived longer and written more.

Discovery

I first encountered "The Letters of Davy Carr" in 1994 or 1995, while researching *The Messenger* for my dissertation on little magazines, modernism, and the Russian Revolution at the University of North Carolina–Chapel Hill, and I only bothered to read it because I was planning to write about a long-running series in the magazine entitled "These 'Colored' United States." Wanting to demonstrate scholarly diligence, I printed out and quickly read the other serializations in the magazine, just to be sure they were unnecessary for the claims I wanted to make. Doing my research in the proto-digital, Netscape era, I had to read most of my primary texts from microfilm. For each of the periodicals I worked on, I would scroll through every page of the magazine's entire run and would then print out the items I felt should be examined more carefully at home; it was at least marginally easier to look at the blurry, blotchy, nickel-a-piece printouts from the microfilm readers than from the dim screens of those ancient machines. When I finally began reading "The Letters of Davy Carr"—which was, as it happened, the very last serialization in my

214   ADAM McKIBLE

stack of perfunctory readings— I realized almost immediately that I had stumbled upon something of great literary and historical value, and I was astonished that it had never been republished and had received no literary or critical attention whatsoever. Being a lowly graduate student with few (read: zero) connections and absolutely no clue about the publishing industry, I made a few tentative contacts with university presses and was greeted only with silence. Kathleen Pfeiffer, who was doing excellent work republishing novels by Carl Van Vechten and Waldo Frank, was an early ally in these efforts (and would later submit the first blurb for the hardback), but I made no headway in finding a publisher.

The grainy, photocopied pages from *The Messenger* languished on various shelves as I finished my degree and then started teaching at John Jay College of Criminal Justice in New York. Along the way, however, I did garner a piece of very useful insight. I had always assumed the novel was viable as an anonymously authored text. But Tanya McKinnon, who would later become my agent for the book, told me that if I did not have the writer's name, my forgotten literary gem would never find a publisher. How could I find the unnamed author? When I first came across "The Letters of Davy Carr" in grad school, I scoured the library and queried my African American literature professors, but no one had ever heard of or mentioned the book. I hired a copyright research agency, and they came up with nothing. The photocopied novel collected more dust after I received Tanya's advice.

A funny thing happened while I was making my various small attempts to locate the novel's author: Google was launched. In the summer of 2001, I asked a former student, Regina Bernard, if she might help me, and Regina did what we all now do when we have a question: she googled "The Letters of Davy Carr" and instantly found Edward Christopher Williams. Because of his historical significance as a Black librarian, Williams was the subject of a number of brief biographies, including one by famed Black librarian and curator, Dorothy Porter, who inaccurately describes "The Letters of Davy Carr" as a series of "articles," but she also suggests they "might well be republished today in novelette form."[6] Once I knew Williams's identity, I started in earnest to find a publisher, and I also had the manuscript transcribed from the nearly illegible photocopied pages of *The Messenger* into a clean typescript that could be sent out to readers.

Publishing and Its Compromises

Two very different houses received the manuscript. I first sent it to a university press, which eagerly accepted the novel for consideration but moved at the snail's pace characteristic of so much academic publishing. I also gave a copy to Tanya McKinnon. At the time, I knew Tanya personally, not professionally, and I had no idea how much moxie she had (and still has) as a literary agent. Within weeks of handing her the manuscript—and while the university press was still waiting to hear back from its outside readers—Tanya had contacted Kelli Martin, an editor at HarperCollins, who was immediately enthusiastic about the book. In July 2002, just eight or nine weeks after Kelli first read it, HarperCollins made an offer on the book; in August, the academic press had still not heard back from its second reader. I signed a contract with HarperCollins in November 2002.

Publishing Williams's novel with a commercial house is a decision that I will probably always second guess. When considering whether or not to sign with the academic press that was still reviewing it, I weighed the benefits of producing a more scholarly edition, but I was ultimately swayed by the advantages afforded by a commercial publisher, namely expediency, wider exposure, and—to be perfectly blunt—financial reward. First, because HarperCollins had already demonstrated the ability to move quickly through the initial approval process, I was hoping both to beat my tenure clock and to allay the nagging fear that another scholar, working with their own set of illegible photocopies, might scoop the novel and publish it first. Indeed, Christina Simmons had already published an article on "The Letters of Davy Carr," working with it as an anonymously authored text.[7] What if someone else got the book out first, and all my efforts came to naught? Speed was an important consideration for me. Also of personal interest, HarperCollins would pay an advance for the book, an irresistible offer for an assistant professor at a public university renting a New York City apartment. Less selfishly, I hoped that a house as large as HarperCollins would be better able to promote and disseminate Williams's novel more widely. I believed then, as I do now, that *When Washington Was in Vogue* deserves the broadest audience possible, and a large commercial house could better afford robust marketing. Just the same, I do wonder if the book would have had a better reception in academia if

216   ADAM MCKIBLE

I had signed with a university press. Almost certainly, the kind of introduction and annotations Chinitz wished for would have been included in such an edition, and perhaps it would have enjoyed more, sustained prominence in both the front and back of a university press catalogue. In the years since I made my decision, another tantalizing alternative future for the novel has become possible. Since 2006, Elda Rotor has helmed Penguin Classics, and her delivery of new Harlem Renaissance editions has been nothing short of extraordinary. Especially in light of the recent publications of Claude McKay's *Amiable with Big Teeth* and *Romance in Marseille* (both of which provide excellent scholarly scaffolding), I can easily imagine a Penguin Classics edition of *The Letters of Davy Carr*, replete with notes on Tosti, Shand, and Stribling's *Birthright*.

Things moved pretty quickly once the contract was signed. After Regina had identified Williams as the author, I started doing my research, and I contacted both Case Western and Howard University for information on Williams. With the contract in hand, I obtained a small grant from my university so I could travel to Washington, DC, scour the archives, prepare my introduction, and attend to processing the typed pages into a usable manuscript. In Founders Library at Howard, I located a few pages of the original manuscript of "Davy Carr," so now I felt certain that Williams was the author. Once I knew the rough outlines of his biography, I also tried to contact his only grandchild, Patricia Ann Williams. I telephoned every Patricia Williams in the DC area, and I also asked a friend who worked with a private detective to locate her, but we had no luck. As far as I could tell, no other living person had control of the novel, and I also wondered if Williams's family line had ended with his granddaughter. (In 2006, however, I received an email from one of Williams's great-grandchildren and was informed that Patricia had passed away in 2000. Williams's great-grandchild only became aware of his forebear's literary output while doing research on his family tree. Williams's novel was as lost to his own family as it was to the rest of us.)

I always believed that my primary role in the production of the codex novel was to produce an accurate version that maintained the integrity of the original text. If I had been Williams's contemporary editor, I might have suggested various cuts or emendations, but because I was dealing with a historical document and could not consult with its author or original editors, I wanted the published novel to be as true to the original as possible. Aside from a few corrected misspellings and other minor imperfections, the text in the book is the same as it appeared in *The Messenger*. For the sake of complete accuracy, however, I must also confess to having introduced an imperfection of my own. In Chapter Five, a letter that should have been dated "Sunday, November 26" was printed as "Sunday, November 2"—a flaw that was caught by one of my perceptive students many years after the book had been in print.[8] HarperCollins supported my efforts to produce an accurate text, but they also insisted on one very substantial alteration: they wanted to rename Williams's novel.

As the book made its way through various departments, a growing in-house consensus developed that "The Letters of Davy Carr: A True Story of Colored Vanity Fair" was not a commercially viable title. There was concern especially that the word "letters" would depress sales, because customers shopping for a novel might mistakenly consider the book a collection of letters by a historical figure, rather than a work of fiction. I do not know if Williams himself created the title, "The Letters of Davy Carr," or if this was provided by *The Messenger*'s editors, and its original subtitle, "A True Story of Colored Vanity Fair," was appended to the serialization several months after its initial installment. I was opposed to changing the title from the beginning, but marketing and editorial were insistent. By late January 2003, Dawn Davis, the Executive Editor of Amistad, proposed "When Washington Was in Vogue," and I ultimately acquiesced. The renaming is certainly clever from a marketing perspective. By riffing on David Levering Lewis's scholarly book, *When Harlem Was in Vogue*—which itself plays on Langston Hughes's chapter in *The Big Sea* entitled "When the Negro Was in Vogue"—the title positions the novel for a number of audiences, including African American readers, an informed general audience, and academics familiar with the 1920s. The literary historical appeal of the title is amplified by one of its two subtitles, "A Lost Novel of the Harlem Renaissance." The other subtitle, "A Love Story," attempts to attract additional readers of lighter romance fiction. In other words, HarperCollins wanted to make a return on its investment, and it tried to appeal to as many different readerships as possible.

When the decision was being made to rename the novel, I objected for as long as I could. In the intervening years, however, I have become

218   ADAM McKIBLE

reconciled and perhaps even fond of the new name. However, although *When Washington Was in Vogue* does have a nice ring to it, I now realize this new title also introduces an unintended irony that undermines its assertion of Black Washington's modishness and modernity in the 1920s. As I noted, the title ultimately derives from Langston Hughes's autobiography and, as it happens, Hughes offers some very unflattering observations about the very same people populating Williams's novel. Hughes describes "the 'better class' Washington colored people" as "on the whole as unbearable and snobbish a group of people as I have ever come in contact with anywhere ... [they] seemed to me altogether lacking in real culture, kindness, or good common sense."[9] For Hughes, the Negro and Harlem were certainly both in vogue in the 1920s, but provincial, small-minded Washington never really was. Although Williams criticizes the "better class" throughout his novel, he portrays this world appreciatively, and even lovingly. Of course, the truth about Black Washington's "vogue" lies somewhere between Hughes's dismissal and Williams's embrace; plenty of evidence supports the idea that the African American community centered around Howard University made significant contributions to the development of the Harlem Renaissance, regardless of either its purported snobbishness or, conversely, its cultural modernity. All the same, Washington was certainly not in vogue, according to Hughes, "when the Negro was in vogue."[10]

Publicity

But, of course, HarperCollins paid me for my work on the book and financed its promotion. To my mind, compromise over the title was compensated for by the attention the book received upon launching. *When Washington Was in Vogue* officially went into production in May 2003, and once the galleys were produced, review copies were sent out and the publicity department began planning its campaign. Throughout my engagement with HarperCollins, I was being coached behind the scenes by my wife, Julie, who also worked in publishing at the time, and her advice at this stage was invaluable. When publicity started planning a tour, they envisioned a fairly cushy, five-city tour that included airplanes and hotel rooms. But HarperCollins's budget priorities changed, and, before long, they were proposing a very truncated visit to only Washington and North Carolina, where I had a built-in audience by virtue of my connection with the University of North Carolina. In light of this limited tour, Julie suggested that I offer to drive myself, rather than fly, and to find my own housing along the way, advice that guaranteed a more extended tour and far more press coverage. Because HarperCollins agreed to pay for gas and a car rental, and with access to friends' guest rooms and couches, I was able to make several more appearances in DC and other cities in North Carolina than originally planned, and I could also visit Atlanta and Detroit. More importantly, the greater flexibility allowed for additional media appearances, so I was able to do more radio interviews for local markets, and I was also interviewed—if ever so briefly—on CNN Headline News.

On the whole, the early reviews of the novel were positive, but I have also sometimes wondered if the book's first review dampened HarperCollins's ardor to promote it with even greater resources. According to *Kirkus*, *When Washington Was in Vogue* lacks any dramatic tension, and although it might interest "historians and Black Studies scholars," the book offers "little engaging power or lift. Meanwhile, Williams's petty snobberies are aggravating enough without the addition of his bad imitation of Jane Austen." The review concludes with a four-word death knell: "Of academic interest only."[11] Fortunately, the *Kirkus* review was the least friendly write-up of the novel. Subsequent appraisals were more positive, and my decisions to go with a commercial press, to dramatize my discovery in the introduction, and to extend the book tour as much as possible seemed to pay off. Through HarperCollins's efforts, *When Washington Was in Vogue* was reviewed in a number of magazines and newspapers, and African American readers, in particular, were reached through pieces in *Honey*, *Essence*, and *Crisis*. In terms of sales, though, the most important reviews were probably by the *Wall Street Journal* and SFGate.com, because their publications coincided with the book's highest rankings on Amazon. Subsequent reviews in local newspapers also followed my book tour.

Julie had counseled me that I should craft my introduction as a marketing tool. Because Williams was long dead and was remembered only by a small circle of library science historians, I would by necessity be the novel's representative, and my story of discovery would be essential to

220 ADAM MCKIBLE

the book's initial reception by the press. Her advice was borne out by the early reviews, many of which draw on my introduction as a way to get into the book itself. I don't want to pretend that self-interest wasn't at work, as well. Every mention of "Adam McKible of John Jay College of Criminal Justice" in the national press was a step closer to my receiving tenure, and I was grateful for that.

Paperback

The next significant phase in the novel's life was the production of the paperback edition, which began in March 2004. The most important decision I was involved in was how the new cover would look. I was surprised when my editor announced that we would be using a new illustration, but she explained that HarperCollins was making a greater effort at marketing the book for larger retail chains. The hardback cover features an illustration by Paul Colin, the French artist whose *Revue Nègre* posters helped launch Josephine Baker's career in Paris. When the art department suggested this illustration for the hardback, I was very happy with it, and I was frankly more concerned at the time with insuring that the words, "Introduction by Adam McKible," were featured, because my name was not included in the original mock-up. Although I did not initiate the decision to pursue a new cover, I was more involved in deciding how the paperback cover would look. The first proposed image was a James VanDerZee photograph of a rather flamboyantly dressed African American flapper who more closely resembles the vampish "Madame X," a minor character who only appears on a handful of pages in the novel. I objected to the photograph strenuously. The HarperCollins photo researcher located another set of VanDerZee photographs, including the one that we ultimately used. In this photograph, an elegant young woman in modern but understated attire looks away from the camera with one hand on her hip and a confident smile on her face. I felt that that the combination of this New Woman's modern confidence and self-assertion balanced by the more old-fashioned gesture of not looking directly into the camera was a nearly perfect visualization of the novel's love interest, Caroline Rhodes. I also felt that the skin tone of VanDerZee's model (the significance and ramifications of African American skin tone is a dominant theme in the novel) resonates with Davy's description of "Caroline, whose vivid coloring, dark skin, and flashing eyes would suggest Spain, or Sicily."[12]

With the March 2005 publication of the paperback edition, my work with HarperCollins was essentially over. For a few months after the release, a very new publicist arranged a few small events, and an even greener publicist was assigned to promote the book a few months after that, but *When Washington Was in Vogue* did not meet market expectations, and its life cycle at the publishing house came to an end. There was a brief uptick in sales with the release of the paperback, and academic interest in the novel started around this time. Despite my continuing hope for a general readership, I now understand that the novel's longevity will owe more to course adoptions and scholarship than to an unexpected—and almost entirely unlikely—surge in popular interest. Fortunately, there has been a small but steady trickle of work on the book, and *When Washington Was in Vogue* is discussed to at least some degree in a handful of theses, dissertations, and articles. Would the novel have fared better with a critical apparatus and the support of an academic press? I don't know if I can ever answer this hypothetical question, but I am at least satisfied that everyone involved in the book's production made good faith efforts to help it succeed, and I am gratified by the number of non-academic readers who have reached out over the years to thank me for making the novel available. I also take heart in *When Washington Was in Vogue*'s affordability and availability. Once they are out of print, republished novels from university presses are often relatively expensive because of their limited runs. The paperback version of *When Washington Was in Vogue*, on the other hand, remains in print, so more readers may yet find it.

Fifteen years after I first looked for *When Washington Was in Vogue* in the vast sea of that Brooklyn Barnes & Noble, I still look through the W's in bookstores large and small, but never with much hope. Occasionally, I find a used copy, but more often I do not, and I have not seen a new copy for sale in a bookstore in years. Perhaps I should take comfort in the idea that the people who buy Williams's novel want to hold onto it rather than sell it, but my sporadic, anecdotal evidence cannot prove this wishful belief. Ultimately, my hope does lie with future scholars and teachers, who may yet help the novel find the audience it so richly deserves. I agreed to write this essay because this is another way to continue publicizing a novel that deserves its place in the American literary canon. Perhaps you will finish reading this, buy your own copy, and then introduce your students to *When Washington Was in Vogue*. In the end, I suppose, this is my letter *for* Davy Carr, and I hope a few of you receive it.

CHAPTER ELEVEN

Editing Claude McKay's
Romance in Marseille
A Groundbreaking Harlem Renaissance Novel Emerges from the Archive

Gary Edward Holcomb

Despite its absence from general access for nearly nine decades, Claude McKay's *Romance in Marseille* has been hiding in plain sight, as scholars have had access to the archival novel since the early 1940s. The reasons for the prevention of the novel's publication are diverse, including objections to the narrative's undissembled portrayal of queer life. During the on-and-off years of writing and revising *Romance in Marseille*, McKay also faced grim existential difficulties that undermined not only the writing process but also his confidence in promoting the project, from French and British colonial harassment while living in Morocco to bleak poverty and disabling infirmity. And not only the surmised lineup of white publishers, editors, and associates thwarted the novel's publication, as even the author himself, at times uncertain of his ability to pull off what he hoped to accomplish, played a role in inhibiting its appearance.

As for approaching the original text and bringing it to a popular readership, William J. Maxwell and I edited the text as closely as possible to the way in which we imagine that McKay's editor would have prepared the text, that is, with a light touch, making changes only when we were certain

224   GARY EDWARD HOLCOMB

McKay had mistyped a word or two, particularly his at times singular treatment of French, or when a sentence simply demanded clarity. As long-time McKay scholars, we felt confident in our knowledge of the author's style.

The story of McKay's writing of and then attempt to get *Romance in Marseille* into print may be as interesting as the text itself. After the success of *Home to Harlem* (1928), McKay was disappointed that the Marseille-based *Banjo: A Story without a Plot* (1929) did not do well.[1] Despite *Banjo*'s mediocre showing, McKay was still committed to going forward with another novel-in-planning set in Marseille, believing he had something new to add on the subject of Black seamen and dockworkers inhabiting the "Bottoms," as he called the Black belt of the city's Vieux Port. Though "The Jungle and the Bottoms" had been planned as another picaresque narrative set in Marseille, moreover, and initially recycled material from *Banjo*, McKay soon began to imagine a vividly different story than that of the previous texts. In both *Home to Harlem* and *Banjo*, McKay generated discursive, dialectical narratives, often the setting being a stage for characters to verbalize ideological perspectives, with the recurring Haitian political exile Ray effectively speaking for the Jamaican émigré author himself. For "The Jungle and the Bottoms," however, McKay would soon fashion a less rhetorically inclined narrative and, in a more objective fashion, turn the spotlight on primary characters based on Black male acquaintances he had made. At the same time, he would hazard beyond the Black male homosocial communities of the two earlier novels to create a dynamic female character along with a complex Black lesbian and a sympathetic queer white male. Most novel, he would move beyond portrayals of robust Black male characters by fleshing out a protagonist with an acute physical disability.

While visiting Barcelona in September 1929, McKay set to work on the novel, yet just a few months into the writing process he was already reconceiving the project.[2] He had sent his literary agent William Aspenwall Bradley a rough draft in late 1929, who responded with reservations about the "unsympathetic" way the protagonist, at that time still called Taloufa (a minor character in *Banjo*) and eventually called Lafala, was portrayed. Responding to Bradley on December 21, 1929, McKay declared his already meditated on intention to "tackle Taloufa's story in another form" and "make a difficult thing of it," that is, complicate the narrative: "I am going to start in afresh on the second part[.] ... I am sure I have a real fine story in hand. The thing is to put it over."[3] He would justify his portrayal of the protagonist and other characters, reassuring his agent that he was planning a novel that would be quite different than the previous, beginning with dispatching an authorial alter ego figure, another character appropriated from *Banjo*: "You see there is and won't be any Ray in the tale. I realized that the form was very awkward and that some of my best scenes, the love ones for instance, would be stifled by it."[4] The character, Malty, a Ray-like figure who apparently spoke for the author in the initial draft, was dismissed so early in the process that he does not appear even in the earliest typescript.

McKay takes Bradley's critique, however, as a suggestion that he make the story of the amputee "sentimental," a proposition he rejects: "Primarily I am not writing a sentimental story about Taloufa. ... To make Taloufa extremely acceptable I should have to write a real sob-sister story and that I just cannot do."[5] Though responding to Bradley, moreover, McKay takes the opportunity to obliquely correct W. E. B. Du Bois, who in *The Crisis* had dismissed *Home to Harlem* for its alleged "filth."[6] McKay's fractious gesture toward Du Bois comes in the form of a reaction to the unexpressed question of whether the novel could perform the duty of "propaganda," an element Du Bois insisted in 1928 New Negro art must assert.[7] "Of the racial stuff in the story," McKay explains, "I felt that that came naturally as the talk and thought of the Negroes, giving a peculiar and definite color to the human story. I never thought of it as propaganda nor felt even the happy-go-lucky Negro does think and feel and talk that way."[8]

In terms of a formal strategy, the letter lays out McKay's plan for transforming the text into a "problem novel," that is, a plotted narrative that explores the tension between characters, and, related to the insertion of a plot, his uncertainty about the versatility of a "picaresque" narrative:

> I don't think a good problem novel of Negro life should not be written. ... I will admit that perhaps Taloufa's state of mind and my analysis of it do not go with the picaresque story—but if I am to go on as a writer my characters beside acting much think and talk some sense and if those characters are mainly Negroes, there

226   GARY EDWARD HOLCOMB

will certainly be in their thinking and talking ideas peculiar to Negroes.[9]

In this way, the text would explore both the particularity of Black experience as well as the universality of human existence: "His [the disabled protagonist's] character is changed by his fortune—but that is also a common human thing. Taloufa excuses himself because he has been amputated but that is also the common human trick."[10] And, ambivalent about generating another picaresque narrative, McKay indicates his plans to concoct a plot: "The climax comes when Taloufa is arrested just when he was about to slip away and Malty and others have to try to get him freed."[11] In a late June 1930 letter to longtime friend Max Eastman, McKay describes the initially revised "The Jungle and the Bottoms" explicitly in terms of formulating a "plot":

> it is a real story with something of a plot, involving a West African young man (who had lost his legs stowing away and received good compensation through the efforts of an ambulance chaser) and a North African Negroid girl. They two represent the "jungle" in the "bottoms" that the girl, who is a whore there, wants to leave to go back to Africa with the man.[12]

By August 1930, however, McKay was already rethinking the draft he had evidently produced after the December 21, 1929 letter, this time writing to Bradley about a pair of characters he has introduced—Big Blonde and "the page"—presumably a reference to a character later named Petit Frère ("Little Brother"), a young, French male hustler whom Big Blonde dotes on. "But I have worried myself about the minor characters of Big Blonde and the page," McKay says, "and wondering if the chances would not be better if I changed them a little!" The exclamation point—in fact, a vertical line penciled-in above a typed period—likely indicates McKay's acknowledgement that Saxton and Bradley have expressed some exasperation with their author at several stages in the reader-evaluation process. McKay hopes that Harper & Brothers editor Eugene Saxton agrees, and will therefore send back the manuscript for a revision of "the two chapters in which they play an important part."[13]

McKay's defense of his project so early in the writing process fore-shadows the obstacles the author encountered over the course of writing, revising, and ultimately trying to publish *Romance in Marseille*. Another objection Bradley offered was to question McKay's decision to recycle the setting and some of the surplus imagery of *Banjo*.[14] McKay's response, posted nine months after his first defense of the novel, was to assert he was structuring a narrative "very different in style and mood from the preceding ones," making the character studies of Lafala and Aslima "more fully realized" than the characters in *Home to Harlem* and *Banjo*.[15] "As the book is a more serious attempt than the others and will set the tone for future work," McKay maintained, "I should like to make it as perfect as I can."[16] McKay ends the letter by stating: "But I don't see where I have gone over the old Banjo ground—I especially tried to avoid that."[17] Neverthe-less, though McKay disputed the idea that he was repeating fundamental aspects of the previous novel, *Banjo*, he anticipated the concerns of Bradley and others, as the original draft of "The Jungle and the Bottoms" refers to Marseille as "Dreamport." McKay's transparent rationale for using the Dreamport contrivance appears in the same June 1930 letter to Eastman: "The scene is the same as 'Banjo,' but I call the town Dreamport as it might have been any of six European ports."[18]

Early on in the process, moreover, "The Jungle and the Bottoms" would adjust its focus more intensely on its female characters than had McKay's previous novels: the Black lesbian prostitute La Fleur Noire ("The Black Flower") and, even more deeply developed, Lafala's love interest, the Moroccan sex worker, Aslima. Writing the initial draft, an excited McKay would relate to Bradley that Aslima was coming close to taking over the narrative: "the Arab girl is growing bigger than I ever dreamed and running away with the book and me."[19]

"The Jungle and the Bottoms" surpasses McKay's previous fiction in its attempt to refine a portrayal of homosexuality, one significant impedi-ment in the way of its publication. McKay biographer Wayne F. Cooper observes, "[I]n 'The Jungle and the Bottoms,' McKay frankly and sympa-thetically discussed for the first time the plight of homosexuals in Western society," and Cooper detects in Harper & Brothers editor Eugene Saxton's reaction to the novel anxiety about its homosexual content.[20] The reaction may not be surprising, as George Hutchinson comments in *The Harlem*

228   GARY EDWARD HOLCOMB

Renaissance in Black and White (1995) that, though Saxton worked to modernize Harper & Brothers, signing iconoclastic authors like Edna St. Vincent Millay, he was known to be "squeamish" about sexually suggestive books.[21] The interesting departure vis-à-vis the homosexuality in "The Jungle and the Bottoms" is that in the embryonic draft of *Romance in Marseille* the queer characters are female: the lesbians La Fleur Noire and her unnamed Greek girlfriend. An unsentimental and, in the world of modern sex subculture, realistic figure, sex laborer La Fleur has no use for men, seeing them as no more than financial opportunities to be exploited. Yet, La Fleur does exhibit classical tragedy. La Fleur, Aslima, and Lafala eventually appear to form a love triangle, as La Fleur's machinations against her archrival, Aslima, seem to be motivated by a furtive ardor for the Moroccan prostitute, feelings Aslima, unaware of, does not reciprocate.

Another significant act McKay undertook during the later stages of revising "The Jungle and the Bottoms" was to add the white queer American character, Big Blonde. As the sobriquet implies, *Big* Blonde is a larger-than-life figure, a stalwart comrade whose social realist double is inscribed in the text. Under photos of Lenin and Marx, a mural on the Communist Party Seamen's Club wall mirrors the monumental labor-class idealism of Big Blonde's heroic heft, significantly united with a Black proletarian colossus: "[A] drawing of two terrible giants, one white, the other black, both bracing themselves to break the chains that bound them. And under the drawing was an exhortation: Workers of the World, Unite to Break Your Chains!" The white deracinated docker enters the novel to prevent a splenetic rabble, egged on by a devious café owner, from giving the *Martiniquais* Communist organizer St. Dominique a beating. As the *e* added to his handle indicates, Big Blonde is openly queer, yet he is so widely esteemed among the international Vieux Port proletarians, Black, white, and straight, that vouching for the besieged Martinican is enough to pacify the agitated Ditch mob.[22]

Unease with a novel's frankly sexual subject matter was for McKay a familiar complication. Following the critical success of *Harlem Shadows* (1922), a poetry collection that assembled such notable sonnets as "If We Must Die" (1919), "The Tropics in New York" (1920), "America" (1921), and "On a Primitive Canoe" (1922), along with a handful of coded if, to a worldly reader, unmistakably queer poems, like the rare example of free verse, "To O.E.A." (1920), McKay decided he should work in another literary genre.[23] From 1923 to 1925, while living in Paris and supported by a Garland Fund grant, the New Negro poet took his first crack at the novel genre, resulting in "Color Scheme," a text that met with criticism of its apparently open sexual nature. In a characteristically blunt remark in defense of the novel's theme and content, McKay wrote to Harlem Renaissance historian and compiler Arthur Schomburg: "I make my Negro characters yarn and backbite and fuck like people the world over."[24]

The lost novel's apparent attempt to present the perspectives of the migrant folk without sentimentality and Black sexuality without judgment—its lack of interest in the idea of art in the service of racial uplift or "propaganda," to use Du Bois's directive for Black art—prefigured the motivation behind the stories, poems, and plays that would be collected in *Fire!!* (1926). Edited by Wallace Thurman and with contributions from additional "*Younger Negro Artists,*" or "*Niggerati,*" including Langston Hughes, Zora Neale Hurston, Countee Cullen, Gwendolyn Bennett, and Richard Bruce Nugent, *Fire!!* was intended to scandalize Black bourgeois tastes, an aim it easily accomplished.[25] Had it been published, "Color Scheme" presumably would be the first queer Black prose text, preceding Nugent's contribution to *Fire!!*, the Black Wildean, elliptical "Smoke, Lilies and Jade."[26] However, all that is known about the contents of McKay's first novel are the scraps that may be gleaned from correspondence. Upon reaching an impasse with his prospective publisher, Alfred A. Knopf, McKay stated that he had burned the sole copy of "Color Scheme."[27]

Still, an editor's anxiety over homosexual characters in "The Jungle and the Bottoms" seems a little curious, considering that both of McKay's previous novels, *Home to Harlem* and *Banjo*, had recognizably gay characters. But a conspicuous difference may be perceived between how the previous novels and "The Jungle and the Bottoms" present their queer characters. In the two earlier novels, the narrative presents the majority of the same-sex characters as urban types in a fringe subculture, as undeveloped "pansies," "fairies," or butch. The only fleshed out major gay character is the Haitian exile Ray, who, embodying modernist alienation, experiences a debilitating Freudian latency. Ray's closeted condition both anticipates and queers Fanon's theories of colonial repression as a form

230   Gary Edward Holcomb

of Black modernist alienation: racist imperialism acting as a form of biopower, the modern state's enforcement, Michel Foucault theorizes, of a repressive heterosexuality.[28]

In contrast, *Romance in Marseille* presents homosexuality as relatively accepted, even normal behavior. The queer characters are represented as an integral part of the Black Diaspora proletarian community, generally *out* in the open. They do not seem to embody either Jazz Age sexual freedom or a modern age-inflected, attenuating closetedness. Just like the heterosexual characters, the queer characters naturalistically people the setting and, rather than occasioning colorful atmosphere, play a key role in the story's action. In contrast with the previous texts, the lesbian La Fleur Noire is a well-developed female character, whose motivation is clearly articulated, and who plays a vital role in the unraveling of tragic events. And the white Big Blonde departs from previous novels' exclusively Black homosexuals.

While unlike "Color Scheme" McKay happily did not destroy "The Jungle and the Bottoms," however, the author struggled with its theme.[29] McKay faced the challenge of developing characters remote from his own personal experience, most alien to him being a severely disabled African. It seems clear that, in addition to appropriating from the tragic experience of a Nigerian man McKay knew in Marseille, Nelson Simeon Dede, McKay's own desperate health problems informed his thoughts while creating Lafala, beginning with a protracted period of treating himself for syphilis with doses of mercury and, most traumatic, a spinal tap surgery he underwent in Berlin after completing "The Jungle and the Bottoms" in June 1930.[30] Nevertheless, it is not difficult to imagine why McKay felt tentative about his abilities to give life to his characters, particularly the disabled Lafala.

By June 1930, when McKay put aside the novel for the first time, he did so in order to start work on a short story collection, which would become *Gingertown* (1932). The act of not continuing with "The Jungle and the Bottoms" seems a little puzzling, as seven months later McKay would describe his plans to revise the Marseille-set novel. Writing to Max Eastman, McKay would say that Harper's editor Eugene Saxton had expressed a lack of enthusiasm for the work, "so I went through the novel again more critically," McKay explained, "and decided that the whole second half could be rearranged for the better."[31] Nevertheless, poet and novelist McKay believed that producing a book of short fiction would prove to critics that he was adept in yet another fiction genre. The short stories, McKay wrote, "will show that I am a writer of many moods and open the way for any book or any theme I may choose to write instead of my being taken solely as a writer of picaresque stories."[32]

With this decision, McKay, however, faced yet another impediment. Saxton and Bradley weighed in again, this time stating that short story collections rarely make money for their authors or their publishers.[33] Judging that "The Jungle and the Bottoms" needed revising but was still viable, Bradley encouraged McKay to continue working on the novel and to abort the plan to produce a book of short fiction.[34] A fervidly independent artist who often displayed an unwillingness to take advice, McKay discounted the warning, and, as predicted, *Gingertown* flopped. Though the book generally did well with critics, some reviews characterized it and McKay as *démodé*. Writing in the *Herald Tribune Books*, Rudolph Fisher, Harlem Renaissance author of the first Black detective novel, *The Conjure-Man Dies* (1932), implied that the long-absent McKay had grown out of touch with Harlem's new generation of Black moderns.[35]

Following the *Gingertown* disappointment, the itinerant Black expat, having enjoyed a short visit to Morocco, returned to Tangier and moved into a small house outside of the French-administered international zone. Rather than resuming "The Jungle and the Bottoms," however, he wrote a new novel set in Jamaica, *Banana Bottom* (1933). The title echoes "The Jungle and the Bottoms," and possibly his unanticipated interest in the female sex worker Aslima informed his decision to focus on *Banana Bottom*'s sexually abused female protagonist, Bita Plant.

In January 1933, as he awaited news of the sales and critical reception of *Banana Bottom*, McKay finally resumed work on the now retitled "Savage Loving," renamed accordingly, one assumes, at least partly due to the necessity not to repeat the *bottom* in the title of the published book. The use of the word in the published novel was possibly also why in the final draft the *Bottoms* would be changed to the "Ditch." Meanwhile, McKay had fallen out with Bradley over the literary agent's lack of enthusiasm for *Gingertown* and taken on John Trounstine, a New York

232   GARY EDWARD HOLCOMB

literary agent he had met in Tangier in the company of Paul Bowles a year earlier.[36] In May 1933, McKay heard the "knock-out blow" news from Trounstine that *Banana Bottom* had fared no better than *Gingertown*.[37] Seeming to anticipate the pastoral-set *Banana Bottom*'s failure, a month earlier McKay had written to Max Eastman: "Evidently my readers prefer my realism of rough slum life than of rural life. If so I can supply the need," a remark which suggests another reason to discard the comparatively bucolic-sounding "The Jungle and the Bottoms," and replace it with the suggestive and, conceivably in McKay's mind, more metropolitan "Savage Loving."[38]

During the "Savage Loving" writing phase, moreover, McKay would explore even further the scheme he had laid out in rethinking the text in December 1929, caught in his letter to Bradley: composing a novel with a more conventional storyline. Unlike *Banjo: A Story without a Plot*, that is, "Savage Loving," even more than "The Jungle and the Bottoms," would be a story *with* a plot. As the text probes the existential clashes between the assortment of Black Diaspora characters, *les dockers noir* and sex workers, in tension with one another as well as in historic conflict with a powerful international capitalist interest and a xenophobic French police state, a plotted rather than episodic narrative made sense. Indeed, he not only revised the second half, but added over a third more.

To exacerbate his desperation, McKay, still a British subject, had been the intermittent target of hostile British secret police abetted by French colonial surveillance since he had settled in Morocco. The French and British accused McKay, a known advocate of Pan-Africanist rights and an admirer of Lenin and Trotsky, of being a "propagandist," of inciting revolutionary ideologies among the colonized Arabs, a not altogether unjustified or at least understandable imputation.[39] The hostility intensified during his final year in French-occupied Morocco to the degree where remaining in the Tangier international colony was becoming no longer tenable.

Meanwhile, McKay's hopes for "Savage Loving" were frustrated. After the failure of *Banana Bottom*, Harper & Brothers refused to sign another contract with him, which meant finding another publisher for the novel.[40] Knopf considered it, but, as if replaying the rejection of "Color Scheme," rebuffed it, saying it seemed out of touch with "depression-ridden New

Deal America."[41] Finding himself at the end of his rope, McKay wrote again to Eastman for advice on how to manage his affairs, including what to do with "Savage Loving."[42] Eastman may also have been hesitant about the merits of the manuscript, while also unsure of his own competence to judge the expectations of contemporary novel publishing, as he turned to Simon and Schuster reader Clifton Fadiman for an objective appraisal. As Trounstine could persuade no publisher to offer McKay a contract for "Savage Loving," moreover, Eastman may have hoped Fadiman would offer advice on how to shape the novel for Simon and Schuster and eventually recommend it to a senior editor. The result was emphatically discouraging, however, as Fadiman fervently disliked "Savage Loving," offering, "I imagine McKay is trying to work a Hemingway on material to which Hemingway is not adapted."[43] Fadiman is apparently at least partly associating McKay's novel of Black nomads with Hemingway's lost generation theme of modern expatriates engaged in primal struggle over romantic liaisons, staged in *The Sun Also Rises* (1926).[44] In the most crushing blow, Fadiman dismissed the novel as "sex hash," mocking the notion of "Savage Loving" being a *literary* novel.[45]

The Simon and Schuster reader's stark perspective reflected a cultivated reaction formed against the emergent, somewhat under-wraps publishing that was taking place during the 1920s and early 1930s, characterized by Boni & Liveright's racier selections and the legal action against the dissemination of D.H. Lawrence's *Lady Chatterley's Lover* (1928).[46] Fadiman's evaluation reflected earlier concerns that the manuscript was, as Hemingway reports Gertrude Stein deemed one of his works of fiction, *"inaccrochable"*—that is, unpublishable due to its sexual candor.[47] During the 1920s, publishers were wary of putting out material that could be branded as offensive. Although policed through such embargos as the 1873 Comstock Act, a law that made it illegal to use the US mail to transmit "obscene" literature, the appetite for underground, erotic writing nevertheless was as pervasive as the thirst for prohibited booze.

The American taste for risqué reading evidently was not enough, however, by 1933 to convince McKay that he could salvage "Savage Loving." On top of relentless harassing by colonial authorities, McKay's last year in Morocco was marked by abject indigence coupled with desperate health problems, and it seemed that no writing project he undertook held the

234 GARY EDWARD HOLCOMB

promise of easing his financial distress. The sole, easily overlooked reference to *Romance in Marseille* in his 1937 memoir, *A Long Way from Home*, is framed as part of an excuse for why he reluctantly, and ultimately regrettably, contributed to Nancy Cunard's massive *Negro: An Anthology* (1934): "Meanwhile I had come to the point of a breakdown while working on my novel in Morocco; and besides I was in pecuniary difficulties."[48] Having absorbed the collective reaction of friends, editors, and agents, McKay finally would lose confidence in and shelve *Romance in Marseille*. Not long after, he would conclude his twelve-year, self-imposed exile and return to the United States.

A Long Way from Home abounds with information about the author's remarkable, restless life, first as a young man in Jamaica, and then an early Harlem Renaissance figure in America, and then as an expatriate in Europe and North Africa. It covers his peripatetic experiences in considerable detail, from interchanges with eminent intellectuals to underground folk, his attendance of such historical events as the Fourth Congress of the Communist International in Moscow, and his past triumphs as an author, from the critically esteemed *Harlem Shadows* to the bestselling *Home to Harlem*. Yet, the memoir's cursory reference—not even mentioning one of the novel's titles—to a book he had invested so much in reveals how little by 1937 he wanted to remember it.

The narrative of the text's provenance and absence over the past nearly ninety years also may be as fascinating as the novel itself. In contrast with the 2009 recovery and eventual publication of McKay's once lost, ca. 1941 *Amiable with Big Teeth* (2017),[49] not one but two versions of the text exist. Among the Beinecke's James Weldon Johnson collection is an eighty-seven-page manuscript of *Romance in Marseille*, and in the archives of the Schomburg Center is a 172-page typescript.[50] How the two versions came to be, and how they came to rest in two fabled African American studies collections, makes for another compelling chapter in the tale of *Romance in Marseille*.

As the examples of "Color Scheme" and particularly *Amiable with Big Teeth* indicate, the author would abandon projects he had spent several years on and then seem to forget about, even promptly.[51] Whereas by the time he would publish his memoir in 1937 McKay still remembered—if not by name—*Romance in Marseille*, a mere four years later he claimed

A Groundbreaking Harlem Renaissance Novel   235

to have forgotten about it. In 1941, the same year McKay was at work on *Amiable with Big Teeth*, Harlem Renaissance enthusiast Carl Van Vechten asked him to donate his manuscripts to Yale University Library's nascent James Weldon Johnson collection.[52] Having lost track of several of his own typescripts, McKay saw the chance to have Van Vechten and Yale Library do the work of retrieving his manuscripts for him.[53] When the Yale archive librarian contacted McKay's publishers and requested the manuscripts, all promptly complied: Harper & Brothers dispatched the original typescript of *Banana Bottom*; Lee Furman passed along *A Long Way from Home*; and Dutton sent the manuscript of the non-fiction work, *Harlem: Negro Metropolis* (1940).[54]

During the process, however, a phantom document turned up—a manuscript referred to as "Lafala." John B. Turner, an editor at Harper's who in a postscript to the Yale librarian noted he once had worked with McKay, was surprised to find "a shorter typescript of 88 pages which was attached to" *Banana Bottom*'s typescript, and Turner sent both manuscripts.[55] The identity of the editor marks another curious detail in the history of *Romance in Marseille*, as the editor was John Trounstine, McKay's literary agent after W. A. Bradley. Trounstine was the agent who in 1933 had sent McKay the grim news that *Banana Bottom* had washed out, and who later could not find a publisher for *Romance in Marseille*. In 1940, the year prior, Trounstine had legally changed his name to "John B. Turner." The "typescript of 88 pages" (actually 87 pages) bore the stamp of "W. A. Bradley" and the agent's Paris address.[56] Moreover, and again intriguingly, all contributors to the correspondence—including McKay—refer to the truncated manuscript as "Lafala," likely because no title appeared on the document. Yale understandably wanted all of the manuscripts, including "Lafala," but when McKay learned of the situation, he wrote back to Van Vechten, demanding that, with the exception of the just-published *Harlem: Negro Metropolis*, he be sent all of the manuscripts: "I especially want to have back Banana Bottom and the unfinished manuscript of Lafala, which I had forgotten about and don't want to be in any collection."[57] Van Vechten wrote to the librarian, asking him to return "Lafala" to McKay immediately, speculating that the always-desperate McKay may hope a benefactor would buy the manuscript from him to donate to the Yale collection.[58]

236   GARY EDWARD HOLCOMB

More likely, McKay intended, once again, to try to publish *Romance in Marseille*. In 1943, Ivie Jackman, sister of Harlem Renaissance cognoscente Harold Jackman, contacted McKay to request material for what would become the Countee Cullen/Harold Jackman Memorial Collection at Atlanta University. McKay replied that aside from a number of letters from James Weldon Johnson, "the only other thing I have here is a novel which I was to work over some day and this is the only copy."[59] McKay almost certainly was referring to "Lafala," that is, *Romance in Marseille*. If so, the author must have regained at least some of his past enthusiasm for the novel, and may have thought of restoring it, with the final chapters and dramatic ending that appear in the longer version.

It therefore is a virtual certainty that the eighty-seven-page Beinecke version is the second draft of "The Jungle and the Bottoms" written in Spain, in 1930, the draft McKay described in his letter to Bradley in December 1929. It is likely not a fragment of a longer version of the novel, since McKay himself refers to it as "unfinished." Near-conclusive evidence suggesting the eighty-seven-page manuscript is the second version of the novel is that Marseille is still referred to as "Dreamport." Moreover, though throughout most of the typescript the protagonist is identified as Lafala, the name Lafala appears handwritten over the redacted name, "Taloufa," eight times in the document, showing that McKay was still making the transition for the protagonist's name.[60] One curious detail is that on the first page of the Beinecke's typescript someone has hand printed "Mac Kay," misspelled with the space between the syllables, and below that, "'New Novel,'" with no title. Meanwhile, the Beinecke typescript is catalogued as "Romance in Marseille" (no *s*) yet this title appears nowhere on the manuscript—indeed, no title appears on the document—suggesting that a librarian, archivist, or another party simply created the top page for filing purposes, which would account for the spelling error. In view of all the above, my coeditor and I consider the eighty-seven-page Beinecke *unfinished* manuscript to be not missing any pages but the draft of the novel that was produced from after December 1929 until June 1930, "The Jungle and the Bottoms," otherwise known as "Lafala."

The 172-page Schomburg manuscript therefore is the final draft, produced from 1932 to 1933 in Tangier, the result of his plan to go through the manuscript "again more critically," as he had written to Eastman in December 1930, particularly resolving "that the whole second half could be rearranged for the better."[61] It is almost certainly "Savage Loving," with the title at some point updated to "Romance in Marseille." On the Schomburg version's title page is typed "ROMANCE IN MARSEILLES," beneath which is "BY CLAUDE McKAY." The added "s" to Marseille might complicate matters except that it should be noted that the title page is the only portion of the document where an *s* is appended. That is, throughout the rest of the text, as in the Beinecke version, "Marseille" appears without an added *s*. It seems likely that, like the top page added to the shorter Beinecke version, the Schomburg version's title page was added later for filing and identification purposes.

Among the most compelling evidence that the 172-page typescript is the final version is that throughout the document the narrative identifies the setting as "Marseille," with no use of the coded Dreamport. Moreover, the Beinecke manuscript's *Bottoms* has become the *Ditch*. We have been unable to determine whether McKay ever recovered the 172-page, *finished* novel manuscript himself, though it seems almost a certainty that he didn't. McKay himself implies that he is thinking of reworking "Lafala" for publication, likely planning to expand the eighty-seven-page manuscript, now in the Beinecke Library, essentially back to the completed version, that is, to the status of the manuscript that is now in the Schomburg. If McKay was planning to restore the unfinished manuscript, he wouldn't have been in possession of the complete version.

Though when compared to the 172-page document the eighty-seven-page manuscript bears some differences, particularly in the second half of the novel, the main distinction between the two is, as the pagination indicates, their length, as McKay added several chapters to the end of the narrative, as well as the character Big Blonde. Indeed, the difference in length between the two is considerable, as the Beinecke manuscript comes to about 24,000 words, while the Schomburg version adds up to about 40,280 words.[62] The Schomburg version's less episodic and more recognizably plotted storyline, moreover, is another compelling reason to conclude that McKay considered the longer document the finished novel, and the manuscripts' two different endings reflect his decision to revise with the classic form in mind. The Beinecke draft terminates with the suggestion

238   Gary Edward Holcomb

of a recognizably modernist ambiguity, as a distressed Lafala eludes the "political police" and vanishes, presumably into the obscure backstreets of the Bottoms, just as McKay describes in his December 1929 letter to Bradley—and likely just as McKay himself dreamed of doing when pursued by British agents and French gendarmes.

Revising the novel in 1932, McKay basically simply added onto his earlier draft; that is, the Beinecke version's ending merely concludes about two-thirds into the Schomburg version. The Schomburg manuscript's final passages follow the ascent and descent of the classic Freytag pyramid, the climax-denouement being Aslima and her pimp Titin engaging in a *Carmen*-like violent encounter, if yet with a dash of modern irony, as the reader has learned that Lafala, under police threat throughout the narrative, has safely embarked for his West African homeland, off stage. The "romantic" title, *Romance in Marseille*, fulfills Black Francophile McKay's intention: a *roman* in the French tradition, a novel that avails itself of both classicism—the use of plot, with a tragic outcome—and modernism in its focus on the trammeling existential circumstances of its characters.

Although the Schomburg typescript is complete, the story of how the center came to acquire it is a little sketchy. The Schomburg finding aid indicates that *Romance in Marseille* came as part of a purchase in 1974 from "Black Sun Inc." Black Sun Books was a leading and highly regarded modern literature rare book and manuscript dealer, started in the early 1970s by Harvey and Linda Tucker.[63] Hope Virtue McKay, McKay's only offspring, appears to have been in possession of the 172-page manuscript in March 1953 when she lent it to the Schomburg for an exhibition, and the document was returned to McKay's last literary agent, Carl Cowl, in 1970.[64] Cowl also represented Hope when she sold her late father's collection to Yale, including, apparently, the earlier draft of the novel, and Cowl evidently sold the original manuscript to the Tuckers.

Finally, why *Romance in Marseille* has not been in print for the past two decades marks another curious chapter in the novel's absence. Around 1993, Cowl apparently agreed to form an arrangement with the University of Exeter Press to publish *Romance in Marseille*, and eight years later Exeter listed Romance in Marseille, *and Three Short Stories* in its catalogue.[65] In the meantime, the McKay estate had contested the right of copyright, and, apparently as a result of the dispute, the UK press was obliged to shelve publishing the book.[66] Although the agreement between Cowl and Exeter specified that the press must publish the novel within a six-month period, the dispute over the property lingered, and for nearly two decades *Romance in Marseille* lay dormant in the archive.

Romance in Marseille's journey to become a Penguin Classic reaches back to the late 1990s. While conducting archival research, I examined the presumed lone manuscript at the Schomburg Center. Amazed by the content, I inquired into its status and learned that the McKay Literary Estate was interceding against University of Exeter Press's move to release it in an omnibus with three of McKay's short stories. The dispute lingered, and the estate wasn't encouraging but said I was welcome to check back periodically. Assuming few scholars would see it in the coming years, I contributed a lengthy chapter on it to my first book, *Claude McKay, Code Name Sasha: Queer Black Marxism and the Harlem Renaissance* (2007). I didn't know then that seeking to publish it would turn into years of frustration. Every year or so I checked in with the estate, and every year was told nothing had changed. About ten years ago, I felt sanguine when negotiations resumed, and invited Bill Maxwell, who had edited the superb McKay recovery project, the *Complete Poems* (2004), to collaborate, but the wrangle persisted.

Five years ago, Exeter Press suddenly withdrew. Being academics, Bill Maxwell and I approached an academic press, which was eager to take on the project. However, in late 2017, the McKay Estate's literary agent proposed first querying commercial publishers, and in spring 2018 Penguin Classics signed *Romance in Marseille* to be their 2020 Black History Month selection. Clearly, Penguin Classics publishing *Amiable with Big Teeth* led to the agreement to publish *Romance in Marseille*. We agreed to submit the transcribed, edited, and annotated primary text and prefatory materials to Penguin by April 2019—an intensive if fulfilling year. For our part, we proposed that the supplemental critical materials should be more expansive than that of the typical Penguin Classic. Our Penguin Classic's thirty pages of notes are intended to deeply contextualize the novel's historical moment, and the thirty-two-page introduction offers a critical approach for reading it. Moreover, where by tradition a Penguin

Classic's "Note on the Text"—an account of a novel's provenance—is a half-page, ours is eleven pages. As well as recounting the narrative of the novel's tangled history and recovery, it also disseminates the news of the Beinecke typescript. So, the timing was right after all.

Coda
Editing as Infrastructural Care

Brigitte Fielder and Jonathan Senchyne

In her 1922 essay in the *Southern Workman*, "Negro Literature for Negro Pupils," Alice Dunbar-Nelson makes an inadvertent case for Black literary editorship. Complaining that "Negro literature is frequently mentioned in whispers as a dubious quantity," she wishes not simply for Black literary production, but its availability for classroom teaching.[1] Imagining an idealized Black schoolroom of the future, she notes, "Assuredly we will teach our boys and girls, not only their own history and literature, but works by their own authors."[2] Her pedagogical aspirations are not only for Black literary representation, but for an acknowledgement of aesthetic value, as she writes that "We will, ourselves, first achieve a sense of pride in our own productions, with a fine sense of literary values which will not allow us to confuse trivialities and trash with literature. We will learn to judge a thing as good, because of its intrinsic value and not because it is a Negro's!"[3] In this early moment of what would become known as the Harlem Renaissance, Dunbar-Nelson's wish for Black literature for Black students presents a common sentiment for Black educators extending from the nineteenth century forward: that Black literature is valuable and that it should be carried forward and made available to future generations. An educator of children as well as a Harlem Renaissance author in her own right, Dunbar-Nelson viewed the reach of her fellow Black authors with a generational scope. She knew, too, that literary creation was not itself sufficient, but that putting this literature into the hands of African American readers would necessitate deliberate effort and careful consideration. Exploring the full range of activities that make up those deliberate efforts gives us a fuller picture of what constitutes editing, and it links various infrastructural labors across time in the project of editing the Harlem Renaissance.

Dunbar-Nelson's aspirations for the study of Black literature speak to the aesthetic values that would conceptualize the Harlem Renaissance for later readers and editors. The project of editing the Harlem Renaissance depends upon a fundamental—though persistently controversial—assertion of literary value. Because African American literature, in any time period, would contend with infrastructural barriers to its production, circulation, preservation, and accessibility, not only recognizing but also articulating that value would be essential to the project of African American literary study. To attend (in any number of ways) to Harlem Renaissance writing is to swing the pendulum of history back toward that era and to carry forward the work of a people whose literary history, productivity, and value have often needed to be established and reestablished as a prerequisite for their consideration. Even as the Harlem Renaissance remains one of the most prominently defined movements of Black literary production and celebration, the editors of this volume recognize that "Some [movements] are not as easily kept alive as others."

It is perhaps for this reason that editorship becomes such a persistently salient and fascinating topic in African American literary studies. As Alice Dunbar-Nelson knew in 1922, making Black literature available to Black students requires not simply Black authorship but also an infrastructural intervention that would make this literature available to subsequent generations. Scholars of African American literary recovery have countered the myth of African American literature's absence in any number of historical moments and generic forms. One might go so far as to say that African American literature, as a visible body of work, has not only been written but edited into our present moment.

Editorship does not create African American literature, but it does deliver it into a particular form for its perpetuated reading. The framing of Black literary genres and movements undoubtedly affects how they and their attending authors and texts are (or are not) carried forward to future

Coda   243

readers. What we have come to call literature of the Harlem Renaissance is, for good or ill, accompanied by a myriad of attendant associations and expectations that inform future reading and reception. As we here consider various instances of editing Harlem Renaissance literature, we also consider the whole, how these individual editorial acts are woven into the larger project of associating them with one another. In this, we might not consider the individual literary creations of the Harlem Renaissance as "midwifed" so much as is the notion of Harlem Renaissance literature itself.

The production of African American literature more generally has historically been marked by such deliberate moments of editorial intervention. Almost a century before Dunbar-Nelson's pedagogical call for Black literature, we see one of the clearest early examples of African American editorial intervention, with Samuel Cornish and John B. Russworm's founding of what is believed to be the first African American owned and operated newspaper, *Freedom's Journal*. Addressing their new readers, they point to the population in which they sought their primary readership, the "FIVE HUNDRED THOUSAND free persons of colour" then living in the United States. Cornish and Russworm argue for the necessity of their paper, noting that "no publication, as yet, has been devoted exclusively to their improvement ... and more important still, that this large body of our citizens have no public channel—all serve to prove the real necessity, at present, for the appearance of the FREEDOM'S JOURNAL."[4] Offering their newspaper as a venue in which a wide variety of content (from what one might call the newsworthy to the more clearly literary) that would be delivered to their Black readership, they frame their editorship as cultivating a Black public.

Publishers, newspaper and literary editors, and writers are not the only people who cultivated and facilitated Black literary and intellectual publics. During the Harlem Renaissance, for example, librarians played a crucial role in facilitating intellectual community, events, and even basic access to space and services for writers and artists in Harlem. Ernestine Rose, Catherine Latimer, and Regina Anderson, among others, were librarians at the 135th Street Branch Library of the New York Public Library, where getting a library card was often the second necessary stop for newly arrived artists in Harlem after securing a room at the

244   BRIGITTE FIELDER AND JONATHAN SENCHYNE

Y.M.C.A. Arna Bontemps and Langston Hughes both recalled their stop at the 135th Street Branch as part of their introductions to Harlem. The librarian Regina Anderson set aside space in the library where Hughes, Claude McKay, and Eric Walrond often worked. Anderson later regularly hosted a salon at her apartment that served as a cornerstone of intellectual life in the community. As Sarah A. Anderson has written, the library and librarians of Harlem rested at a "confluence of interests and a mission whose time had come. The library provided a space in which people ... could explore what it meant to be [B]lack. ... It became a sphere for public discourse; within this domain, voices representing a wide range of political and aesthetic viewpoints found expression and audience."[5]

Because librarianship involves selection and recommendation, it bears some resemblance to what is usually called editorship. But it is worth dwelling near the more mundane aspects of service that these "Harlem Renaissance librarians" provided—access to space to work, regular occasions to gather, access to books—and asking why not include it in the domain of editing? What would it mean to include this work of everyday facilitation within the realm of possible understandings of editorship? Maintaining good space for people to work and offering services such as access to books within a community establish the conditions which make writing and thinking possible. Acts of infrastructural building and maintenance are too often invisibilized, or obscured, behind more prominent acts of selection and publication commonly called editing but needn't be. In "Maintenance and Care," Sharon Mattern proposes stewardship and maintenance as "corrective framework[s]" that focus needed attention on "traditions of women's work, domestic and reproductive labor, and ... acts of preservation and conservation, formal and informal" that too often fail to register in scholarship and organizing work.[6]

Incorporating maintenance, care, and infrastructural work into our concept of editing is also crucially important for linking the work Harlem Renaissance editors to the various labors of students, librarians, and researchers working in digital humanities projects that study, curate, circulate, analyze, and build community around African American literature. Projects that build databases of African American periodicals, organize full-text transcription efforts, or provide greater access to digitized primary materials ought to be claimed as part of the genealogy of editing reaching back through generations of African American editors and other facilitators of African American written and visual expression. Once editing is approached as part of the larger frame of maintenance and care work, then a fuller range of people, acts, and works become available for our scholarly attention (like the Harlem Renaissance librarians and the places where current generations of editors are doing this work). There are hundreds of digital projects where this kind of work is being done, including the Colored Conventions Project and the Black Press Research Collective (to name only two very prominent editorial and infrastructure building networks), drawing on the expertise of so many who may not at first consider themselves or be considered by others as editors. Just like the librarians making space and providing access to materials through the 135th Street Branch, today's editors maintain internet infrastructures, lead community scholarship efforts, teach students and project volunteers about metadata, and create high-resolution scans of primary source materials.

Scholars of African American studies have considered what it means or takes for a people, a public, a literature, or a movement to be carried forward as legible and valuable for future academic study or readerly exploration. Editors of African American literature have participated directly in that work to various ends. In his discussion of the mid-nineteenth-century periodical, the *Anglo-African Magazine,* Ivy G. Wilson examines the early Black press in terms of what he calls "the genealogies of African American editorial practices."[7] Tracing this genealogy back to early Black newspaper editors, Wilson offers an alternative to author-centered examinations of African American literary production. This alternative allows for a less individualized and more comprehensive understanding of African American literary production, more broadly.

The chapters in this volume take us through various ways of rethinking editorial genealogies and futures for the Harlem Renaissance. In doing so, we can consider these texts and authors alongside what has been a historically collective effort to create and sustain Black literature. In a move that recalls the work of early Black newspaper editors to usher forth what we now recognize as early African American literature, John K. Young considers magazines as editions in their own right. Examining the influence of white financers of Black literary production, Adam Nemmers

246   BRIGITTE FIELDER AND JONATHAN SENCHYNE

explores how work might bear the mark of factors beyond (and even potentially at odds with) aesthetic choice. Taking up questions of authorship and ownership of Harlem Renaissance material, Darryl-Dickson Carr raises questions about writing as an individual endeavor that can be cleanly separated from the larger influences of community and conversation. Considering both what is written and unwritten, Shawn Anthony Christian reads the role of the folk in the editorial work of anthologizing Black voices, and Joshua M. Murray notes tensions between the written and unwritten editorial work of autobiography. These understandings of editorship consider Harlem Renaissance writing beyond the careful crafting of individual authors.

Just as attention to editorial practices allows us to think beyond the individuality of authors, it also demands that we extend our scope beyond the immediacy of contemporary contexts and readers. In the introduction to their edited collection *Post-Bellum, Pre-Harlem: African American Literature and Culture,* Caroline Gebhard and Barbara McCaskill note forward-glancing toward this period by writers of this earlier period.[8] Though not yet demarcated as a specific period of African American literature, what would only later become known as the Harlem Renaissance was not simply produced after the fact or even produced *ex nihilo* by the authors associated with it but emerges from the longer genealogies that produced a future for Black literature. This earlier moment of Black literary production and framing anticipates later movements and moments for conceiving Black literature. Even if we do not understand this explicitly as a premonition of what we now call the Harlem Renaissance, it is an expectant gesture, an understanding of Black literary futures even beyond its purview.

Editors of the Harlem Renaissance make similarly forward-looking gestures, as they imagine, present, or suggest new possibilities, alternative futures for the literature that would fall under the broad umbrella of this movement. Jayne Marek notes this, extending the reach of this literature beyond its intended audience, even in its own time. Adam McKible's discussion of the republication and re-presentation of texts for later audiences (academic and otherwise) and Gary Edward Holcomb's on publishing a manuscript text for the public for the first time similarly trace the future-glancing of these editorial glances. We see here how different possibilities and alternative futures for reading might be produced, as Emanuela Kucik has it, by the framing work of introductions or, as Ross K. Tangedal shows, the alternative endings that appear in different textual editions. Korey Garibaldi's discussion of segregation's extension from print to digital literary culture extends concerns about literary futures beyond the texts themselves and to the media structures by which they are circulated and accessed.

These considerations of editorial histories and possibilities ask us to look at Harlem Renaissance literature with an eye toward not only the individual authors of this literary movement, but also the attendant efforts that have made this movement legible as a body. The essays in this volume explore how the Harlem Renaissance has been, and continues to be, brought into existence through the work of many hands. It helps us to gain a more complex understanding of the avenues through which we continue to encounter expressions of the Harlem Renaissance, as well as of what constitutes editing itself.

Notes

Introduction: Editing the Harlem Renaissance
Joshua M. Murray and Ross K. Tangedal

1. Langston Hughes, *The Big Sea* (New York: Alfred A. Knopf, 1940; repr. New York: Hill & Wang, 1993), 17.
2. Arna Bontemps, "Introduction to the 1968 Edition," in *Black Thunder* (New York: Macmillan, 1936; repr. Boston: Beacon Hill Press, 1968 and 1992), xxi.
3. Bontemps, "Introduction to the 1968 Edition," xxix.
4. Hughes, *The Big Sea*, 218.
5. Alain Locke, "The New Negro," in *The New Negro*, ed. Alain Locke (New York: Albert & Charles Boni, 1925; repr. New York: Simon & Schuster, 1997), 3.
6. Locke, "New Negro," 3.
7. Alain Locke, "Negro Youth Speaks," in *The New Negro*, 50.
8. Locke, "Negro Youth Speaks," 51.
9. W.E.B. Du Bois, "Criteria of Negro Art," *The Crisis* 32, no. 6 (1926): 296.
10. Du Bois, "Criteria of Negro Art," 296.

Chapter One: The Renaissance Happened in (Some of) the Magazines   John K. Young

1. This was, until its recent redesign, the slogan of the Modernist Journals Project (modjourn.org), a joint venture of Brown University and The University of Tulsa, which has been an invaluable resource for

250   NOTES TO PAGES 15–16

any study of modernism and magazines. Robert Scholes and Clifford Wulfman make a related claim in their discussion of modernism and modernity: "Modernism began in the magazines, and the magazines in which it began were—all of them—shaped by modernity." *Modernism in the Magazines: An Introduction* (New Haven, CT: Yale University Press, 2010), 43.

2   Though I focus on magazines in this chapter, for studies of African American literature in newspapers of the period, see especially John Lowe, "Newsprint Masks: The Comic Columns of Finley Peter Dunne, Alexander Posey, and Langston Hughes," in *Beyond the Binary: Reconstructing Cultural Identity in a Multicultural Context*, ed. Timothy B. Powell (New Brunswick, NJ: Rutgers University Press, 1999); Martha Patterson, "'Chocolate Baby, a Story of Ambition, Deception, and Success': Refiguring the New Negro Woman in the *Pittsburgh Courier*," in *The New Woman International: Representations in Photography and Film, 1890s–1930s*, ed. Elizabeth Otto and Vanessa Rocco (Ann Arbor, MI: University of Michigan Press, 2011); Zoe Trodd, "The Black Press and the Black Chicago Renaissance," in *Writers of the Chicago Black Renaissance*, ed. Steven C. Tracy (Urbana, IL: University of Illinois Press, 2011); and Juliet E.K. Walker, "The Promised Land: The *Chicago Defender* and the Black Press in Illinois, 1862–1970," in *The Black Press in the Middle West, 1865–1985*, ed. Henry Lewis Suggs (Westport, CT: Greenwood Press, 1996). For a historical overview of additional African American magazines of the 1920s, see Abby Ann Arthur Johnson and Ronald M. Johnson, "Forgotten Pages: Black Literary Magazines in the 1920s," *Journal of American Studies* 8.3 (1974): 363–82.

3   George Hutchinson, *The Harlem Renaissance in Black and White* (Cambridge, MA: Belknap Press, 1995), 128, 132–33. Hutchinson notes further examples of Harlem Renaissance writers appearing in "white" periodicals, including W.E.B. Du Bois, Langston Hughes, and Eric Walrond (128). While such a contribution might well be the only one from a Black writer in a particular issue, Hutchinson finds that publishing in white magazines remained appealing, "not only because they reached a larger white audience than black magazines but also because they encouraged types of ideological and artistic freedom the African American editors either shied away from or did not appreciate" (129). On Larsen as the first African American author in *Forum*, see George Hutchinson, *In Search of Nella Larsen: A Biography of the Color Line* (Cambridge, MA: Belknap Press, 2006), 343. Suzanne Churchill notes, "modernism was not always divided along the color line: Fenton Johnson published poems in the largely white avant-garde magazine *Others*, Claude McKay and Mike Gold co-edited the *Liberator*, and William Stanley Braithwaite's 1918 *Anthology of Magazine Verse* included war poems by Jesse Fauset

NOTES TO PAGES 16–18   251

and William Rose Benét" ("Modernism in Black & White," *Modernism/ modernity* 16, no. 3 [2009]: 490). For further discussion of these kinds of cultural intersections, see my "African American Magazine Modernism," in *African American Literature in Transition, 1920–1930*, ed. Rachel Farebrother and Miriam Thaggert (Cambridge: Cambridge University Press, forthcoming).

4   Claude McKay, *Collected Poems*, ed. William Maxwell (Urbana, IL: University of Illinois Press, 2004).

5   Peter Shillingsburg, *Resisting Texts: Authority and Submission in Constructions of Meaning* (Ann Arbor, MI: University of Michigan Press, 1997), 77–80.

6   Sean Latham, "Unpacking My Digital Library: Programs, Modernisms, Magazines," in *Making Canada New: Editing, Modernism, and New Media*, ed. Dean Irvine, Vanessa Lent, and Bart Vautour (Toronto: University of Toronto Press, 2017), 38.

7   I elaborate on this issue, though without specific reference to the Harlem Renaissance, in "The Editorial Ontology of the Periodical Text," *Ecdotica* 15 (2019): 89–128.

8   For further scholarship on the Harlem Renaissance and magazine culture, see Anne Elizabeth Carroll, *Word, Image, and the New Negro: Representation and Identity in the Harlem Renaissance* (Bloomington, IN: Indiana University Press, 2005); Shawn Anthony Christian, *The Harlem Renaissance and the Idea of a New Negro Reader* (Amherst, MA: University of Massachusetts Press, 2016); Suzanne Churchill, "Little Magazines and the Gendered, Racialized Discourse of Women's Poetry," in *A History of Twentieth-Century Women's Poetry*, ed. Linda A. Kinnahan (Cambridge: Cambridge University Press, 2016); Suzanne Churchill, "Modernism in Black & White," *Modernism/modernity* 16, no. 3 (2009): 489–92; Eurie Dahn, "*Cane* in the Magazines: Race, Form, and Global Periodical Networks," *Journal of Modern Periodical Studies* (2012): 119–35; Cynthia Dobbs, "Mapping Black Movement, Containing Black Laughter: Ralph Ellison's New York Essays," *American Quarterly* (2016): 907–29; Michel Fabre, "Oubliés par la *NRF*?: Marginalité du modernisme noir," *Romanic Review* 99, nos. 1–2 (2008): 133–42; Caroline Goeser, *Picturing the New Negro: Harlem Renaissance Print Culture and Modern Black Identity* (Lawrence, KS: University Press of Kansas, 2007); George Hutchinson, *The Harlem Renaissance in Black and White*; Robert Johnson, "Globalizing the Harlem Renaissance: Irish, Mexican, and 'Negro' Renaissances in *The Survey* and *Survey Graphic*," in *Other Renaissances: A New Approach to World Literature*, ed. Brenda Deen Schildgen, Gang Zhou, and Sander Gilman (New York: Palgrave Macmillan, 2006); Jayne Marek, "Women Editors and Little Magazines in the Harlem Renaissance," in *Little Magazines and Modernism: New Approaches*, ed. Suzanne Churchill and Adam

252 NOTES TO PAGES 18–23

McKible (London: Ashgate, 2007); Martha Nadell, "'Devoted to younger artists': *Fire!!* (1926) and *Harlem* (1928)," in *The Oxford Critical and Cultural History of Modernist Magazines*, vol. 2, *North America, 1894–1960*, ed. Peter Brooker and Andrew Thacker (New York: Oxford University Press, 2012); Nadell, *Enter the New Negroes: Images of Race in American Culture* (Cambridge, MA: Harvard University Press, 2004); Kirsten Bartholomew Ortega, "Accessing the Harlem Renaissance through *The Crisis*," *Pedagogy* 15, no. 2 (2015): 378–82; John K. Young, "The Roots of *Cane*: Jean Toomer in *The Double Dealer* and Modernist Networks," in *Race, Ethnicity, and Publishing*, ed. Cecile Cottenet (New York: Palgrave Macmillan, 2014); and essays focused on specific magazines as noted below. James L.W. West III's edition of F. Scott Fitzgerald's magazine fiction, *The Lost Decade: Stories from Esquire, 1936–1941* (Cambridge: Cambridge University Press, 2008) offers an instructive model for editions based on magazine publications vs. book productions. For a discussion of the affordances of this edition, see my "Editorial Ontology," 102–4.

9   Hans Walter Gabler, *Text Genetics in Literary Modernism and Other Essays* (Cambridge: Open Book Publishers, 2018), 171.

10 For a discussion of the concept of the work in a musical context, see Lydia Goehr, *The Imaginary Museum of Musical Works: An Essay in the Philosophy of Music* (Oxford: Clarendon Press, 1992). Paul Eggert discusses the ontology of the work across aesthetic registers, partially in response to Goehr's ideas, in *The Work and the Reader in Literary Studies: Scholarly Editing and Book History* (Cambridge: Cambridge University Press, 2019), 31–33. Jacqueline Goldsby traces the textual history of *Ex-Colored Man* in the introduction to her 2015 Norton Critical Edition of the novel.

11 Jean Toomer, "Kabnis," *Broom* 5, no. 2 (1923): 83.

12 Jean Toomer, *The Letters of Jean Toomer, 1919–1924*, ed. Mark Whalan (Knoxville, TN: University of Tennessee Press, 2006), 44.

13 Daniel Ferrer, "Genetic Criticism with Textual Criticism: From Variant to Variation," *Variants* 12–13 (2013): 58.

14 Eggert, *Work and the Reader*, 33. Here Eggert returns to a conception of the work as a regulative ideal advanced in his *Securing the Past: Conservation in Art, Architecture and Literature* (Cambridge: Cambridge University Press, 2009), chap. 10.

15 For a more complete history of this magazine, see my "Midwestern Magazine Modernism: Recovering Samuel Pessin and *The Milwaukee Arts Monthly/Prairie*," forthcoming in *Journal of Modern Periodical Studies*.

16 Peter Shillingsburg, "Text as Matter, Concept, and Action," in *Resisting Texts*, 76, 77.

17 Shillingsburg, "Text as Matter," 77.

18 Patrick Collier, "What Is Modern Periodical Studies?" *Journal of Modern Periodical Studies* 6, no. 2 (2015): 109. On magazines as ergodic objects

NOTES TO PAGES 23–27   253

and the editorial questions arising from this condition, see Latham, "Unpacking My Digital Library," 53.

19 Margaret Beetham, "Open and Closed: The Periodical as a Publishing Genre," *Victorian Periodicals Review* 22, no. 3 (1989): 98.

20 Hutchinson, *Harlem Renaissance*, 433.

21 Rachel Farebrother, *The Collage Aesthetic in the Harlem Renaissance* (London: Ashgate 2019), 51.

22 Peter Shillingsburg, *Textuality and Knowledge: Essays* (University Park, PA: Penn State University Press, 2017), 59.

23 Shillingsburg, *Textuality and Knowledge*, 123, 125.

24 Eggert, *Work and the Reader*, 10–11.

25 Eggert, *Work and the Reader*, 114–15. For a more wide-ranging and nuanced discussion of the editorial concept of the work, see the cluster of essays organized by Barbara Bordalejo as "Work and Document," in *Ecdotica* 10 (2013).

26 Margaret Beetham, "Toward a Theory of the Periodical as a Publishing Genre," in *Investigating Victorian Journalism*, ed. Laurel Brake, Aled Jones, and Lionel Madden (New York: St. Martin's, 1990), 24.

27 Farebrother, *Collage Aesthetic*, 2.

28 Kinohi Nishikawa, "Race, Thick and Thin," *Arcade: Literature, Humanities, and the World*: http://arcade.stanford.edu/content/race-thick-and-thin. Mar. 16, 2015 (original emphasis).

29 Mark W. Turner, "Time, Periodicals, and Literary Studies," *Victorian Periodicals Review* 39, no. 6 (2006): 315. For an example of readings of individual magazine issues within a broader sense of the periodical as a genre, see Latham, "Unpacking My Digital Library."

30 "If the edition is to be seen as an argument then it is necessarily one that is addressed *to* an audience *in respect of* the documents gathered and analysed for the editorial project, usually documents deemed to witness the textual transmission," Eggert writes (*Work and the Reader*, 82; original emphasis).

31 Peter Brooker and Andrew Thacker, "General Introduction," *The Oxford Critical and Cultural History of Modernist Magazines*, vol. 1, *Britain and Ireland, 1880–1955* (New York: Oxford University Press, 2009), 6 (original emphasis).

32 Philpotts offers a refinement of Brooker and Thacker's periodical codes, subdividing these into temporal codes (a magazine's longevity and regularity of publication); material codes (size and quality of binding and printing); economic codes (print run, price, subscription rate); social codes (the network of editorial and production staff, along with contributing authors and readers); and compositional codes (a mixture of text, illustrations, and other design elements) as evidenced in a given issue or run of issues. See Philpotts, "Defining the Thick Journal: Periodical

254   NOTES TO PAGES 27–35

Codes and Common Habitus": https://seeeps.princeton.edu/wp-content/uploads/sites/243/2015/03/mla2013_philpotts.pdf.

33   Rachel Farebrother, "*The Crisis* (1910–34)," in Brooker and Thacker, *Oxford Critical and Cultural History of Modernist Magazines*, 2:106. On *The Crisis*, see also Carroll, *Word, Image, and the New Negro*; Russ Castronovo, "Beauty Along the Color Line: Lynching, Aesthetics, and the *Crisis*," *PMLA* 121, no. 5 (2006): 1443–59; Goeser, *Picturing the New Negro*; Hutchinson, *Harlem Renaissance*, chap. 5; and Amy Helene Kirschke, *Art in Crisis: W.E.B. Du Bois and the Struggle for African American Identity and Memory* (Bloomington, IN: Indiana University Press, 2007).

34   The magazine's prices had increased from rates of 10 cents per copy and $1.00 per year as of September 1919 (Farebrother, "*The Crisis*," 103).

35   I am using the copy of the magazine available through the Modernist Journals Project, at https://modjourn.org/issue/bdr514203/.

36   On Williams's career, see Camille F. Forbes, "Dancing with 'Racial Feet': Bert Williams and the Performance of Blackness," *Theatre Journal* 56, no. 4 (2004): 603–25.

37   Eurie Dahn, "Forgotten Manuscripts: 'Lex Talionis: A Story,' by Robert W. Bagnall," *African American Review* 51, no. 4 (2018): 279.

38   Dahn, "Forgotten Manuscripts," 281.

39   Dahn, "*Cane* in the Magazines," 133 n. 32. Dahn discusses "Song of the Son" in relation to the issue's contents, especially in its focus on anti-lynching activity (127–29).

40   Mortimer G. Mitchell, "Pride," *The Crisis* (Apr. 1922): 265.

41   Madeline G. Allison, "The Horizon," *The Crisis* (Apr. 1922): 266.

42   William Henry Harrison, Jr., *Colored Girls' and Boys' Inspiring United States History and a Heart to Heart Talk about White Folks* (Allentown, PA: [Searle & Dressler Co.], 1921), 150.

43   Noting that her awareness of "Lex Talionis" came from her research into Toomer's periodical publications, Dahn observes: "The contingent juxtapositions within periodicals hold the promise of textual recovery." Dahn, "Forgotten Manuscripts," 282 n. 4.

44   George B. Hutchinson, "Organizational Voices: *The Messenger* (1917–28) and *Opportunity* (1923–49)," in Brooker and Thacker, *Oxford Critical and Cultural History of Modernist Magazines*, 2:785. On *The Messenger*, see also Hutchinson, *Harlem Renaissance*, chap. 10; Theodore Kornweibel, *No Crystal Stair* (Westport, CT: Greenwood Press, 1975); and Adam McKible, "Our(?) Country: Mapping 'These "Colored" United States' in *The Messenger*," in *The Black Press: New Literary and Historical Essays*, ed. Todd Vogel (New Brunswick, NJ: Rutgers University Press, 2001).

45   Hutchinson, "Organizational Voices," 784, 785.

46   The magazine's pattern of female cover photographs returns with the subsequent issue, alternating with other kinds of illustrations, such as

Aaron Douglas's "Steelworks" on the October 1927 cover, over the next several months.

47 Arnold Rampersad, ed., *The Collected Poems of Langston Hughes* (New York: Random House, 1994), 630.

48 Coleman published short fiction and poetry in *The Crisis, Opportunity, Half-Century Magazine*, and *The Messenger*, among other journals, during this period, with two volumes of poetry appearing in the ensuing decades. See Mary E. Young, "Anita Scott Coleman: A Neglected Harlem Renaissance Writer," *CLA Journal* 40, no. 3 (1997): 271–87.

49 "Since it is from the materiality of the documents alone that the authoriality behind them may be discerned," Gabler writes, "we may legitimately declare 'authoriality' a function of the documents" (*Text Genetics*, 169). This chapter was originally published as "Beyond Author-Centricity in Scholarly Editing," *Journal of Early Modern Studies* 1, no. 1 (2012): 15–35.

50 Robert E. Hemenway, *Zora Neale Hurston: A Literary Biography* (Urbana, IL: University of Illinois Press, 1977), 68–70. See also Valerie Boyd, *Wrapped in Rainbows: The Life of Zora Neale Hurston* (New York: Scribner, 2003), 139–41.

51 On the Van Vechten review in the context of Thurman's career, see Michael Nowlin, *Literary Ambition and the African American Novel* (Cambridge: Cambridge University Press, 2019), 111–18. On Thurman's reviews more generally, see the introduction to Part Four, "Literary Essays and Reviews," in *The Collected Writings of Wallace Thurman: A Harlem Renaissance Reader*, ed. Amritjit Singh and Daniel M. Scott (New Brunswick, NJ: Rutgers University Press, 2003).

52 Richard Digby-Junger, "*The Guardian, Messenger, Crisis*, and *Negro World*: The Early 20th-Century Black Radical Press," *Howard Journal of Communications* 9 (1998): 279.

53 Digby-Junger, "The Early 20th-Century Black Radical Press," 271.

54 While not considering this topic in quite these terms, two articles by Matthew Philpotts offer a conceptual foundation from which notions of editorial intentionality might develop: "The Role of the Periodical Editor: Literary Journals and Editorial Habitus," *Modern Language Review* 107, no. 1 (2012): 39–64; and "Through Thick and Thin: On the Typology and Agency of Literary Journals," *International Journal of the Book* 7, no. 4 (2010): 55–64.

55 Cornelius L. Bynum, "The New Negro and Social Democracy during the Harlem Renaissance, 1917–1937," *Journal of the Gilded Age and Progressive Era* 10, no. 1 (2011): 93.

56 Bynum, "The New Negro and Social Democracy," 97, 99.

57 Wallace Thurman, "A Stranger at the Gates," *The Messenger* (Sept. 1926): 279.

256   NOTES TO PAGES 39–43

58   See Matthew Philpotts, "Dimension: Fractal Forms and Periodical Texture," *Victorian Periodicals Review* 48, no. 3 (2015): 415–23.
59   See Stephanie P. Browner and Kenneth M. Price, "Charles Chesnutt and the Case For Hybrid Editing," *International Journal of Digital Humanities* 1, no. 2 (2019): 165–78.
60   Hutchinson estimates that "Schuyler published more in *American Mercury* between 1924 and 1934 than anyone but its editors" (*Harlem Renaissance*, 509 n. 47). Faye Hammill and Karen Leick consider Mencken's support for Harlem Renaissance authors, especially men, "a particularly important element of the literary and cultural work performed by *The American Mercury*." Faye Hammill and Karen Leick, "Modernism and the Quality Magazines: *Vanity Fair* (1914–36); *American Mercury* (1924–81); *New Yorker* (1925–); *Esquire* (1933–)," in Brooker and Thacker, *Oxford Critical and Cultural History of Modernist Magazines*, 2:184.
61   Hutchinson, *Harlem Renaissance*, 336.
62   Hammill and Leick, "Modernism and the Quality Magazines," 182.
63   Hammill and Leick, "Modernism and the Quality Magazines," 182.
64   For a history of *Accent*, see Frederick Jefferson Hendricks's Ph.D. dissertation: "'Accent' 1940–1960: The History of a Little Magazine," University of Illinois, 1984.
65   Adam McKible and Suzanne Churchill, "Introduction: In Conversation: The Harlem Renaissance and the New Modernist Studies," *Modernism/modernity* 20, no. 3 (2013): 428. In addition to this issue, for examples of studies extending the boundaries of the "Harlem Renaissance," see especially Davarian L. Baldwin and Minkah Makalani, eds., *Escape from New York: The New Negro Renaissance Beyond Harlem* (Minneapolis, MN: University of Minnesota Press, 2013); Brent Hayes Edwards, *The Practice of Diaspora: Literature, Translation, and the Rise of Black Internationalism* (Cambridge, MA: Harvard University Press, 2003); and Lawrence P. Jackson, *The Indignant Generation: A Narrative History of African American Writers and Critics, 1934–1960* (Princeton, NJ: Princeton University Press, 2011).
66   See Hazel Rowley, *Richard Wright: The Life and Times* (Chicago: University of Chicago Press, 2001), 262–63.
67   Julia Istomina includes some comparisons between the draft and published versions in "The Terror of Ahistoricity: Reading the Frame(-up) Through and Against Film Noir in Richard Wright's 'The Man Who Lived Underground,'" *African American Review* 49, no. 2 (2016): 111–27.
68   Seaver and Wright became friends while both were writing for the *Daily Worker* in the 1930s, with Seaver positively reviewing "Big Boy Leaves Home" for the newspaper in 1936. See Jerry W. Ward, Jr. and Robert J. Butler, eds., *The Richard Wright Encyclopedia* (Westport, CT:

NOTES TO PAGES 43–47   257

Greenwood Press, 2008), 340–41. For an overview of Seaver's career, see Gordon B. Neavill, "So Far, So Good: Recollections of a Life in Publishing: Edwin Seaver," *Library Quarterly* 58, no. 2 (1988), 214–15; and Jackson, *Indignant Generation*, 178–79.

69 Barbara Foley, "Questionnaire Responses," *Modernism/modernity* 20, no. 3 (2013): 439.

70 For a full discussion of modernist magazine advertising and editorial responses to it, see Scholes and Wulfman, *Modernism in the Magazines*, chap. 8.

Chapter Two: The Pawn's Gambit: Black Writers, White Patrons, and the Harlem Renaissance   *Adam Nemmers*

1   Mario Biagioli, *Galileo, Courtier: The Practice of Science in the Culture of Absolutism* (Chicago: University of Chicago Press, 1993), 15.

2   Jeffrey C. Stewart, *The New Negro: The Life of Alain Locke* (New York: Oxford University Press, 2018), 616–17.

3   Langston Hughes, *The Big Sea* (New York: Alfred A. Knopf, 1940; repr. New York: Hill & Wang, 1993), 228.

4   For example, not only did Charlotte Osgood Mason encourage and fund Langston Hughes's composition of *Not Without Laughter*, but she also sent him "a 24-page, chapter-by-chapter critique of the novel" after the first draft was completed. See Arnold Rampersad, *The Life of Langston Hughes*, vol. 1, *1902–1941: I, Too, Sing America* (New York: Oxford University Press, 1986), 172.

5   Ralph D. Story, "Patronage and the Harlem Renaissance: You Get What You Pay For," *CLA Journal* 32, no. 3 (1989): 285.

6   Amritjit Singh, "Black–White Symbiosis: Another Look at the Literary History of the 1920s," *The Harlem Renaissance*, ed. Harold Bloom (Broomall, PA: Chelsea House, 2004), 23.

7   David Levering Lewis, *When Harlem Was in Vogue* (New York: Knopf, 1981), 152, 95.

8   Rodney Trapp, "Whose Renaissance Was It Really: Black Art Patronage of the 1920s and 1930s," *American University Graduate Review* 5 (1993): 94.

9   Rampersad, *Life of Langston Hughes*, 1:200.

10 Stewart, *The New Negro*, 618.

11 Story, "Patronage," 289.

12 Sharon L. Jones, *Rereading the Harlem Renaissance: Race, Class, and Gender in the Fiction of Jessie Fauset, Zora Neale Hurston, and Dorothy West* (Westport, CT: Greenwood Press, 2002), 68.

13 Robert E. Hemenway, *Zora Neale Hurston: A Literary Biography* (Urbana, IL: University of Illinois Press, 1977), 107.

258   NOTES TO PAGES 47–52

14 Robert C. Hart, "Black–White Literary Relations in the Harlem Renaissance," *American Literature* 44, no. 1 (1973): 627–28.

15 See John Sekura, "Black Message/White Envelope: Genre, Authenticity, and Authority in the Antebellum Slave Narrative," *Callaloo* 32 (Summer 1987): 482–515.

16 Stephanie M. H. Camp, *Closer to Freedom: Enslaved Women and Everyday Resistance in the Plantation South* (Chapel Hill, NC: University of North Carolina Press, 2004), 1.

17 Cary D. Wintz, *Black Culture and the Harlem Renaissance* (College Station, TX: Texas A&M University Press, 1996), 177.

18 Wintz, *Black Culture*, 177.

19 Wintz, *Black Culture*, 178.

20 Carla Kaplan, *Miss Anne in Harlem* (New York: Harper, 2013), 195.

21 Wintz, *Black Culture*, 177–78.

22 Stewart, *The New Negro*, 623.

23 Wintz, *Black Culture*, 179.

24 Lewis, *When Harlem Was in Vogue*, 99.

25 Arna Bontemps, "The Awakening: A Memoir," in *The Harlem Renaissance Remembered*, ed. Arna Bontemps (New York: Dodd, Mead & Company, 1972), 11.

26 Warrington Hudlin, "The Renaissance Re-examined," originally published in Bontemps, *The Harlem Renaissance Remembered*; reprinted in Bloom, *Harlem Renaissance*, 9.

27 Wintz, *Black Culture*, 179.

28 Lewis, *When Harlem*, 152.

29 Rampersad, *Life of Langston Hughes*, 1:276.

30 Like Mason, Cunard was childless, suggesting that she and other "Miss Annes" (to borrow a term from Carla Kaplan's volume) were in some sense exercising a sort of surrogate "maternalism" in adopting young Black artists as their "children."

31 Wintz, *Black Culture*, 185.

32 Wintz, *Black Culture*, 186.

33 Yuval Taylor, *Zora and Langston: A Story of Friendship and Betrayal* (New York: W.W. Norton, 2019), 89.

34 Kaplan, *Miss Anne*, 173.

35 Kaplan, *Miss Anne*, 172.

36 Lewis, *When Harlem*, 154.

37 Locke had, according to a notebook entry by Mason, exchanged this sentiment with Hughes within earshot of someone who then relayed it to Mason. See Stewart, *The New Negro*, 557.

38 Hudlin, "Renaissance Re-examined," 10.

39 Melinda Booth, "Charlotte Osgood Mason: Politics of Misrepresentation," *Oakland Journal* 10 (2006): 50.

NOTES TO PAGES 52–58   259

40 Trapp, "Whose Renaissance," 96.
41 Bruce Kellner, "White Patronage in the Harlem Renaissance," in *Harlem Renaissance Re-examined*, ed. Victor A. Kramer and Robert A. Russ (Troy, NY: Whitson Publishing, 1997), 123.
42 Steven Watson, *The Harlem Renaissance: Hub of African-American Culture, 1920–1930* (New York: Pantheon, 1995), 146.
43 For a prime and predominant example of self-essentialism, see Locke's 1925 essay "The New Negro."
44 Cheryl Wall, *Women of the Harlem Renaissance* (Bloomington, IN: Indiana University Press, 1995), 154.
45 Bruce Kellner, ed., *The Harlem Renaissance: A Historical Dictionary for the Era* (Westport, CT: Greenwood Press, 1984), 237.
46 Rampersad, *Life of Langston Hughes*, 1:170.
47 Rampersad, *Life of Langston Hughes*, 1:170.
48 Bontemps, "The Awakening," 23.
49 Stewart, *The New Negro*, 617.
50 Taylor, *Zora and Langston*, 136.
51 Kaplan, *Miss Anne*, 242.
52 Kaplan, *Miss Anne*, 246.
53 Wall, *Women of the Harlem Renaissance*, 158.
54 Qtd. in Henry Louis Gates, Jr., *The Signifying Monkey: A Theory of African-American Literary Criticism* (New York: Oxford University Press, 1988), 54.
55 Winifred Morgan, *The Trickster Figure in American Literature* (New York: Palgrave Macmillan, 2013), 15.
56 Qtd. in Gates, *Signifying Monkey*, 67.
57 Qtd. in Gates, *Signifying Monkey*, 68.
58 Morgan, *Trickster Figure*, 23–24.
59 Gates, *Signifying Monkey*, 70.
60 Rampersad reports, "When Mrs. Mason grumbled about Zora's letters, [Hughes] urged Hurston to write more often and in a different tone." See Rampersad, *Life of Langston Hughes*, 1:183. Stewart writes similarly that Hughes "was advising Hurston about how to manipulate the situation" with Mason. See Stewart, *The New Negro*, 610.
61 Stewart, *The New Negro*, 576.
62 Taylor, *Zora and Langston*, 158.
63 Qtd. in Rampersad, *Life of Langston Hughes*, 1:187.
64 Deborah G. Plant, "Afterword" to Zora Neale Hurston, *Barracoon: The Story of the Last "Black Cargo,"* ed. Deborah G. Plant (New York: Amistad, 2018), 118.
65 Rebecca Panovka, "A Different Backstory for Zora Neale Hurston's 'Barracoon,'" *Los Angeles Review of Books*, July 7, 2018: https://lareviewofbooks.org/article/different-backstory-for-zora-neale-hurstons-barracoon/.

260   NOTES TO PAGES 58–65

66   Frank A. Salamone, "His Eyes Were Watching Her: Papa Franz Boas, Zora Neale Hurston, and Anthropology," *Anthropos* 109, no. 1 (2014): 221.
67   Salamone, "His Eyes," 221.
68   Deborah G. Plant, "Introduction" to Hurston, *Barracoon*, xx.
69   Panovka, "A Different Backstory."
70   Stewart, *The New Negro*, 586.
71   Qtd. in Stewart, *The New Negro*, 587.
72   Qtd. in Taylor, *Zora and Langston*, 138.
73   Panovka, "A Different Backstory."
74   Panovka, "A Different Backstory."
75   Panovka, "A Different Backstory."
76   Deborah G. Plant, "Editor's Note," in Hurston, *Barracoon*, xxviii.
77   Hurston, *Barracoon*, 1.
78   Panovka, "A Different Backstory."
79   Plant, "Afterword" to Hurston, *Barracoon*, 123.

Chapter Three: Clad in the Beautiful Dress One Expects: Editing and Curating the Harlem Renaissance Text   *Ross K. Tangedal*

An earlier version of this chapter appeared as "I'm Inclined to Believe: Editing Uncertainty in the Ending(s) to Nella Larsen's *Passing*," *South Atlantic Review* 84, nos. 2–3 (2019): 205–23, as part of a special issue on *Passing* at ninety. The author is indebted to Donavan Ramon and Joshua Murray for suggestions on early versions of that essay as well as editors R. Barton Palmer and M. Alison Wise for permission to reprint portions of that essay here.

1   Charles Willis Thompson, "The Negro Question," *New York Times* (Oct. 16, 1927): 14, 16.
2   "Bibliography Defined," Bibliographical Society of America: https://bibsocamer.org/about-us/bibliography-defined/: "Bibliography is the branch of historical scholarship that examines any aspect of the production, dissemination, and reception of handwritten and printed books as physical objects. ('Books' is shorthand here for various kinds of text-bearing objects, including pamphlets and single leaves.) Among the characteristic activities of this field are the following: analyzing physical clues in specific books in order to reveal details of the underlying production process; describing the paper (or parchment), letterforms, design, illustrations, structure, binding, and post-publication features of specific books; determining the relationship among books that carry texts of the same works (texts both verbal and nonverbal, such as musical and choreographic notation); writing narrative histories and technical studies of papermaking, paper use, ink, handwriting, type faces, type manufacture, book design, typesetting procedures, graphic processes, bookbinding, printing, publishing, bookselling, book collecting, libraries, provenance,

NOTES TO PAGES 65–70   261

and the role of the physical book in society and culture—along with biographies of the persons involved in these stories."

3   "Guidelines for Editors of Scholarly Editions: 1.2.2. The Editor's Theory of Text." www.mla.org: "Editorial perspectives range broadly across a spectrum from an interest in authorial intention, to an interest in the process of production, to an interest in reception, and editors may select a given methodology for a variety of reasons. In very general terms, one could see copy-text, recensionist, and best-text editing as being driven by an interest in authorship—but best-text editing might also be driven by an interest in the process of production, along with 'optimist,' diplomatic, scribal, documentary, and social-text editing. Social-text editing might also be driven by an interest in reception—as 'versioning' and variorum editing might be. And, of course, an editing practice that is primarily interested in authorship might very well be interested in production or reception or both—any good editor will be aware of the importance of all these things. However, when an editor has to choose what to attend to, what to represent, and how to represent it, there should be a consistent principle that helps in making those decisions."

4   Zafar's set includes new printings of *Cane* (Jean Toomer), *Home to Harlem* (Claude McKay), *Quicksand* (Nella Larsen), *Plum Bun* (Jessie Redmon Fauset), *The Blacker the Berry ...* (Wallace Thurman), *Not Without Laughter* (Langston Hughes), *Black No More* (George Schuyler), *The Conjure-Man Dies* (Rudolph Fisher), and *Black Thunder* (Arna Bontemps).

5   G. Thomas Tanselle, "Problems and Accomplishments in the Editing of the Novel," reprinted in *Textual Criticism and Scholarly Editing* (Richmond, VA: University of Virginia Press, 1990), 189.

6   G. Thomas Tanselle, "A Description of Descriptive Bibliography," *Studies in Bibliography* 45 (1992): 8.

7   Tanselle, "A Description of Descriptive Bibliography," 29.

8   Most of these bibliographies were published as part of a series by the University of Pittsburgh Press. Unfortunately, that series is no longer active.

9   See John K. Young, *Black Writers, White Publishers: Marketplace Politics in Twentieth-Century African American Literature* (Jackson, MS: University Press of Mississippi, 2006).

10 Tanselle, "A Description of Descriptive Bibliography," 3.

11 For example, see Roland Barthes, "The Death of the Author," in *Image, Music, Text* (London: Fontana, 1977); W.K. Wimsatt, Jr. and Monroe C. Beardsley, "The Intentional Fallacy," in *The Verbal Icon: Studies in the Meaning of Poetry* (Lexington, KY: University of Kentucky Press, 1954).

12 Mark J. Madigan, "'Then everything was dark'? The Two Endings of Nella Larsen's *Passing*," *Papers of the Bibliographical Society of America* 83, no. 4 (1989): 523.

262   NOTES TO PAGES 70–75

13 Nella Larsen, *Passing*, ed. Carla Kaplan (New York: W.W. Norton, 2007 [1929]), 79. When quoting from the novel, I use Kaplan's edition, which, to date, remains the most reliable edition of the book.

14 Fredson Bowers, "Regularization and Normalization in Modern Critical Texts," *Studies in Bibliography* 42 (1989): 81–82.

15 Elizabeth L. Eisenstein, "The Unacknowledged Revolution," *The Printing Press as an Agent of Change* (Cambridge: Cambridge University Press, 1979), reprinted in *The Broadview Reader in Book History*, eds. Michelle Levy and Tom Mole (Peterborough, ON: Broadview Press, 2015), 226.

16 G. Thomas Tanselle, *A Rationale of Textual Criticism* (Philadelphia, PA: University of Pennsylvania Press, 1989), 25.

17 Young, *Black Writers, White Publishers*, 56.

18 Madigan, "'Then everything was dark'?," 522.

19 Young, *Black Writers, White Publishers*, 45.

20 Young, *Black Writers, White Publishers*, 51.

21 Martha J. Cutter, "Sliding Significations: Passing as a Narrative and Textual Strategy in Nella Larsen's Fiction," *Passing and the Fictions of Identity*, ed. Elaine K. Ginsburg (Durham, NC: Duke University Press, 1996), 84.

22 Deborah E. McDowell, *"The Changing Same": Black Women's Literature, Criticism, and Theory* (Bloomington, IN: Indiana University Press, 1995), 79–80.

23 Judi M. Roller, *The Politics of the Feminist Novel* (Westport, CT: Greenwood Press, 1986), 102.

24 Joshua M. Murray, "Just Passing Through: The Harlem Renaissance Woman on the Move," *Critical Insights: Harlem Renaissance*, ed. Christopher Allen Varlack (Hackensack, NJ: Salem Press, 2015), 179, 181.

25 There are three biographies of Nella Larsen: Charles R. Larson's *Invisible Darkness: Jean Toomer & Nella Larsen* (Iowa City, IA: University of Iowa Press, 1993); Thadious M. Davis's *Nella Larsen, Novelist of the Harlem Renaissance: A Woman's Life Unveiled* (Baton Rouge, LA: Louisiana State University Press, 1994); and George Hutchinson's *In Search of Nella Larsen: A Biography of the Color Line* (Cambridge, MA: Belknap Press, 2006).

26 Larson, *Invisible Darkness*, 211.

27 Davis, *Nella Larsen*, 464.

28 Hutchinson, *In Search of Nella Larsen*, 482.

29 Larsen, *Passing*, 72.

30 Young, "Versions of *Passing*," *Approaches to Teaching the Novels of Nella Larsen*, ed. Jacquelyn Y. McLendon (New York: Modern Language Association of America, 2016), 153.

31 Young, "Versions," 153.

32 Young, "Versions," 154 (original emphasis).

NOTES TO PAGES 75–91   263

33 Young, "Versions," 154.

34 Nella Larsen, *Quicksand* and *Passing*, ed. Deborah E. McDowell (New Brunswick, NJ: Rutgers University Press, 1986), xxxviii.

35 Larsen, *Quicksand* and *Passing*, 246.

36 Larsen, *Passing*, ed. Thadious M. Davis (New York: Penguin, 1997 [1929]), xxxv.

37 Larsen, *The Complete Fiction of Nella Larsen*, ed. Charles R. Larson (New York: Anchor Books, 2001), xxii.

38 Larsen, *Passing*, critical foreword and notes by Mae Henderson (New York: Modern Library, 2002 [1929]), 203–4.

39 Larsen, *Passing*, ed. Kaplan, xxxi.

40 Davis, *Nella Larsen*, 322.

41 See Young, *Black Writers, White Publishers*, 50.

42 Davis, *Nella Larsen*, 306–7.

43 Hutchinson, *In Search of Nella Larsen*, 294.

44 Kaplan, "Nella Larsen's Erotics of Race," "Introduction" to Larsen, *Passing*, ed. Kaplan, xi.

45 Johnson, preface to the first edition of *Book of American Negro Poetry*, vii.

46 Tanselle, *A Rationale of Textual Criticism*, 35.

Chapter Four: The Two Gentlemen of Harlem: Wallace Thurman's *Infants of the Spring*, Richard Bruce Nugent's *Gentleman Jigger*, and Intellectual Property   *Darryl Dickson-Carr*

Portions of this chapter first appeared in Darryl Dickson-Carr, *Spoofing the Modern: Satire in the Harlem Renaissance* (Columbia, SC: University of South Carolina Press, 2015).

1 Thomas Wirth, "Introduction" to *Gay Rebel of the Harlem Renaissance: Selections from the Work of Richard Bruce Nugent*, ed. Thomas Wirth (Durham, NC: Duke University Press, 2002), 7.

2 Elonore van Notten, *Wallace Thurman's Harlem Renaissance* (Amsterdam: Rodopi, 1994), 173–75. This account is reproduced in almost precisely the same terms in Richard Bruce Nugent, *Gentleman Jigger*, ed. Thomas Wirth (Philadelphia, PA: Da Capo, 2008), 20–21.

3 Wallace Thurman, letter to Claude McKay, Feb. 3, 1928, Langston Hughes Papers, James Weldon Johnson Collection, Beinecke Rare Book and Manuscript Library, Yale University, New Haven, Connecticut. Hereinafter cited as JWJ.

4 Wallace Thurman, "This Negro Literary Renaissance," in *The Collected Writings of Wallace Thurman*, Amritjit Singh and Daniel M. Scott III (New Brunswick, NJ: Rutgers University Press, 2004), 242.

5 Wallace Thurman, "Nephews of Uncle Remus," in *Collected Writings of Wallace Thurman*, 202.

264   NOTES TO PAGES 91–99

6   Thurman, "Nephews," "Nephews of Uncle Remus," in *Collected Writings of Wallace Thurman*, 202–3.
7   Van Notten, *Wallace Thurman's Harlem Renaissance*, 244.
8   Van Notten, *Wallace Thurman's Harlem Renaissance*, 245.
9   Qtd. in Van Notten, *Wallace Thurman's Harlem Renaissance*, 245.
10 Van Notten, *Wallace Thurman's Harlem Renaissance*, 246.
11 Qtd. in Van Notten, *Wallace Thurman's Harlem Renaissance*, 247.
12 Peter Stallybrass, "Against Thinking," *PMLA* 122, no. 5 (Oct. 2007): 1581.
13 Stallybrass, "Against Thinking," 1581.
14 See, for example, Geoffrey Sanborn, "'People Will Pay to Hear the Drama': Plagiarism in *Clotel*," *African American Review* 45, nos. 1/2 (2012): 65–82.
15 Zora Neale Hurston, letter to Langston Hughes, Jan. 18, 1931, reprinted in *Zora Neale Hurston: A Life in Letters*, ed. Carla Kaplan (New York: Doubleday, 2002), 201–4.
16 Arnold Rampersad, *The Life of Langston Hughes*, vol. 1, *1902–1941: I, Too, Sing America* (New York: Oxford University Press, 1986), 194–98. For an updated and lengthier analysis of Hurston and Hughes's friendship and the *Mule Bone* controversy, see Yuval Taylor, *Zora and Langston: A Story of Friendship and Betrayal* (New York: W.W. Norton, 2019).
17 Langston Hughes, *The Big Sea*, 1940 (New York: Thunder's Mouth, 1986), 234.
18 Thomas Wirth, "Introduction" to Nugent, *Gentleman Jigger*, xiv.
19 Abby Arthur Johnson and Ronald Maberry Johnson, *Propaganda and Aesthetics: The Literary Politics of African-American Magazines in the Twentieth Century* (Amherst, MA: University of Massachusetts Press, 1979), 77.
20 Qtd. in Taylor, *Zora and Langston*, 80.
21 Wallace Thurman, letter to Alain Locke, Oct. 3, 1928, Moorland-Spingarn Collection, Howard University Libraries, Washington, DC.
22 Wallace Thurman, letter to Langston Hughes, undated, ca. Oct. 1926: "Just one more complication and I will be ready to blow up. Have had two bad checks which I had to make good to The World Tomorrow. Fire is certainly burning me." JWJ, MS 26, Box 155, Folder 2877.
23 Wallace Thurman, letter to Langston Hughes, undated, ca. Oct. 1926.
24 Granville Hicks, "The New Negro: An Interview with Wallace Thurman," *The Churchman* 30 (Apr. 1927): 10.
25 Wallace Thurman, *Infants of the Spring*, 1932 (Boston, MA: Northeastern University Press, 1992), 144–45.
26 Thurman, *Infants*, 228.
27 Thurman, *Infants*, 233–35.
28 Singh and Scott, *Collected Writings of Wallace Thurman*, xv; Bernard W. Bell, *The Afro-American Novel and its Tradition* (Amherst, MA: University of Massachusetts Press, 1987), 133.

NOTES TO PAGES 99–111   265

29 Thurman, *Infants*, 236. A reference to Cullen's "ambivalence that vacillates between African ancestralism and Western classicism" in addition to Cullen's skeptical view of religion and superstition in his only novel, *One Way to Heaven* (Bell, *Afro-American Novel*, 134).

30 Thurman, *Infants*, 237.

31 Thurman, *Infants*, 242–45.

32 Thurman, *Infants*, 277.

33 Thurman, *Infants*, 280.

34 Thurman, *Infants*, 280–81.

35 Thurman, *Infants*, 284.

36 Nugent explained to Thomas Wirth that Paul Arbian's death was "the only way Wallie could think of to end the book." Wirth, "Introduction" to *Gay Rebel of the Harlem Renaissance*, 15.

37 Nugent, *Gentleman Jigger*, 160.

38 Nugent, *Gentleman Jigger*, 160, 162–63.

39 Nugent, *Gentleman Jigger*, 160–61.

40 Nugent, *Gentleman Jigger*, 172, 112–13.

41 Wirth, "Introduction" to Nugent, *Gentleman Jigger*, xiii.

42 David Levering Lewis, interview with Bruce Nugent, Sept. 11, 1974, "Voices from the Renaissance," David Levering Lewis Collection, Schomburg Center for Research in Black Culture, New York Public Library.

43 Nugent, *Gentleman Jigger*, 13–18.

44 Nugent, *Gentleman Jigger*, 108.

45 Indeed, Nugent's interviews with Wirth and with David Levering Lewis, the latter of which reside in the archives of Harlem's Schomburg Center for Research in Black Culture reveal someone with a sharply accurate memory of the movement's events; his accounts may be corroborated via letters from and interviews with the movement's other major figures.

46 Nugent, *Gentleman Jigger*, 62–63.

Chapter Five: Editorial Collaboration and Creative Conflict in *Outline for the Study of the Poetry of American Negroes* Shawn Anthony Christian

1 Sterling A. Brown, letter to James Weldon Johnson, Dec. 14, 1930, James Weldon Johnson and Grace Nail Johnson Papers (1850–2005), Beinecke Rare Book and Manuscript Library, Yale University, New Haven, Connecticut. Hereinafter cited as JWJ. MS 49, Series 1: Correspondence, 1896–1972, Box 4, Folder 66.

2 James Weldon Johnson, *Along This Way: The Autobiography of James Weldon Johnson* (New York: The Viking Press, 1933), 377.

3 James Weldon Johnson, *Book of American Negro Poetry* (New York: Harcourt, Brace, and Company, Inc., 1922), vii–viii.

266   Notes to pages 111–13

4 Harcourt, Brace, and Company, letter to "Dear Friend," Apr. 19, 1922, JWJ, MS 49, Box 9, Folder 193.
5 Harcourt, Brace, and Company, letter to "Dear Friend," Apr. 19, 1922.
6 Todd Carmody, "Sterling Brown and the Dialect of New Deal Optimism," *Callaloo* 33, no. 3 (2010): 822.
7 Robert G. O'Meally, "Sterling A. Brown's Literary Essays: The Black Reader in the Text," *Callaloo* 21, no. 4 (Sterling A. Brown: A Special Issue) (1998): 1017.
8 Sterling A. Brown, letter to James Weldon Johnson, Feb. 17, 1932, JWJ, MS 49, Box 9, Folder 66.
9 Brown to Johnson, letter, Feb. 17, 1932.
10 Sterling A. Brown's four-year appointment as Editor for Negro Affairs at the Federal Writer's Project allows him to deepen his editorial work and sustain his critical advocacy of truthful representations of African American life or, as he argues, "All references on Negroes came from our office. I was editing there all day. Then a long distance call would come. Somebody would run into some kind prejudicial treatment, and I'd have to take it up. My job was very comprehensive and very complex. Meanwhile, we were editing." Charles H. Rowell, "'Let Me Be with Ole Jazzbo': An Interview with Sterling A. Brown," in *After Winter: The Art and Life of Sterling A. Brown*, ed. John Edgar Tidwell and Steven C. Tracy (New York: Oxford University Press, 2009), 300.
11 George Bornstein, *Palimpsest: Editorial Theory in the Humanities* (Ann Arbor, MI: University of Michigan Press, 1993), 4.
12 James Weldon Johnson, letter to Sterling A. Brown, Feb. 22, 1932, JWJ, MS 49, Box 9, Folder 66.
13 Johnson, letter to Brown, Feb. 22, 1932.
14 James Weldon Johnson, "Introduction" to *Southern Road: Poems by Sterling A. Brown* (New York: Harcourt, Brace, and Company, Inc., 1932), xv.
15 Noelle Morrissette, *James Weldon Johnson's Modern Soundscapes* (Iowa City, IA: University of Iowa Press, 2013), 120.
16 Johnson, "Introduction" to *Southern Road*, xiii.
17 Johnson, "Introduction" to *Southern Road*, xiv.
18 Johnson, "Introduction" to *Southern Road*, xv.
19 Joanne V. Gabbin, *Sterling A. Brown: Building the Black Aesthetic Tradition* (Charlottesville, VA: University of Virginia Press, 1985), x.
20 Sterling A. Brown, letter to James Weldon Johnson, Jan. 13, 1931, JWJ, MS 49, Box 9, Folder 66.
21 Brown, letter to Johnson, Jan. 13, 1931.
22 James Weldon Johnson, letter to Sterling A. Brown, Nov. 14, 1930, JWJ, MS 49, Box 9, Folder 66.
23 Ben Glaser, "Folk Iambics: Prosody, Vestiges, and Sterling Brown's *Outline for the Study of the Poetry of American Negroes*," *PMLA* 129,

NOTES TO PAGES 113–17   267

no. 3 (May 2014): 423. Michael Nowlin makes a related observation about Johnson's parallel study of "modern poetry" while preparing the first edition of *Book*. See "Race Literature, Modernism, and Normal Literature: James Weldon Johnson's Groundwork for an African American Literary Renaissance, 1912–20," *Modernism/modernity* 20, no. 3 (2013): 513.

24 Zora Neale Hurston, letter to Langston Hughes, Jan. 18, 1931, in *Mule Bone: A Comedy of Negro Life by Langston Hughes and Zora Neale Hurston*, ed. George Houston Bass and Henry Louis Gates, Jr. (New York: Harper Perennial, 1991), 213–14.

25 Gates, Jr., "A Tragedy of Negro Life," in *Mule Bone*, 18.

26 W. Lawrence Hogue, *Discourse and the Other: The Production of the Afro-American Text* (Durham, NC: Duke University Press, 1986), 7.

27 James Weldon Johnson, preface to the revised edition, *Book of American Negro Poetry* (New York: Harcourt, Brace, and Company, Inc., 1931), 3.

28 Johnson, preface to the revised edition, *Book of American Negro Poetry*, 3.

29 Johnson, preface to the revised edition, *Book of American Negro Poetry*, 4; Brent Hayes Edward, *The Practice of Diaspora: Literature, Translation, and the Rise of Black Internationalism* (Cambridge, MA: Harvard University Press, 2003), 45.

30 Johnson, letter to Brown, Nov. 14, 1930.

31 Johnson, letter to Brown, Nov. 14, 1930.

32 Sterling A. Brown, *Outline for the Study of the Poetry of American Negroes* (New York: Harcourt, Brace, and Company, 1931), 1–2.

33 Brown, *Outline*, 1, 3.

34 Johnson, letter to Brown, Nov. 14, 1930.

35 Sterling A. Brown, letter to James Weldon Johnson, Dec. 14, 1930, JWJ, MS 49, Box 9, Folder 66.

36 James Weldon James, letter to Harcourt, Brace, and Company, July 21, 1922, JWJ, MS 49, Box 9, Folder 193.

37 Harcourt, Brace, and Company, letter to James Weldon Johnson, Apr. 6, 1931, JWJ, MS 49, Box 9, Folder 193.

38 Sterling A. Brown, letter to James Weldon Johnson, July 21, 1930, JWJ, MS 49, Box 9, Folder 66.

39 Myron T. Pritchard and Mary White Ovington, *The Upward Path* (New York: Harcourt, Brace, and Howe, 1920); Otelia Cromwell, Lorenzo Dow Turner, and Eva Beatrice Dykes, eds., *Readings from Negro Authors* (New York: Harcourt, 1931).

40 Brown, *Outline*, 3.

41 Cromwell, Turner, and Dykes, *Readings*, 3–54; 313–25.

42 Cromwell, Turner, and Dykes, *Readings*, 313–25.

43 Cromwell, Turner, and Dykes, *Readings*, 313.

44 Brown, *Outline*, 24–25.

268 NOTES TO PAGES 118–24

45 Glaser, "Folk Iambics," 424.

46 Johnson, letter to Brown, Nov. 14, 1930.

47 Elizabeth Lay Green, *The Negro in Contemporary American Literature* (Chapel Hill, NC: University of North Carolina Press, 1928), 3.

48 Green, *The Negro*, 7; Johnson, preface to the first edition of *Book of American Negro Poetry*, xxxiii–xxxiv.

49 Green, *The Negro*, 8.

50 Brown, *Outline*, 8.

51 Brown, *Outline*, 8.

52 Brown, *Outline*, 9.

53 Brown, *Outline*, 9.

54 Brown, *Outline*, 10.

55 Johnson, revised edition of *Book of American Negro Poetry*, 64, 75.

56 Brown, *Outline*, 13.

57 Brown, *Outline*, 13.

58 Brown, *Outline*, 13.

59 Johnson, preface to the revised edition of *Book of American Negro Poetry*, 3.

60 Johnson, preface to the revised edition of *Book of American Negro Poetry*, 5.

61 Brown, *Outline*, 3.

62 Brown, *Outline*, 3.

63 Johnson, preface to first edition of *Book of American Negro Poetry*, xl; Johnson, preface to the revised edition of *Book of American Negro Poetry*, 3, 7.

64 Mark Sanders, "African American Folk Roots and Harlem Renaissance Poetry," *The Cambridge Companion to the Harlem Renaissance*, ed. George Hutchinson (Cambridge: Cambridge University Press, 2007), 96.

65 Johnson, preface to first edition of *Book of American Negro Poetry*, xix.

66 Letter, Brown to Johnson, Feb. 17, 1932.

67 Johnson, revised edition of *Book of American Negro Poetry*, 247.

68 Brown, *Outline*, 35.

69 Brown, *Outline*, 35.

70 Brown, *Outline*, 36.

71 Sanders, "African American Folk Roots," 97.

72 Brown, *Outline*, 18–19.

73 Brown, "James Weldon Johnson," revised edition of *Book of American Negro Poetry*, 116.

74 Brown, letter to Johnson, January 13, 1931.

75 Johnson, preface to revised edition of *Book of American Negro Poetry*, 6

76 Johnson, preface to revised edition of *Book of American Negro Poetry*, 6.

77 Brown, *Outline*, 20.

78 Brown, *Outline*, 19.

NOTES TO PAGES 124–28   269

79 Johnson, preface to first edition of *Book of American Negro Poetry*, xix.
80 Sanders, "African American Folk Roots," 105.
81 Rowell, "'Let Me Be,'" 304.
82 Sterling A. Brown, Arthur P. Davis, and Ulysses Lee, eds., *Negro Caravan* (New York: The Dryden Press, 1941), 277.
83 Brown, Davis, and Lee, *Negro Caravan*, 279.
84 Johnson, preface to the first edition of *Book of American Negro Poetry*, xli.

Chapter Six: Jessie Fauset and Her Readership: The Social Role of *The Brownies' Book*   Jayne E. Marek

1 Carol J. Batker locates in Fauset's journalistic efforts a "political significance" that has been overlooked. See her *Reforming Fictions: Native, African, and Jewish American Women's Literature and Journalism in the Progressive Era* (New York: Columbia University Press, 2000), 53. Katherine Capshaw Smith remarks that "Fauset applied her inclusive aesthetic to her editorship of *The Brownies' Book*, welcoming a variety of visions on the issue of crafting a progressive [B]lack identity through children's literature." *Children's Literature of the Harlem Renaissance* (Bloomington, IN: Indiana University Press, 2004), 26. Fauset's contributions to both *The Brownies' Book* and *The Crisis* have sometimes been credited to Du Bois, although a number of scholars recognize Fauset's editorial primacy at *The Brownies' Book*. Cheryl A. Wall, *Women of the Harlem Renaissance* (Bloomington, IN: Indiana University Press, 1995), 53, designates Fauset as *The Brownies' Book*'s "managing editor." Wall also notes that Fauset managed *The Crisis* "frequently" while Du Bois traveled (47, 55). See also Carolyn Wedin Sylvander, who notes that Du Bois often ceded *Crisis* editorship to Fauset. *Jessie Redmon Fauset, Black American Writer* (Albany, NY: Whitston, 1981), 56–57. Smith summarizes several scholars' opinions in this regard (25).
2 Davarian L. Baldwin, *Chicago's New Negroes: Modernity, the Great Migration, and Black Urban Life* (Chapel Hill, NC: University of North Carolina Press, 2007), 38–39. See also Cameron McWhirter, *Red Summer: The Summer of 1919 and the Awakening of Black America* (New York: Henry Holt and Company, 2011), 117–19 and Kevin K. Gaines, *Uplifting the Race: Black Leadership, Politics, and Culture in the Twentieth Century* (Chapel Hill, NC: University of North Carolina Press, 1996), 88–90.
3 Smith, *Children's Literature*, xvi–xvii.
4 Minkah Makalani, "Black Women's Intellectual Labor and the Social Spaces of Black Radical Thought in Harlem," in *Race Capital?: Harlem as Setting and Symbol*, ed. Andrew M. Fearnley and Daniel Matlin (New York: Columbia University Press, 2019), 145. See also Elizabeth McHenry, *Forgotten Readers: Recovering the Lost History of African American*

270 NOTES TO PAGES 128–31

Literary Societies (Durham, NC: Duke University Press, 2002), 50, 63, 82, 99–100.

5   Shawn Anthony Christian, *The Harlem Renaissance and the Idea of a New Negro Reader* (Amherst, MA: University of Massachusetts Press, 2016), 3.

6   Smith, *Children's Literature*, 2.

7   "The Children's Number," *The Crisis* 20, no. 2 (1920), 72.

8   Smith, *Children's Literature*, 25. Fauset's shaping of this new print venue created lively interest that brought new work by Black authors to public attention. As Emily Wojcik notes, Fauset was "[d]eeply invested in the cultivation of a new generation of [B]lack readership … [and] laid the groundwork for a child's continued engagement with [B]lack voices, introducing a base of supporters to newer, more experimental, and at times revolutionary literature from 'their' people in the hopes that such an interest would continue into adulthood—and perhaps lead to a new generation of writers as well." "Editing Children of the Sun: Jessie Redmon Fauset, Little Magazines, and the Cultivation of the New Negro," in *Communal Modernisms: Teaching Twentieth-Century Literature and Culture in the Twenty-First-Century Classroom*, ed. Emily M. Hinnov, Laurel Harris, and Lauren M. Rosenblum (New York: Palgrave Macmillan; 2013), 84–85.

9   See Peter Brooker and Andrew Thacker, eds., *The Oxford Critical and Cultural History of Modernist Magazines*, 3 vols. (Oxford: Oxford University Press, 2012), 1:6.

10 See Wojcik's summary of this phrase from a Fenton Johnson poem and its resonances within Fauset's editorial project. "Editing Children of the Sun," 84–85.

11 Advertisement for *The Brownies' Book*, *The Crisis* 18, no. 4 (Aug. 1919).

12 Smith identifies cross writing in portions of *The Crisis*, in which "by alluding to children the magazine also undoubtedly compels their involvement" in learning about racist culture; generally *The Crisis's* "militancy" pushed children "to be at the forefront of resistance." *Children's Literature*, 9. In *The Brownies' Book*, Fauset's editorial choices did not deny political awareness but couched it in a more entertaining, varied, and appealing format.

13 Smith, *Children's Literature*, 25.

14 McHenry, *Forgotten Readers*, 232–33. See also Gaines, *Uplifting the Race*, 1–5.

15 Smith notes that Fauset understood how tales provide essential means of conveying norms and ideas. *Children's Literature*, 30. See also my discussion of "The Judge" in "Women Editors and Little Magazines in the Harlem Renaissance," in *Little Magazines and Modernism: New Approaches*, ed. Suzanne Churchill and Adam McKible (London: Ashgate, 2007), 103–18.

16 "Over the Ocean Wave," *The Brownies' Book* 1, no. 1 (Jan. 1920): 9–10.

NOTES TO PAGES 132–41   271

17 "The Grown-Ups' Corner," *The Brownies' Book* 1, no. 4 (Apr. 1920): 109.

18 Fauset's "The Looking Glass" in *The Crisis* compiled informative excerpts about education, the arts, religion, politics, and other matters from a range of large and small publications. See Sylvander, *Jessie Redmon Fauset*, 53 and Wall, *Women of the Harlem Renaissance*, 45. Wall states that "As the Crow Flies" in *The Brownies' Book* was prepared by *Crisis* editor Du Bois whereas Fauset conveyed her social views through "The Judge" (53–54).

19 Dianne Johnson-Feelings, ed., *The Best of the Brownies' Book* (New York: Oxford University Press, 1996), 19, 14.

20 "The Judge," *The Brownies' Book* 1, no. 4 (Apr. 1920): 108.

21 "The Judge," *The Brownies' Book* 1, no. 5 (May 1920): 138.

22 "The Judge," *The Brownies' Book* 1, no. 5 (May 1920): 139.

23 "The Judge," *The Brownies' Book* 1, no. 6 (June 1920): 176.

24 "The Judge," *The Brownies' Book* 1, no. 6 (June 1920): 177.

25 James Alpheus Butler, Jr., "The Jury," *The Brownies' Book* 1, no. 7 (July 1920): 215.

26 "The Judge," *The Brownies' Book* 2, no. 8 (Aug. 1921): 224.

27 As Smith puts it, "The Judge's" treatment of Africa was a complicated, even "conflicted," locus of meanings. *Children's Literature*, 35–36.

28 Abby Arthur Johnson, "Literary Midwife: Jessie Redmon Fauset and the Harlem Renaissance," *Phylon* 39, no. 2 (1978): 149.

29 McHenry, *Forgotten Readers*, 232–33.

30 McHenry, *Forgotten Readers*, 235.

31 Jessie Fauset, "After School," *The Brownies' Book* 1, no. 1 (Jan. 1920): 30.

32 Smith, *Children's Literature*, xx.

33 Lillie Buffum Chace Wyman, "Brave Brown Joe and Good White Men," *The Brownies' Book* 2, no. 11 (Nov. 1921): 318–20.

34 "As the Crow Flies," *The Brownies' Book* 2, no. 8 (Aug. 1921): 225.

35 Julia Lee, *Our Gang: A Racial History of The Little Rascals* (Minneapolis, MN: University of Minnesota Press, 2015), 22–32.

36 "'Sunshine Sammy' Would Never Do This in Real Life, But It's All Right in the Movies" [photo], *The Brownies' Book* 2, no. 7 (July 1921): 203.

37 "Little People of the Month," *The Brownies' Book* 2, no. 2 (Feb. 1921): 60–61.

38 A four-minute fragment of "Whirl o' the West" survives and has been digitized. *Whirl o' the West* [fragment], *YouTube*, 2016. www.youtube.com/watch?v=roUE2rcpjK4.

39 See, for example, the summary remarks in Gaines, *Uplifting the Race*, 281 n. 27, 282 n. 32.

40 Lillian A. Turner, "How Lilimay 'Kilt' the Chicken," *The Brownies' Book* 2, no. 9 (Sept. 1921): 251–52.

41 "The Judge," *The Brownies' Book* 2, no. 10 (Oct. 1921): 294.

42 Smith, *Children's Literature*, 43.

272   NOTES TO PAGES 142–49

43 W.E.B. Du Bois, "Valedictory," *The Brownies' Book* 2, no. 12 (Dec. 1921): 354; W.E.B. Du Bois, "Editing *The Crisis*," *The Crisis* 77, no. 9 (Nov. 1970): 370; W.E.B. Du Bois, "Opinion: The Children," *The Crisis* 24, no. 6 (Oct. 1922): 247.
44 "The Judge," *The Brownies' Book* 2, no. 12 (Dec. 1921): 341.
45 "The Jury," *The Brownies' Book* 2, no. 12 (Dec. 1921): 348.
46 Wall, *Women of the Harlem Renaissance*, 69.
47 Wall, *Women of the Harlem Renaissance*, 48, 52–53.

Chapter Seven: Pure Essence without Pulp: Editing the Life of Langston Hughes   *Joshua M. Murray*

1 Langston Hughes, "To Arna Bontemps," Apr. 26, 1956, in *Selected Letters of Langston Hughes*, ed. Arnold Rampersad and David Roessel (New York: Knopf, 2015), 334.
2 Sidonie Smith and Julia Watson, *Reading Autobiography: A Guide for Interpreting Life Narratives*, 2nd ed. (Minneapolis, MN: University of Minnesota Press, 2010), 72.
3 Smith and Watson, *Reading Autobiography*, 72.
4 Smith and Watson, *Reading Autobiography*, 77.
5 Smith and Watson, *Reading Autobiography*, 77.
6 Langston Hughes, "To Arthur Spingarn," Jan. 20, 1940, in *Selected Letters of Langston Hughes*, 214.
7 Arnold Rampersad, *The Life of Langston Hughes*, vol. 1, *1902–1941: I, Too, Sing America* (New York: Oxford University Press, 1988), 388.
8 Smith and Watson, *Reading Autobiography*, 284–85.
9 J.D. Scrimgeour posits that "the book does not seem to be nearly as much about who Hughes is as what he has seen." See J.D. Scrimgeour, "Casting the Nets: Audience and Selfhood in Langston Hughes's *The Big Sea*," *a/b: Auto/Biography Studies* 13, no. 1 (1998): 98.
10 Smith and Watson, *Reading Autobiography*, 42.
11 Smith and Watson, *Reading Autobiography*, 42.
12 Smith and Watson, *Reading Autobiography*, 92–93.
13 Rampersad, *Life of Langston Hughes*, 1:370.
14 Langston Hughes, "To Noël Sullivan," May 27, 1939, in *Selected Letters of Langston Hughes*, 210.
15 "MILAGE [*sic*] TRAVELLED—1931–1933," undated, Langston Hughes Papers, James Weldon Johnson Collection, Beinecke Rare Book and Manuscript Library, Yale University, New Haven, Connecticut. Hereinafter cited as JWJ. MS 26, Box 304, Folder 4997.
16 Joseph McLaren, "The Creative Voice in the Autobiographies of Langston Hughes," in *Critical Insights: Langston Hughes*, ed. R. Baxter Miller (Ipswich, MA: Salem Press, 2013), 121.

NOTES TO PAGES 150–55   273

17 Rampersad, *Life of Langston Hughes*, 1:376.
18 Brian Loftus, "In/Verse Autobiography: Sexual (In)Difference and the Textual Backside of Langston Hughes's *The Big Sea*," *a/b: Auto/Biography Studies* 15, no. 1 (2000): 142.
19 While Hughes uses the name S.S. *Malone* in his autobiography, the ship was actually the *West Hesseltine*. See Rampersad, *Life of Langston Hughes*, 1:71.
20 Hughes did not truly toss all of his books into the sea; the one book he saved was his copy of Walt Whitman's *Leaves of Grass*. See Rampersad, *Life of Langston Hughes*, 1:72, 377.
21 Langston Hughes, *The Big Sea* (New York: Alfred A. Knopf, 1940; repr. New York: Hill & Wang, 1993), 4, 16, 26.
22 Langston Hughes, letter to Ing Zdenko Alexy, July 9, 1951, JWJ, MS 26, Box 279, Folder 4581.
23 Hughes, *Big Sea*, 11.
24 Linda M. Carter, "Langston Hughes (1902–1967)," in *African American Autobiographers: A Sourcebook*, ed. Emmanuel S. Nelson (Westport, CT: Greenwood Press, 2002), 199.
25 Scrimgeour, "Casting the Nets," 97.
26 Langston Hughes, "To Blanche Knopf," Feb. 8, 1940, in *Selected Letters of Langston Hughes*, 215.
27 Rampersad, *Life of Langston Hughes*, 1:379.
28 Hughes, *Big Sea*, 228.
29 Typed paper scrap discussing *The Big Sea*, undated, JWJ, MS 26, Box 278, Folder 4574.
30 Rampersad, *Life of Langston Hughes*, 1:390.
31 Rampersad, *Life of Langston Hughes*, 1:388, 393.
32 Rampersad, *Life of Langston Hughes*, 1:388–89.
33 Arnold Rampersad, *The Life of Langston Hughes*, vol. 2, *1941–1967: I Dream a World* (New York: Oxford University Press, 1988), 113.
34 Hughes, *Big Sea*, 335.
35 Matthew J. Bruccoli, "Postscript" to William Charvat, *The Profession of Authorship in America, 1800–1870*, ed. Matthew J. Bruccoli (Columbus, OH: Ohio State University Press, 1968; repr. New York: Columbia University Press, 1992), xx.
36 Charvat, *The Profession of Authorship*, 3.
37 Rampersad, *Life of Langston Hughes*, 2:224.
38 Langston Hughes, "To Carl Van Vechten," Nov. 8, 1941, in *Selected Letters of Langston Hughes*, 233.
39 Hughes, "To Arna Bontemps," Apr. 26, 1956, in *Selected Letters of Langston Hughes*, 334.
40 Arnold Rampersad, "Introduction" to Langston Hughes, *I Wonder as I Wander* (New York: Hill & Wang, 1993), xv.

274   NOTES TO PAGES 156–61

41   Juan J. Rodriguez Barrera, "'Tightrope of Words': Self-Censorship in Langston Hughes' Account of the Spanish Civil War in *I Wonder as I Wander*," *Science & Society* 81, no. 2 (2017): 174.

42   R. Baxter Miller, *The Art and Imagination of Langston Hughes* (Lexington, KY: University Press of Kentucky, 2006 [1989]), 20.

43   "Brief Resume of I WONDER AS I WANDER by Langston Hughes," undated, JWJ, MS 26, Box 310, Folder 5033.

44   Rampersad, *Life of Langston Hughes*, 2:258.

45   "POSSIBLE BLURB MATERIAL," undated, JWJ, MS 26, Box 310, Folder 5034.

46   "Possible Publicity Ideas," Sept. 7, 1956, JWJ, MS 26, Box 310, Folder 5035.

47   "AN IDEAL CHRISTMAS GIFT," 1956, JWJ, MS 26, Box 310, Folder 5035.

48   Invitation for Autographing Party, 1956, JWJ, MS 26, Box 310, Folder 5035.

49   J. Saunders Redding, "I Wonder as I Wander (1956)," in *Langston Hughes: Critical Perspectives Past and Present*, ed. Henry Louis Gates, Jr. and K.A. Appiah (New York: Amistad, 1993), 36.

50   Langston Hughes, letter to Arna Bontemps, May 23, 1943, in *Arna Bontemps–Langston Hughes Letters, 1925–1967*, ed. Charles H. Nichols (New York: Dodd, Mead & Company, 1980), 127.

51   Rampersad, *Life of Langston Hughes*, 2:258–59.

52   Langston Hughes, "To Maxim Lieber," Sept. 17, 1956, in *Selected Letters of Langston Hughes*, 336.

53   Langston Hughes, "To Roy Blackburn," Nov. 6, 1956, in *Selected Letters of Langston Hughes*, 339.

54   Langston Hughes, "To Arna Bontemps," July 17, 1954, in *Selected Letters of Langston Hughes*, 325.

55   Langston Hughes, letter to Arna Bontemps, Mar. 4, 1962, in *Arna Bontemps–Langston Hughes Letters, 1925–1967*, 432–33.

56   Langston Hughes, "To Arna Bontemps," Apr. 11, 1963, in *Selected Letters of Langston Hughes*, 387.

57   Miller, *Art and Imagination*, 8–32.

58   James A. Emanuel, *Langston Hughes* (New York: Twayne Publishers, 1967), 178.

59   The adjacent paper scrap appears to indicate that L.G. refers to Lloyd K. Garrison.

60   "I WONDER (As Christmas gifts)," 1956, JWJ, MS 26, Box 310, Folder 5038.

61   Rampersad, "Introduction" to *Selected Letters of Langston Hughes*, x.

62   "Possible Titles," 1955, JWJ, MS 26, Box 306, Folder 5008.

63   "Chronology," undated, JWJ, MS 26, Box 310, Folder 5040.

NOTES TO PAGES 161–67   275

64 Wire to Bob Sylvester, Feb. 6, 1957, JWJ, MS 26, Box 310, Folder 5040.
65 "DON'T WORRY ABOUT THE SUNSET GUN," undated, JWJ, MS 26, Box 310, Folder 5042.
66 Miller, *Art and Imagination*, 20.

Chapter Eight: Desegregating the Digital Turn in American Literary History   *Korey Garibaldi*

1 James Briggs Murray, "Democratizing Education at the Schomburg: Catalog Development and the Internet," *Journal of Internet Cataloging* 3, no. 1 (2000): 94.
2 For a recent call to acknowledge these texts and incorporate them into the classroom, see Nicole J. Aljoe, Eric Gardner, and Molly O'Hagan Hardy, "The *Just Teach One: Early African American Print* Project," in *Teaching with Digital Humanities: Tools and Methods for Nineteenth-Century American Literature*, ed. Jennifer Travis and Jessica DeSpain (Urbana, IL: University of Illinois Press, 2018), 117–32. For a much broader sample of recently compiled resources on African American literature and culture in the digital humanities, see @CCP_org: "Black Digital Humanities Projects, Resources, Events, and Anything Else," *Fire!!!* 4, no. 1: 21st Century Black Studies: Digital Publications (Part Two) (2015): 134–39.
3 See, for example, Lee Skallerup Bessette, "It's About Class: Interrogating the Digital Divide," *Hybrid Pedagogy* (blog), July 2, 2012: https://hybrid pedagogy.org/its-about-class-interrogating-the-digital-divide/; Ernesto Priego, "Various Shades of Digital Literacy: The New Digital Divides," *Inside Higher Ed* (blog), Dec. 6, 2012: www.insidehighered.com/blogs/ university-venus/various-shades-digital-literacy-new-digital-divides.
4 See, for example, H.B. Wonham, ed., *Criticism on the Color Line: Desegregating American Literary Studies* (New Brunswick, NJ: Rutgers University Press, 1996); Shelley Fisher Fishkin, "Desegregating American Literary Studies," in *Aesthetics in a Multicultural Age*, ed. Emory Elliott, Louis Freitas Caton, and Jeffrey Rhyne (New York: Oxford University Press, 2002), 121–34.
5 Howard Rambsy II, "African American Scholars and the Margins of DH," *PMLA* 135, no. 1 (2020): 152.
6 Despite renewed attention to related separatist tendencies, even Rambsy's critiques do not emphasize either segregation or desegregation. For another recent example of related scholarship investigating "diversity" and "marginalization" in the field, see Alan Liu, "Toward a Diversity Stack: Digital Humanities and Diversity as Technical Problem," *PMLA* 135, no. 1 (2020): 130–51.
7 The most influential study of related interracialism was published slightly before the ascent of digitization's impact on related literary history.

276   NOTES TO PAGES 167–69

See George Hutchinson, *The Harlem Renaissance in Black and White* (Cambridge, MA: Harvard University Press, 1995).

8   See, for example, Lauren Klein, "The Image of Absence: Archival Silence, Data Visualization, and James Hemings," *American Literature* 85, no. 4 (2013): 661–88; Molly O'Hagan Hardy, "'Black Printers' on White Cards: Information Architecture in the Data Structures of the Early American Book Trades," in *Debates in the Digital Humanities 2016*, ed. Matthew K. Gold and Lauren F. Klein (Minneapolis, MN: University of Minnesota Press, 2016), 377–83; Amy E. Earhart, "Can Information Be Unfettered? Race and the New Digital Humanities Canon," in *Debates in the Digital Humanities*, ed. Matthew K. Gold (Minneapolis, MN: University of Minnesota Press, 2012), 309–32.

9   Consider, for example, a recent conference titled "Intentionally Digital, Intentionally Black," Oct. 18–20, 2018, AAIHS: African American History, Culture and Digital Humanities: https://aadhum.umd.edu/conference/. Joel Bergholtz has offered an astute critique of the racialized divisions of labor that frameworks like these might perpetuate. "If we understand recovery projects as recovering Black history, and we see it as the work and main contribution of black scholars, then white people are potentially free to remove themselves from the work in two key ways: (1) this is a history of black people for black people, and thus it is not my history, (2) as a white person I do not need to, and indeed should not attempt to, do recovery projects that look at oppressed groups, because that work belongs to them." Bergholtz, "Whose Job is it Anyway? 'Black Digital Humanities,'" *FSU Digital Scholars* (blog), Nov. 14, 2017: https://digitalscholars.word-press.com/2017/11/14/whose-job-is-it-anyway-black-digital-humanities/.

10   For an excellent model of innovative scholarship reminding humanists and others of the importance of this work, see Leah Henrickson, "The Darker Side of Digitization," *Leah Hendrickson* (blog), Mar. 20, 2014: https://bhilluminated.wordpress.com/2014/03/20/google-book-scanners/.

11   Alain Locke, letter to Claude McKay, Apr. 29, 1927, Claude McKay Collection, Beinecke Rare Book and Manuscript Library, Yale University, New Haven, Connecticut. Hereinafter cited as CMC. Box 5, Folder 138.

12   Most scholarship on interracial literature in the United States focuses on the nineteenth century. The most notable cultural material in this vaguely defined genre includes prefatory material of slave narratives, and in some cases white authorship of entire slave narratives. For a broad chrono-logical and transnational overview of related texts, see Werner Sollors, *Neither Black Nor White Yet Both: Thematic Explorations of Interracial Literature* (New York: Oxford University Press, 1997).

13   Alfred Kazin, "The Jew as American Writer," *Commentary* 41, no. 4 (1966): www.commentarymagazine.com/articles/alfred-kazin-2/the-jew-as-american-writer/.

NOTES TO PAGES 170–74 277

14 Alfred Holt Stone, *Studies in the Race Problem* (New York: Doubleday, 1908), 41–42. For an example of scholarship investigating related literature and literary criticism, see Holly Jackson, "Identifying Emma Dunham Kelley: Rethinking Race and Authorship," *PMLA* 122, no. 3 (2007): 728–41.

15 Richard Jean So and Edwin Roland, "Race and Distance Reading," *PMLA* 135, no. 1 (2020): 59. Also see Richard Jean So, Hoyt Long, and Yuancheng Zhu, "Race, Writing, and Computation: Racial Difference and the US Novel, 1880–2000," *Journal of Cultural Analytics* (Jan. 11, 2019).

16 Langston Hughes, letter to Wallace Thurman, Letter Four [ca. 1929], Wallace Thurman Collection, Beinecke Rare Book and Manuscript Library, Yale University. Hereinafter cited as WTC. Box 1, Folder 3.

17 Langston Hughes letter to Wallace Thurman, Letter Five [ca. 1929], WTC, Box 1, Folder 3.

18 Langston Hughes letter to Wallace Thurman, Letter Four [ca. 1929], WTC, Box 1, Folder 3. Hughes also addressed another letter to Thurman in Folder 3 with an eerily accurate prediction that scholars were going to try and decipher his coded writing in the future: "Monday July 29, 1929 (full date for benefit of literary historian) Lincoln University, Pa., Box 36, (full place, ditto)."

19 Langston Hughes letter to Wallace Thurman, July 29, 1929, WTC, Box 1, Folder 3.

20 Langston Hughes letter to Wallace Thurman, Letter Four, [ca. 1929], WTC, Box 1, Folder 3.

21 Sinclair Lewis letter to Roger Baldwin, June 19, 1925, CMC, Box 5, Folder 135.

22 Moya Z. Bailey, "All the Digital Humanists Are White, All the Nerds Are Men, but Some of Us Are Brave," *Journal of Digital Humanities* 1, no. 1 (2011): http://journalofdigitalhumanities.org/1-1/all-the-digital-humanists-are-white-all-the-nerds-are-men-but-some-of-us-are-brave-by-moya-z-bailey/; Tara McPherson, "Why Are the Digital Humanities So White? or Thinking the Histories of Race and Computation," in *Debates in the Digital Humanities* (2012), 139–60.

23 Nan Z. Da's "The Computational Case against Computational Literary Studies," *Critical Inquiry* 45, no. 3 (2019): 602. A relatively accessible and popular distillation of this essay's major points was published around the same time as Da, "The Digital Humanities Debacle: Computational Methods Repeatedly Come Up Short," *Chronicle of Higher Education* (Mar. 27, 2019): www.chronicle.com/article/The-Digital-Humanities-Debacle/245986.

24 See, for example, Maurizio Ascari, "The Dangers of Distant Reading: Reassessing Moretti's Approach to Literary Genres," *Genre* 47, no. 1 (2014): 1–19.

25 For a small yet representative example of critical responses to Da's *Critical Inquiry* and *Chronicle of Higher Education* essays, see Chris Beausang, "Some Thoughts on Nan Z. Da's 'The Computational Case Against Computational Literary Criticism' or; 'Against Articles Beginning with the word "Against",'" *Medium* (Mar. 14, 2019): https://web.archive.org/web/20190402093003/https://medium.com/@differengenera/some-thoughts-on-nan-z-17a12445eb3f; Mark Algee-Hewitt, "Criticism, Augmented," *Critical Inquiry* (blog) (Apr. 1, 2019): https://critinq.wordpress.com/2019/04/01/computational-literary-studies-participant-forum-responses/; Matthew Lavin, Letter to the Editor: "The Interestingness of the Digital Humanities," *Chronicle of Higher Education* (blog) (Apr. 3, 2019): www.chronicle.com/blogs/letters/the-interestingness-of-the-digital-humanities/.

26 Katherine Bode, Response: "Computational Literary Studies: A Critical Inquiry Online Forum," *Critical Inquiry* (blog) (Mar. 31, 2019): https://critinq.wordpress.com/2019/03/31/computational-literary-studies-a-critical-inquiry-online-forum/.

27 Echoing, and citing, Da's critiques of computation's shortcomings, Daniel Shore observes that in efforts to study the linguistic importance of "Black Lives Matter," "[t]he 'bag of words' methods [e.g. text mining algorithms] that have held center stage in the digital humanities ... are especially inapposite." Daniel Shore, "The Form of Black Lives Matter," *PMLA* 135, no. 1 (2020): 178.

28 Jacqueline Wernimont and Elizabeth Losh, eds., *Bodies of Information: Intersectional Feminism and the Digital Humanities* (Minneapolis, MN: University of Minnesota Press, 2018), ix. For a nuanced discussion of Losh and Wernimont's scholarship in a broader overview of feminist, Black, and intersectional work in the digital humanities, see Sharon Block, "#DigEarlyAm: Reflections on Digital Humanities and Early American Studies," *William and Mary Quarterly* 76, no. 4 (2019): 615–20.

29 Lisa Spiro, "'This Is Why We Fight': Defining the Values of the Digital Humanities," in *Debates in the Digital Humanities* (2012), 16–34. Examples of more recent scholarship include: Alex Lothian, "From Transformative Works to #transformDH: Digital Humanities as (Critical) Fandom," *American Quarterly* 70, no. 3 (2018): 371–93; Dorothy Kim and Jesse Stommel, "Disrupting the Digital Humanities: An Introduction," in *Disrupting the Digital Humanities*, ed. Dorothy Kim and Jesse Stommel (Santa Barbara, CA: Punctum Books, 2018).

30 Armand Marie Leroi, "Digitizing the Humanities," *New York Times* (Feb. 14, 2015): www.nytimes.com/2015/02/14/opinion/digitizing-the-humanities.html.

31 Neal, quoted in Kim Gallon, "Making a Case for the Black Digital Humanities," in *Debates in the Digital Humanities 2016*, 45–46.

NOTES TO PAGES 176–88   279

32 Eric Weiskott, "There is No Such Thing as 'the Digital Humanities,'" *Chronicle of Higher Education* (Nov. 1, 2017): www.chronicle.com/article/ There-Is-No-Such-Thing-as/241633.

33 Michael Piotrowski, "Ain't No Way Around It: Why We Need to Be Clear About What We Mean by 'Digital Humanities.'" *SocArXiv*, Apr. 14, 2020. doi:10.31235/osf.io/d2kb6.

34 Sara Ahmed, "The Nonperformativity of Antiracism," *Meridians* 7, no. 1 (2006): 104–26.

35 Todd Presner, "Digital Humanities 2.0: A Report on Knowledge," OpenStax CNX (June 8, 2010): http://cnx.org/contents/2742bb37-7c47-4bee-bb34-0f35bda760f3@6.

36 Project on the History of Black Writing: 2010–2012 Report: https:// hbw.ku.edu/sites/hbw.drupal.ku.edu/files/docs/HBW%20Biennial%20 Report%202010-12.pdf.

37 Tara McPherson, "U.S. Operating Systems at Mid-Century: The Inter-twining of Race and UNIX," in *Race After the Internet*, ed. Lisa Nakamura and Peter Chow-White (New York: Routledge, 2012), 24.

38 Newman White, "American Negro Poetry," *South Atlantic Quarterly* 20 (1917): 305.

39 Alan Liu, "Toward a Diversity Stack: Digital Humanities and Diversity as Technical Problem," *PMLA* 135, no. 1 (2020): 138.

40 "A Prize Winner in Mississippi," attributed to the *S.W. Christian Advocate*, and reprinted in *The American Missionary* 68, no. 10 (Oct. 1914): 415.

41 "New Negro Magazine to Be Published Here," *Nashville Banner* (Feb. 5, 1915).

42 "To Contributors," *The Champion* 1, no. 1 (1916): 37.

Chapter Nine: (Re-)Framing Black Women's Liberation in the Classroom: Nella Larsen, Zora Neale Hurston, and Twenty-First-Century Editorial Frameworks   *Emanuela Kucik*

1 Carla Kaplan, "Nella Larsen's Erotics of Race," Introduction to Nella Larsen, *Passing* (New York: W.W. Norton, 2007 [1929]), ix.

2 The biographical information in this section is drawn from two of the most famous accounts of Larsen's life: Thadious M. Davis's *Nella Larsen, Novelist of the Harlem Renaissance: A Woman's Life Unveiled* (Baton Rouge, LA: Louisiana State University Press, 1994) and George Hutchin-son's *In Search of Nella Larsen: A Biography of the Color Line* (Cambridge, MA: Belknap Press, 2006). For a recent look into the social and cultural impact of Larsen's *Passing*, see Lynn Domina's *The Historian's Passing: Reading Nella Larsen's Classic Novel as Social and Cultural History* (Santa Barbara, CA: Praeger, 2018).

3 Domina, "The Many Lives of Nella Larsen," *The Historian's Passing*, 15.

280 NOTES TO PAGES 188–200

4 See Domina, *The Historian's Passing*.

5 The biographical information in this section is drawn from the most famous account of Hurston's life: Robert Hemenway's *Zora Neale Hurston: A Literary Biography* (Urbana, IL: University of Illinois Press, 1977). For further information on Hurston's life, see Carla Kaplan's *Zora Neale Hurston: A Life in Letters* (New York: Anchor Books, 2002).

6 For scholarship on the role of sexuality in Larsen's *Passing*, see, among others, Claudia Tate's "Nella Larsen's *Passing*: A Problem of Interpretation," *Black American Literature Forum* 14, no. 4 (1980): 142–46; Deborah E. McDowell's "Introduction" to Nella Larsen, *Quicksand* and *Passing* (New Brunswick, NJ: Rutgers University Press, 1986); Ann duCille's *The Coupling Convention: Sex, Text, and Tradition in Black Women's Fiction* (New York: Oxford University Press, 1993); Judith Butler's "Passing, Queering: Nella Larsen's Psychoanalytic Challenge," in *Bodies that Matter: On the Discursive Limits of "Sex"* (New York: Routledge, 1993); and Johanna M. Wagner's "In the Place of Clare Kendry: A Gothic Reading of Race and Sexuality in Nella Larsen's *Passing*," *Callaloo* 34, no. 1 (2011): 143–57. For scholarship on the role of class in the novel, see, among others, Jennifer DeVere Brody's "Clare Kendry's 'True' Colors: Race and Class Conflict in Nella Larsen's *Passing*," *Callaloo* 15, no. 4 (1992): 1053–65 and Mary Mabel Youman's "Nella Larsen's *Passing*: A Study in Irony," *CLA Journal* 18, no. 2 (1974): 235–41.

7 Kaplan, "Nella Larsen's Erotics of Race," ix.

8 Kaplan, "Nella Larsen's Erotics of Race," ix.

9 Kaplan, "Nella Larsen's Erotics of Race," xi; emphases in original.

10 Kaplan, "Nella Larsen's Erotics of Race," xiii.

11 Kaplan, "Nella Larsen's Erotics of Race," xx.

12 Kaplan, "Nella Larsen's Erotics of Race," xxi.

13 Kaplan, "Nella Larsen's Erotics of Race," xxii. See McDowell, "Introduction," ix–xxxi.

14 Zora Neale Hurston, *Their Eyes Were Watching God* (ebook) (New York: HarperCollins, 2004), 8.

15 Hurston, *Their Eyes Were Watching God*, 9.

16 Hurston, *Their Eyes Were Watching God*, 9.

17 Hurston, *Their Eyes Were Watching God*, 9.

18 Hurston, *Their Eyes Were Watching God*, 10–11.

19 Edwidge Danticat, "Foreword" to Hurston, *Their Eyes Were Watching God*, 14.

20 Danticat, "Foreword," 15.

21 Danticat, "Foreword," 15.

22 Danticat, "Foreword," 18.

23 Danticat, "Foreword," 18–19.

24 Danticat, "Foreword," 19.

NOTES TO PAGES 201–10   281

25 Mary Helen Washington, "Foreword" to Hurston, *Their Eyes Were Watching God*, 23–24.
26 Washington, "Foreword," 25.
27 Washington, "Foreword," 29–30.

Chapter Ten: Editing Edward Christopher Williams: From "The Letters of Davy Carr" to *When Washington Was in Vogue*   Adam McKible

1   David Chinitz, "The New Harlem Renaissance Studies," *Modernism/modernity* 13, no. 2 (2006): 377.
2   Michael Nowlin, "Race Literature, Modernism, and Normal Literature: James Weldon Johnson's Groundwork for and African American Literary Renaissance, 1912–20," *Modernism/modernity* 20, no. 3 (2013): 504.
3   Langston Hughes, *The Big Sea*, "Introduction" by Arnold Rampersad (New York: Hill & Wang, 1993 [1940]), 233.
4   Hughes, *The Big Sea*, 236.
5   Edward Christopher Williams, *When Washington Was in Vogue* (New York: Amistad, 2004), 118.
6   Dorothy B. Porter, "Phylon Profile, XIV: Edward Christopher Williams," *Phylon* 8 (1947): 320.
7   Christina Simmons, "'Modern Marriage' for African Americans, 1920–1940," *Canadian Review of American Studies* 30, no. 3 (2000): 273–300.
8   Williams, *Washington*, 98.
9   Hughes, *The Big Sea*, 206–7.
10 Hughes, *The Big Sea*, 223.
11 "*When Washington Was in Vogue*," *Kirkus Reviews* 71, no. 20 (Oct. 15, 2003): 1251.
12 Williams, *Washington*, 75.

Chapter Eleven: Editing Claude McKay's *Romance in Marseille*: A Groundbreaking Harlem Renaissance Novel Emerges from the Archive   Gary Edward Holcomb

1   See Claude McKay, *Home to Harlem* (Boston, MA: Northeastern University Press, 1987; orig. pub. New York: Harper & Brothers, 1928). See *Banjo: A Story Without a Plot* (New York: Harcourt Brace, 1970; orig. pub. New York: Harper & Brothers, 1929).
2   Two spring 1930 letters from McKay's Harper & Brothers editor, Eugene Saxton, suggest that McKay sent Saxton an "outline" or truncated version of "The Jungle and the Bottoms." Eugene Saxon letters to McKay (Mar. 19, 1930 and June 2, 1930), Claude McKay Papers, Schomburg Center for Research in Black Culture, New York Public Library.

282   NOTES TO PAGES 212–28

3   McKay, letter to W.A. Bradley, Dec. 21, 1929, William A. Bradley Literary Agency Records, 1909–1982, Harry Ransom Center, University of Texas, Austin. Hereinafter cited as BLAR.

4   McKay, letter to Bradley, Dec. 21, 1929.

5   McKay, letter to Bradley, Dec. 21, 1929. Also, for Bradley's response to McKay regarding "sentimentality," see W.A. Bradley letter to McKay, Feb. 23, 1930, BLAR.

6   W.E.B. Du Bois, "The Browsing Reader," *The Crisis* (June 1928): 202.

7   Possibly his most controversial statement, in "Criteria of Negro Art," W.E.B. Du Bois wrote: "all Art is propaganda and ever must be, despite the wailing of the purists. ... I do not care a damn for any art that is not used for propaganda." W.E.B. Du Bois, *Writings: The Suppression of the African Slave-Trade, Souls of Black Folk, Dusk of Dawn, Essays and Articles* (New York: Penguin, 1986), 1000.

8   See McKay, letter to W.A. Bradley, Dec. 21, 1929, BLAR.

9   See McKay, letter to W.A. Bradley, Dec. 21, 1929, BLAR.

10   See McKay, letter to W.A. Bradley, Dec. 21, 1929, BLAR.

11   See McKay, letter to W.A. Bradley, Dec. 21, 1929, BLAR.

12   McKay, letter to Max Eastman, June 27, 1930, Claude McKay Papers, Lilly Library Manuscript Collections, Indiana University, Bloomington, Indiana. Hereinafter cited as CMP.

13   McKay, letter to W.A. Bradley, Aug. 28, 1930, BLAR.

14   McKay, letter to W.A. Bradley, Dec. 21, 1929, BLAR.

15   McKay, letter to W.A. Bradley, Dec. 21, 1929, BLAR.

16   McKay, letter to W.A. Bradley, Dec. 21, 1929, BLAR.

17   McKay, letter to W.A. Bradley, Dec. 21, 1929, BLAR.

18   McKay, letter to Max Eastman, June 27, 1930, 27 CMP. "Dreamport" appears in the Beinecke version of the manuscript, though redacted, with "Marseille" written above it. James Weldon Johnson Collection, Beinecke Rare Book and Manuscript Library, Yale University, New Haven, Connecticut. Hereinafter cited as JWJ.

19   McKay, letter to W.A. Bradley, Dec. 21, 1929, BLAR.

20   Wayne F. Cooper, *Claude McKay, Rebel Sojourner in the Harlem Renaissance: A Biography* (Baton Rouge, LA: Louisiana State University Press, 1987), 268.

21   George Hutchinson, *The Harlem Renaissance in Black and White* (Cambridge, MA: Harvard University Press, 1995), 378.

22   The handle *Big Blonde* also may carry the significance of a literary allusion: the reiterating of the title of Dorothy Parker's famed 1929 short story "Big Blonde." Admitting that though she had reservations about *Home to Harlem*'s literary merit, the influential critic praised the novel as "a vitally important addition to American letters" and laudable for "putting even further in their place the writings of Mr. Carl Van Vechten." Dorothy Parker,

NOTES TO PAGES 228–31   283

"Review of *Home to Harlem*," *The Portable Dorothy Parker* (New York: Penguin, 1973), 503. Parker unquestionably had in mind Van Vechten's *Nigger Heaven* (1926), controversial because the white author presumed to write a Harlem Renaissance novel, and McKay no doubt appreciated the distinction. In his first memoir, *A Long Way from Home* (1937), McKay chafed at the onetime allegation that the publication of *Nigger Heaven* had anything to do with writing *Home to Harlem*, pointing out he had written a short story of the same title a year before the appearance of Van Vechten's novel, adding, "I never saw the book until the late spring of 1927 ... And by that time I had nearly completed *Home to Harlem*." McKay, *A Long Way from Home*, ed. with introduction by Gene Andrew Jarrett (New Brunswick, NJ: Rutgers University Press, 2007); originally published as *A Long Way from Home* (New York: Lee Furman, 1937). See also Carl Van Vechten, *Nigger Heaven* (Urbana, IL: University of Illinois Press, 2000 [1926]).

23 McKay, *Harlem Shadows: The Poems of Claude McKay* (New York: Harcourt, Brace, 1922). Also, see McKay, *Complete Poems*, ed. with introduction by William J. Maxwell (Urbana, IL: University of Illinois Press, 2004).

24 McKay, letter to A.A. Schomburg, July 17, 1925, Arthur A. Schomburg Papers, Schomburg Center for Research in Black Culture, New York Public Library.

25 See Wallace Thurman, ed., *Fire!! A Quarterly Devoted to the Younger Negro Artists* 1, no. 1 (1926). Thurman satirized the Black bourgeois reaction to the *Fire!!* poets and artists, referring to themselves as the "Niggerati," in *Infants of the Spring*, 1932 (Boston, MA: Northeastern University Press, 1992).

26 See Richard Bruce [Nugent], "Smoke, Lilies and Jade," *Fire!! A Quarterly Devoted to the Younger Negro Artists* 1, no. 1 (1926): 33–40.

27 Cooper, *Claude McKay, Rebel Sojourner*, 222, 404 n. 64.

28 Michel Foucault, *The History of Sexuality*, vol. 1, *An Introduction*, trans. Robert Hurley (New York: Vintage, 1990 [1978]), 140–41.

29 McKay, letter to W.A. Bradley, June 25, 1930, BLAR; McKay, letter to Max Eastman, June 27, 1930, CMP.

30 McKay, letter to W.A. Bradley, July 4, 1930, BLAR; McKay, letter to Max Eastman, Dec. 1, 1930, CMP.

31 McKay, letter to Max Eastman, Dec. 1, 1930, CMP.

32 McKay, letter to W.A. Bradley, Sept. 18, 1930, BLAR.

33 See Cooper, *Claude McKay, Rebel Sojourner*, 267, 412 n. 16.

34 See Cooper, *Claude McKay, Rebel Sojourner*, 267, 412 n. 16.

35 Rudolph Fisher, "White, High Yellow, Black" [Review of *Gingertown*], *New York Herald Tribune Books*, Mar. 27, 1932: 3. See also Fisher, *The Conjure-Man Dies: A Mystery Tale of Dark Harlem*, 1932 (Ann Arbor, MI: University of Michigan Press, 1992).

284   NOTES TO PAGES 232–35

36   Both McKay and Bowles wrote about their Tangier encounter, McKay accusing Bowles of precipitating his troubles with the French colonial administration: Bowles, *Without Stopping* (New York: Putnam, 1972), 147–49 and McKay, letter to Max Eastman, [May 1933], CMP. See also Gary Edward Holcomb, *Claude McKay, Code Name Sasha: Queer Black Marxism and the Harlem Renaissance* (Gainesville, FL: University Press of Florida, 2007), 66.

37   McKay, letter to Max Eastman, Apr. 21, 1933, CMP.

38   McKay, letter to Eastman, Apr. 21, 1933.

39   McKay, letters to Eastman, Dec. 1, 1930 and [May 1933], CMP.

40   McKay, letter to Eastman, [May 1933], CMP.

41   Cooper, *Claude McKay, Rebel Sojourner*, 288.

42   McKay, letter to Eastman, [May 1933].

43   Clifton Fadiman, letter to Max Eastman, Sept. 12, 1933, CMP.

44   Ernest Hemingway, *The Sun Also Rises* (New York: Scribner, 1926).

45   Fadiman, letter to Eastman, Sept. 12, 1933, CMP.

46   See Holcomb, *Claude McKay, Code Name Sasha*, 174.

47   Ernest Hemingway, *A Moveable Feast*, restored ed. (New York: Scribner, 2010 [1964]), 15.

48   McKay, *A Long Way*, ed. Jarrett, 261. Thanks to Jack Bruno for noting the reference. See also Nancy Cunard, ed., *Negro: An Anthology* (London: Wishart & Co., 1934).

49   Jean-Christophe Cloutier and Brent Hayes Edwards, eds., "Introduction" to Claude McKay, *Amiable with Big Teeth: A Novel of the Love Affair between the Communists and the Poor Black Sheep of Harlem* (New York: Penguin, 2017), ix–xxxviii, xliii.

50   The pagination of both manuscripts is unstable. The Beinecke manuscript ends with page 88, but is actually 87 typed pages, as the document has no page 25. McKay, or more likely someone else, attempted to correct the problem of the pagination. Written over the "5" in the typed "25" (on what follows as p. 25) is a "6," thereby identifying the leaf as page 26, and over the "6" (on p. 26) is a "7," indicating that the sheet is meant to be page 27. Meanwhile, pages 28 to 88 show no signs of attempted correction. In contrast, the Schomburg manuscript ends at page 171, but actually numbers 172 pages, as it contains two pages numbered 99, the second marked "99a."

51   Cloutier and Edwards, "Introduction" to *Amiable with Big Teeth*, ix.

52   McKay, letter to Carl Van Vechten, Sept. 11, 1941, Carl Van Vechten Papers, Manuscripts and Archives Division, New York Public Library. Hereinafter cited as CVVP.

53   McKay, letter to Van Vechten, Oct. 26, 1941, CVVP.

54   Bernhard Knollenberg, letter to McKay, Oct. 10, 1941, CVVP.

55   John B. Turner, letter to Knollenberg, Oct. 3, 1941, CVVP.

NOTES TO PAGES 235–44   285

56 See n. 31, above.

57 McKay, letter to Van Vechten, Oct. 26, 1941, CVVP.

58 Van Vechten, letter to Knollenberg, Oct. 27, 1941, CVVP.

59 McKay, letter to Ivie Jackman, Sept. 15, 1943, Countee Cullen/Harold Jackman Memorial Collection, Robert W. Woodruff Library, Atlanta University Center, Atlanta, Georgia. Thanks to Jean-Christophe Cloutier for suggesting that in the letter to Ivie Jackman, McKay may be referring to *Romance in Marseille*. The editors of *Amiable with Big Teeth*, Cloutier and Edwards, note McKay's letter to Ivie Jackman in their introduction, theorizing that the manuscript McKay may have been referring to in 1943 was "Amiable with Big Teeth." Cloutier and Edwards, "Introduction" to *Amiable with Big Teeth*, xxxviii, and 285 n. 104. But in an email to the editors dated Sept. 19, 2018, Cloutier states that, on reflection, he suspects that the typescript McKay is referring to is "Lafala," or *Romance in Marseille*, given that McKay likely was not in possession of the "Amiable with Big Teeth" manuscript when he wrote the letter. In 1943, the sole copy of "Amiable with Big Teeth" was almost certainly in the hands of Samuel Roth, the publisher who acquired the manuscript, and among whose papers "Amiable with Big Teeth" was found.

60 See n. 5, above.

61 McKay, letter to Max Eastman, Dec. 1, 1930, CMP.

62 The document contains redactions and other effects that render the notion of an absolute word count abstruse.

63 The editors again are indebted to Professor Cloutier for sharing information about Black Sun Books. Cloutier email to editors, Sept. 19, 2018.

64 Diana Lachatanere, email to Gary Holcomb, Oct. 6, 2018.

65 Lachatanere, email to Holcomb, Oct. 6, 2018.

66 The Schomburg Center for Research in Black Culture represented the McKay estate until 2015.

Coda: Editing as Infrastructural Care
Brigitte Fielder and Jonathan Senchyne

1 Alice Dunbar-Nelson, "Negro Literature for Negro Pupils," *Southern Workman* 51, no. 2 (Feb. 1922): 60.

2 Dunbar-Nelson, "Negro Literature," 63.

3 Dunbar-Nelson, "Negro Literature," 63.

4 Samuel Cornish and John B. Russworm, "Editors," "To Our Patrons," *Freedom's Journal* 1, no. 1 (Mar. 16, 1827): 1.

5 For more on how the 135th Street Branch and its librarians served as catalysts of intellectual and artistic production, see Ethelene Whitmire, *Regina Anderson Andrews: Harlem Renaissance Librarian* (Urbana, IL: University of Illinois Press, 2014), 32–47 and Sarah A. Anderson, "'The

286 NOTES TO PAGES 244–48

Place to Go': The 135th Street Branch Library and the Harlem Renaissance," *The Library Quarterly: Information, Community, Policy* 73, no. 4 (2003): 383–421.

6 Sharon Mattern, "Maintenance and Care: A Working Guide to the Repair of Rust, Dust, Cracks, and Corrupted Code in Our Cities, Our Homes, and Our Social Relations," *Places Journal* (Nov. 2018): https://places-journal.org/article/maintenance-and-care/.

7 Ivy G. Wilson, "The Brief Wondrous Life of the *Anglo-African Magazine*: Or, Antebellum African American Editorial Practice and Its Afterlives," in *Publishing Blackness: Textual Constructions of Race Since 1850*, ed. George Hutchison and John K. Young (Ann Arbor, MI: The University of Michigan Press, 2013), 19.

8 Caroline Gebhard and Barbara McCaskill, "Introduction" to *Post-Bellum, Pre-Harlem: African American Literature and Culture, 1877–1919*, ed. Caroline Gebhard and Barbara McCaskill (New York: New York University Press, 2006), 1–16.

Contributors

Editing the Harlem Renaissance

Shawn Anthony Christian is Associate Professor of English at Florida International University. He is the author of *The Harlem Renaissance and the Idea of a New Negro Reader* (2016). His other writings on the Harlem Renaissance and African American literary and print culture appear in *CLAJ, MAWA Review, Ethnic Studies Review, Legacy: A Journal of American Women Writers*, and the volumes *Reading African American Experiences in the Obama Era* (2012) and *The Harlem Renaissance Revisited* (2010). As a public humanities advocate, he has also served on the board for the Rhode Island Council for the Humanities and is a member of the Annual Langston Hughes Community Poetry Reading Committee in Providence, Rhode Island.

Darryl Dickson-Carr is Professor of English at Southern Methodist University. He is the author of *Spoofing the Modern: Satire in the Harlem Renaissance* (2015), *The Columbia Guide to Contemporary African American Fiction* (2005), and *African American Satire: The Sacredly Profane Novel* (2001).

Brigitte Fielder is Associate Professor of Comparative Literature at the University of Wisconsin–Madison. She is co-editor (with Jonathan Senchyne) of *Against a Sharp White Background: Infrastructures of African American Print* (2019). She is the author of *Relative Races: Genealogies of*

287

288   Editing the Harlem Renaissance

Interracial Kinship in Nineteenth-Century America (2020) and is currently working on a second book on racialized human–animal relationships in the long nineteenth century.

Korey Garibaldi is Assistant Professor in the Department of American Studies at the University of Notre Dame. He is working on a manuscript tentatively titled *Before Black Power: The Rise and Fall of Interracial Literary Culture, 1908–1968*. Most recently, he has written a short essay, "De/Provincializing Europe," published online by *Contending Modernities*, and an article reconnecting Henry James and Gertrude Stein that appeared in *The Henry James Review*. A book chapter, "Sketching in an Age of Anxiety: Henry James's Morganatic Baroness in *The Europeans*," in *Reading Henry James in the Twenty-First Century: Heritage and Transmission* (2019), reflects his latest research interests in both interracial literary culture and the Jamesian canon.

Gary Edward Holcomb is Professor of African American Literature and Studies in the Department of African American Studies, Ohio University. With William J. Maxwell, he is co-editor of Claude McKay's ca. 1933 novel, *Romance in Marseille* (2020), a project he worked on for nearly twenty years, now published for the first time as a Penguin Classic and reviewed widely in such venues as the *New Yorker*, the *New York Times Book Review*, and *New York* magazine's "Vulture" section. His other books are *Claude McKay, Code Name Sasha: Queer Black Marxism and the Harlem Renaissance* (2007), *Hemingway and the Black Renaissance* (2012), and *Teaching Hemingway and Race* (2018). He is co-editor of the forthcoming *English Language Notes* special issue devoted to the release of *Romance in Marseille* and is co-editing the McKay letters for Columbia University.

Emanuela Kucik is Assistant Professor of English and Africana Studies and the Co-Director of Africana Studies at Muhlenberg College. In her scholarship and teaching, she examines the intersections of race, genocide, and human rights violations through the study of twentieth-century and contemporary literature(s). She is a scholar of twentieth- and twenty-first-century African American and American literature; global Black literature; holocaust literature; genocide literature; literature of human rights violations; and comparative race and ethnic studies. She received her Ph.D. in English from Princeton University in 2018, along with a Doctoral Graduate Certificate in African American Studies. She received her M.A. in English from Princeton University in 2014 and her B.A. with Highest Distinction (*Summa Cum Laude*, Phi Beta Kappa) in English from the University of North Carolina at Chapel Hill in 2012.

Jayne E. Marek is Professor Emerita of English at Franklin College. She is the author of *Women Editing Modernism: "Little" Magazines and Literary History* (1995), and she compiled the 1912–88 Index to *Poetry Magazine*. Her studies of literary history appear in volumes published by Cambridge, Blackwell, Ashgate, Illinois, and Rutgers, and she received two fellowships from the National Endowment for the Humanities for literary scholarship. She has published five volumes of poetry, won the Bill Holm Witness Poetry Contest, and was nominated for Best of the Net and Pushcart Prizes.

Adam McKible is Associate Professor of English at John Jay College of Criminal Justice. He is the author of *The Space and Place of Modernism: The Russian Revolution, Little Magazines, and New York* (2002), and he edited and introduced Edward Christopher Williams's *When Washington Was in Vogue* for HarperCollins (2004), a previously lost novel of the Harlem Renaissance. He is also co-editor of a special issue of *Modernism/ modernity* devoted to the Harlem Renaissance and of the collection, *Little Magazines and Modernism: New Approaches* (2016). His essays appear in a number of books and journals, including *The Oxford Handbook of Modernisms, Teaching the Harlem Renaissance: Course Design and Classroom Strategies, The Black Press, African American Review, American Periodicals, The Journal of Modern Periodical Studies,* and *Modernism/ modernity*. His current project is tentatively titled *Jim Crow Modernism, George Horace Lorimer, and the* Saturday Evening Post.

Joshua M. Murray is Assistant Professor of English at Fayetteville State University, a constituent institution of the University of North Carolina. He specializes in African American literature with emphasis on the Harlem Renaissance, transnationalism, and autobiography and life

290   EDITING THE HARLEM RENAISSANCE

writing. His work has appeared in the *Journal of West Indian Literature*, *Atlantic Studies*, *Teaching Hemingway and Race* (2018), and *Critical Insights: Harlem Renaissance* (2015), among others. His current research project examines the prominence of transnational and diasporic themes within key works of the Harlem Renaissance by analyzing the sociohistorical significance of the way extranational sites captivated the literary imagination of the period. When not teaching African American literature, he also teaches courses on video game storytelling and legal studies.

Adam Nemmers is Assistant Professor of English at Lamar University, where he teaches courses in American literature. He is the author of *American Modern(ist) Epic: Novels to Refound a Nation* (Clemson University Press, 2021). His research focuses on modernism and multi-ethnic American literature, including recent essays and articles on Nella Larsen, Richard Wright, William Faulkner, and radio drama. Aside from his monograph, his forthcoming published work will include essays and articles on American protest literature, Southern matriarchy, and the Midwestern ecogothic, as well as an anthology of Transatlantic literature across the long nineteenth century.

Jonathan Senchyne is Associate Professor of Book History and Print Culture in the Information School and Director of the Center for the History of Print and Digital Culture at the University of Wisconsin–Madison. He is co-editor (with Brigitte Fielder) of *Against a Sharp White Background: Infrastructures of African American Print* (2019) and the author of *The Intimacy of Paper in Early Nineteenth-Century American Literature* (2020).

Ross K. Tangedal is Assistant Professor of English and Director of the Cornerstone Press at the University of Wisconsin–Stevens Point, where he specializes in American print and publishing culture, textual editing, bibliography, book history, and the profession of authorship. He is the author of *The Preface: American Authorship in the Twentieth Century* (2021), and his articles have been published in *The Papers of the Bibliographical Society of America*, *South Atlantic Review*, *The Hemingway Review*, *The F. Scott Fitzgerald Review*, *Authorship*, and *MidAmerica*, as well as in various edited collections. He serves as a consulting editor for the Hemingway Letters Project, where he is associate editor of volume 6, *The Letters of Ernest Hemingway (1934–1936)* (2022).

John K. Young is Professor of English at Marshall University, where he studies and teaches twentieth- and twenty-first-century American, British, and anglophone literatures, especially in relation to the material history of textual production. He is the author of *Black Writers, White Publishers: Marketplace Politics in Twentieth-Century African American Literature* (2006), *How to Revise a True War Story: Tim O'Brien's Process of Textual Production* (2017), and co-editor, with George Hutchinson, of *Publishing Blackness: Textual Constructions of Race since 1850* (2013). His chapter draws on a current research project tracing the periodical roots of Jean Toomer's *Cane*. Young serves as the executive director of the Society for Textual Scholarship.

Index

Accent (magazine) 18, 25, 40–43, 256n64
Aesop 134
African Times and Orient Review
    (journal) 180–81
Alexy, Ing Zdenko 150
Alfred A. Knopf (publisher) 40, 49,
    63–64, 76–78, 81, 153, 229, 232
Ali, Dusé Mohamed 180
Allen, Devere 50
Allen, Frederick 50
Allison, Madeline G. 29–30
American Mercury (magazine) 15, 18, 25,
    39–40, 256n60
American Missionary (magazine) 181
Amistad (imprint of HarperCollins) 208,
    217
Amussen, Theodore 158
Anchor Books 77
Anglo-African Magazine (magazine) 245
Armstrong, Henry 159

Bagnall, Robert W. 18, 28–30
    "Lex Talionis" 18, 28–29, 254n43
Baker, Josephine 220
Baldwin, James 169
Bambara, Toni Cade 195
Barthes, Roland 78–79

Bartlett, Walter 50
Benét, William Rose 251n3
Bennett, Gwendolyn 50, 105, 229
Bentley, Eric 41
Berryman, John 67
Black Sun Books 238, 285n63
Blackburn, Roy 160
Blackmur, R.P. 19, 41–42
Boas, Franz 58–59, 104
Boni & Liveright 20–21, 40, 48, 233
Bonner, Marita 67
Bontemps, Arna 1, 11, 49, 67, 145, 154,
    156, 160, 244
    Black Thunder 1, 261n4
The Bookman (journal) 37, 90
Bowles, Paul 231, 284n36
Bradley, William Aspenwall 224–27,
    231–32, 235–36, 238
Braithwaite, William Stanley (W.S.) 119,
    168, 170, 181
    Anthology of Magazine Verse 250n3
    "The Negro in American Literature"
    119
Brawley, Benjamin 28
    *A Social History of the American
    Negro* 29
Brecht, Bertolt 41

293

294   INDEX

Brinnin, John Malcolm 41
Brook, Cleanth 41
Broom (magazine) 15–16, 20, 21
Brown, Sterling A. 8, 11, 109–26, 201, 266n10
    "Long Gone" 122
    The Negro Caravan (with Arthur P. Davis and Ulysses Lee) 41, 112, 125
    The Negro in American Fiction 112
    Negro Poetry and Drama 112
    "Odyssey of the Big Boy" 122
    "Our Literary Audience" 110
    Outline for the Study of the Poetry of American Negroes (w/ James Weldon Johnson) 8, 109–26
    "Southern Road" 122, 125
    Southern Road 109, 112–13, 121, 125
Brown, William Wells 93
    Clotel, or the President's Daughter 94
The Brownie's Book (magazine) *see* Fauset, Jessie Redmon
Burke, Kenneth 19, 41–43

Campbell, James Edwin 120
Cather, Willa 67
The Champion (magazine) 181
Chandler, Raymond 67
Charles Scribner's Sons 41
Chesnutt, Charles 109, 182
    The Conjure-Man Tales 23
The Chicago Defender (newspaper) 142, 159
Coleman, Anita Scott 35, 255n48
Colin, Paul 220
Colored American Magazine 143
Commentary (magazine) 169
Competitor (magazine) 135
Cornish, Samuel, and John B. Russworm 243
Corrothers, James David 120
Cowl, Carl 238–39
Cozzens, James Gould 67

The Crisis (magazine) 2, 8, 15–16, 18, 25, 27–34, 36–38, 40, 96, 127–31, 133, 135–36, 142, 181, 219, 225, 254n34, 255n48, 269n1, 270n12, 271n18
Crosswaith, Frank 37–38
Cullen, Countee 39, 49–51, 56, 67, 99, 229, 265n29
    The Ballad of the Brown Girl 40
    One Way to Heaven 88, 106, 265n29
Cummings, E.E. 41
Cunard, Nancy 50–51, 258n30
    Negro: An Anthology 23, 25, 50, 234

Daily Worker (newspaper) 256n68
Dandridge, Ray Garfield 120
Danticat, Edwidge 10, 194, 198–203, 210
Davis, Daniel Webster 120
Davis, John P. 105
The Dial (magazine) 15
Dickey, James 67
Dorland, William Alexander Newman 209
Douglas, Aaron 46, 50, 52, 64, 97, 101, 103, 105, 255n46
Du Bois, W.E.B. 2, 4–5, 11, 27–28, 38–39, 67, 103–104, 135–36, 141, 181, 225, 229, 250n3, 269n1, 271n18
    "As the Crow Flies" 133
    "Criteria of Negro Art" 4, 282n7
    "The World and Us" 28
    The Quest for the Silver Fleece 211
Dumas, Alexandre 170–71, 177
Dunbar, Paul Laurence 109, 115, 117–21, 123–25, 135, 141
Dunbar-Nelson, Alice 241–43
    "Negro Literature for Negro Pupils" 241

Eastman, Max 226–27, 230, 232–33, 237
Elegbara, Esu 56
Eliot, T.S.
    "Tradition and the Individual Talent" 90

Ellison, Ralph 43
E.P. Dutton (publisher) 235
The Etude (magazine) 135

Fadiman, Clifton 233
Fauset, Jessie Redmon 2, 8, 11, 27, 29,
  50, 67, 82, 103–104, 127–43, 168,
  170, 250n3, 269n1, 270n8, 270n10,
  270n12, 270n15, 271n18
  The Brownies' Book 8, 127–43, 269n1,
    270n12, 271n18
  Plum Bun 65, 261n4
Fire!! (magazine) 15–16, 37, 89–91,
  94–97, 101, 105, 143, 172, 229,
  264n22, 283n25
Fisher, Isaac 168, 181
  Negro Farmer 181
Fisher, Rudolph 11, 99, 103, 106, 231
  The Conjure-Man Dies 231, 261n4
  Walls of Jericho 54, 88–89
Fitzgerald, F. Scott 67
  The Great Gatsby 211–12
Forum Magazine (magazine) 16, 250n3
Frank, Waldo 20, 40, 214
Freedom's Journal (newspaper) 243
Frost, Robert 41

Garvey, Marcus 38, 136
G.K. Hall (publisher) 178
Gladwell, Malcolm 171
Gold, Mike 250n3
Gordon, Eugene 40
Green, Elizabeth Lay
  *The Negro in Contemporary
    American Literature: An Outline
    for Individual and Group Study*
  118

Half-Century Magazine (magazine)
  255n48
Hammett, Dashiell 67
Handy, W.C. 37
Harcourt Brace 41, 109, 111, 113,
  116–17
Harlem (magazine) 90–91, 96, 143

Harper & Brothers 226–28, 232, 235
HarperCollins 60, 189–90, 194–96,
  208–10, 215, 217–21
Hayes, Roland 51
Hays, H.R. 41
Heartman, Charles 179
Heller, Joseph 67
Hemingway, Ernest 67, 233
  The Sun also Rises 233
Hicks, Granville 97
Hopkins, Pauline 143
Huebsch, B.W. 40
Hughes, Langston 1–3, 8–9, 11, 15, 18,
  35–37, 39, 43, 46, 48, 50–52, 54–57,
  59, 64, 67, 82, 89, 94–95, 97, 99,
  103–104, 107, 114, 145–62, 171–73,
  182–83, 212, 218, 229, 244, 250n3,
  257n4, 258n37, 259n60, 264n16,
  273n19, 273n20, 277n18
  "Autumn Note" 35
  The Big Sea 1, 8–9, 95, 106, 147,
    149–56, 159–61, 212, 217
  Collected Poems 36
  Fine Clothes to the Jew 89
  "For Dead Mimes" 35
  "Formula" 35
  I Wonder as I Wander 8–9, 145, 147,
    149, 153–61
  Mule Bone (with Zora Neale
    Hurston) 55, 94, 114, 264n16
  "The Negro Artist and the Racial
    Mountain" 15, 94
  Not Without Laughter 257n4, 261n4
  Selected Letters (Rampersad and
    Roessel, eds.) 160
  The Ways of White Folks 54, 65, 83
  The Weary Blues 64, 89
Hurst, Fannie 50
Hurston, Zora Neale 3, 6, 9–11, 25, 36,
  47, 49–61, 67, 94–95, 97, 99, 103–104,
  114, 185–90, 194–05, 229, 259n60,
  264n16, 280n5
  *Barracoon: The Story of the Last
    "Black Cargo"* 2, 57, 61–62, 188,
    208

296 INDEX

"Cudjoe's Own Story of the Last
  African Slaver" 58
Dust Tracks on a Road 36, 54, 195
"The Eatonville Anthology" 18, 35–36
From Sun to Sun 55
The Great Day 55–56
"How It Feels to be Colored Me" 15, 17
*I Love Myself When I am
  Laughing ... and Then Again
  When I Am Looking Mean and
  Impressive* 17
Jonah's Gourd Vine 61
Mule Bone (with Langston Hughes)
  55, 94, 114, 264n16
Mules and Men 36, 56, 61, 201
Seraph on the Sewanee 36
Singing Steel 55
Their Eyes Were Watching God 9–10,
  36, 61, 83, 185–87, 189, 194–205,
  210
Hyman, Stanley Edgar 43

The Independent (magazine) 37

J.B. Lippincott (publisher) 41
Jackman, Harold 92, 236
Jackson, Shirley 43
Johnson, Charles Bertram 120
Johnson, Charles S. 50, 104
  Ebony and Topaz 89
Johnson, Fenton 181, 250n3, 270n10
Johnson, Georgia Douglas 18
  Bronze 23
  "Three Poems" 35
Johnson, Helene 103
Johnson, James Weldon 8, 11, 25, 63–64,
  67, 70, 82, 109–26, 209–10, 213, 236,
  267n23
  *The Autobiography of an Ex-Colored
    Man* 19, 63–65, 70, 83, 213
  The Book of American Negro Poetry
    8, 63–64, 82, 109–12, 114–15,
    118–21
  *The Book of American Negro
    Spirituals* 89, 110

"The Dilemma of the Negro Author"
  15, 18, 39–40
God's Trombones 89, 121, 123–25
"A Negro Look at Politics" 40
*Outline for the Study of the Poetry
  of American Negroes* (w/
  Sterling A. Brown) 8, 109–26,
  266–67n23
*The Second Book of American Negro
  Spirituals* 110
"Sence You Went Away" 124

Kazin, Alfred 169–71
Kellogg, Paul 50
Kipling, Rudyard 135
Kirchwey, Freda 50
Kreymborg, Alfred 41

Lardner, Ring 67
Larsen, Nella 6–7, 9–11, 16, 67–83, 103,
  168, 170, 172, 185–94, 200, 203–205,
  250n3, 262n25, 279n2
  The Complete Fiction of Nella Larsen
    77
  Passing 6–7, 9–10, 49, 65, 68–83,
    185–94, 203–205, 280n6
  Quicksand 40, 73, 76, 78, 89, 185,
    261n4
  "Sanctuary" 16, 73
Lawrence, D.H. 233
Levin, Harry 42
Lewis, Cudjoe 57–61, 188
Lewis, Sinclair 173
Lewis, Theophilus 35, 37, 92
Liberator (magazine) 16, 17
Library of America 65–66
Lieber, Maxim 160
Literary Digest (magazine) 135
The Little Review (magazine) 15–16
Liveright, Horace 50
Locke, Alain 2–5, 38, 46, 49–53, 55, 57,
  59–60, 67, 96, 98–99, 101, 103–104,
  168, 201, 258n37
  The New Negro: An Interpretation 3,
    16, 23, 25, 89, 99, 119, 143, 259n43

Lowell, Robert 41
Loy, Mina 41

Mac Low, Jason 19, 42–43
Macleod, Norman 43
Macmillan (publisher) 76–77
Mailer, Norman 43
Mason, Charlotte Osgood 6, 46–47, 50–61, 104, 257n4, 258n30, 258n37, 259n60
McClure, John 40
McDonald, Ross 67
McKay, Claude 3, 10–11, 50–52, 65, 67, 82, 90, 168, 170, 173, 182, 223–40, 244, 250n3, 281n2, 283n22, 284n36
  A Long Way from Home 234–35, 283n22
  Amiable with Big Teeth 2, 65, 208, 216, 234–35, 239, 285n59
  Banana Bottom 231–32, 235
  Banjo: A Story without a Plot 224–25, 227, 229, 232
  Collected Poems 17, 239
  "Color Scheme" 229–30, 232, 234
  "Dreamport" 227, 236–37, 282n18
  Gingertown 230–32
  Harlem: Negro Metropolis 235
  Harlem Shadows 228–29, 234
  Home to Harlem 40, 65, 89, 224–25, 227, 229, 234, 261n4, 282–83n22
  "The Jungle and the Bottoms" 224, 226–32, 236, 281n2
  "Lafala" 235–37, 285n59
  Long Way from Home 234–35
  Romance in Marseille 2, 10, 65, 208, 216, 223–40, 282n18, 285n59
  "Savage Loving" 231–33, 237
  "The Tired Worker" 117–18
  "White House" 101
Mencken, H.L. 15, 39–40, 104, 256n60
The Messenger (magazine) 10, 15, 18, 25, 27, 30, 35–38, 89, 92, 96, 104, 143, 208, 211–14, 217, 254–55n46, 255n48
Meyer, Annie Nathan 50–51
  Black Souls 51

Millay, Edna St. Vincent 228
Miller, Arthur 43, 67
Miller, Henry 41
Mitchell, Mortimer G. 29
Modern Library (imprint of Random House) 77, 79
Modern Quarterly (magazine) 16
Modernist Journals Project (MJP) 18, 22, 31–34, 181, 249–50n1, 254n35
Moore, George 37
Moore, Marianne 67
Morrison, Ernest 139–40
Mother Goose (fairy tales) 135

The Nation (magazine) 15–16
Negro Story (journal) 15
New Directions 41
New Masses (magazine) 16
New Era (magazine) 143
The New Negro: An Interpretation see Locke, Alain
New Negro Magazine (magazine) 181
The New Republic (magazine) 37
Newsome, Mary Effie Lee 29
Norris, Frank 67
Nugent, Richard Bruce 7, 87–89, 91–97, 99–107, 172, 229, 265n36, 265n45
  Gentleman Jigger 7, 87, 89, 92, 95, 101–107
  "Smoke, Lilies, and Jade" 96, 103, 229

O'Connor, Flannery 41
O'Hara, John 67
O'Neill, Eugene 67
Opportunity (magazine) 15–16, 30, 37–38, 96, 110, 112, 143, 201, 239, 255n48
Others (magazine) 250n3
Owen, Chandler 37, 89

Parker, Dorothy 161, 282–83n22
  "Big Blonde" 282n22
Penguin Random House 65, 76–77, 216, 239

298 INDEX

Poetry Journal (journal) 181
Pollard, "Snub" 140
Porter, Katherine Anne 19, 41–43
Prairie (magazine) 16, 21, 22
Project on the History of Black Writing
  (HBW) 166, 177, 182
Pullman Porters' Review (journal) 181
Pushkin, Alexander 170, 177

Quinn, J. Kerker 40–41

Randolph, A. Philip 35, 37–38, 89, 212
  "A New Negro—A New World" 38
Randolph, Jeanette 97
Random House 41
Rapp, William Jourdan 91–92
  Harlem (w/ Wallace Thurman) 102
Readings from Negro Authors (Cromwell,
  et al.) 116–17
Reynal & Hitchcock 41
Rilke, Rainer Maria 41
Robeson, Paul 51
Roche, Emma Langdon 58
Rogers, J.A. 35, 37
Roth, Samuel 285n59
Rukeyser, Muriel 41
Rutgers University Press 65, 73, 76–77
Rutledge, Archibald 162

Saxton, Eugene 226–28, 230–31, 281n2
Schomburg, Arturo (aka Arthur)
  165–68, 170, 179, 182, 229
  *Bibliographical Checklist of American
    Negro Poetry* 179
Schomburg Center for Research in Black
  Culture 165, 177–78, 234, 237–39,
  265n45, 285n66
Schuyler, George 11, 15, 35, 37, 39, 89,
  256n60
  Black No More 261n4
  "Keeping the Negro in His Place"
    40
  "The Negro-Art Hokum" 15, 90
  "Our White Folks" 40
Schwartz, Delmore 19, 42–43

Seaver, Edwin 42–43, 256–57n68
Shapiro, Karl 41
Shaw, Irwin 42
Simon and Schuster 233
Smith, Lilian 41
Stein, Gertude 170–71, 182, 233
  Three Lives 170
Stephansson, Jan Harold 97
Stevens, Wallace 41, 67
Stevenson, Robert Louis 135
Stone, Alfred Holt 170–71, 177
Stribling, Thomas Sigismund 37, 209,
  216
Sullivan, Noël 50, 149
Survey Graphic (journal) 2, 16, 143

Taggard, Genevieve 41
Tagore, Rabindranath 29
Tarkington, Booth 135
Tate, Allen 42
Thompson, Louise 52, 103
Thurman, Wallace 3, 7, 11, 16, 35–38,
  87–108, 171–73, 183, 229, 255n51,
  277n18
  Aunt Hagar's Children 91
  The Blacker the Berry ... 88, 106, 171,
    261n4
  "Cordelia the Crude" 96
  Harlem (with William Jourdan Rapp)
    102
  Infants of the Spring 7, 87, 91–92, 95,
    97–107, 283n25
  "Nephews of Uncle Remus" 90
  Porgy 92
  "This Negro Literary Renaissance"
    90
Toomer, Jean 16, 20–22, 25, 29, 36, 51,
  67, 103, 107, 168, 170, 254n43
  "Blood-Burning Moon" 21, 22
  Cane 16, 17, 19–22, 25, 30, 65, 211,
    261n4
  "Carma" 17
  "Kabnis" 20
  "Karintha" 20, 21
  "Song of the Son" 18, 29–31, 36

Trounstine, John (aka Turner, John) 231–33, 235
Tully, Jim 40
Twain, Mark 135
  Huckleberry Finn 135

"Uncle Remus" (story) 145
The Upward Path: A Reader for Colored Children (Pritchard and Ovington) 116–17

Van Doren, Carl 50
Van Vechten, Carl 35–37, 49, 58, 61, 103–104, 154, 214, 235, 255n51, 282–83n22
  Nigger Heaven 35–38, 81, 89, 283n22
VanDerZee, James 220

W.W. Norton (publisher) 65, 78, 82, 189–90, 194, 251n10
Walker, Alice 188–89, 195, 199
  "In Search of Zora Neale Hurston" 189
Walrond, Eric 50, 99, 103, 244, 250n3
  Tropic Death 89
Warren, Robert Penn 41, 67
Welty, Eudora 42
West, Dorothy 99
Wharton, Edith 67
Whirl o' the West (film) 140, 271n38
White, Newman 179

White, Walter 11, 50, 67
  The Fire in the Flint 65
  Flight 37
Whitman, Walt 273n20
Wilber, Richard 41
Williams, Edward Christopher 10, 207–22
  "The Letters of Davy Carr" 2, 10, 207, 209, 211–17
  When Washington Was in Vogue 2, 10, 207–12, 215, 217–22
Williams, Oscar 41
Williams, Tennessee 67
Williams, William Carlos 41
Wilson, Edmund 42
Wirth, Thomas 95, 102, 105, 107, 265n36, 265n45
Wolfe, Thomas 42, 67
Woodson, Carter G. 28, 58
The World Tomorrow (magazine) 15, 17, 89, 97, 264n22
Wright, Richard 16, 25, 42–43, 107, 188, 201, 256n68
  "The Man Who Lived Underground" 19, 40, 42
  Native Son 42, 153
  "Two Excerpts from a Novel" 42
Wylie, I.A.R. 37
Wyman, Lilli Buffum Chace 138

Yerby, Frank 171
Young, Marguerite 41

Printed in the USA
CPSIA information can be obtained
at www.ICGtesting.com
CBHW031502021224
18317CB00001B/47